ANTHROPOLOGICAL WITNESS

ANTHROPOLOGICAL WITNESS

Lessons from the Khmer Rouge Tribunal

Alexander Laban Hinton

CORNELL UNIVERSITY PRESS ITHACA AND LONDON

First published 2022 by Cornell University Press

Library of Congress Cataloging-in-Publication Data

Names: Hinton, Alexander Laban, author.
Title: Anthropological witness: lessons from the Khmer Rouge tribunal / Alex Laban Hinton.
Description: Ithaca [New York]: Cornell University Press, 2022. | Includes bibliographical references and index.
Identifiers: LCCN 2022001476 (print) | LCCN 2022001477 (ebook) | ISBN 9781501765681 (hardcover) | ISBN 9781501765698 (paperback) | ISBN 9781501765711 (pdf) | ISBN 9781501765704 (epub)
Subjects: LCSH: Nuon Chea, 1926—Trials, litigation, etc. | Extraordinary Chambers in the Courts of Cambodia. | Forensic anthropology. | Evidence, Expert—Cambodia. | Trials (Genocide)—Cambodia. | Trials (Crimes against humanity)—Cambodia. | Cambodia—Politics and government—1975–1979.
Classification: LCC KZ1208.C36 H56 2022 (print) | LCC KZ1208.C36 (ebook) | DDC 341.6/90268—dc23/eng/20220531
LC record available at https://lccn.loc.gov/2022001476
LC ebook record available at https://lccn.loc.gov/2022001477

In loving memory of my mother, Darlene Hinton

Contents

Acknowledgments

"You have to write about it!" Many people said this to me as soon as I finished testifying at the Khmer Rouge Tribunal, particularly given my exchange with "Brother Number Two" Nuon Chea. I knew I would do so. However, the path took a bit longer than expected and had some twists and turns. First, there was the Trump presidency, which set me on course to write another book, *It Can Happen Here*, with which this book was originally intertwined and shares echoes. Eventually I came to see that I was taking on two different but interrelated projects.

The second event was the pandemic, when I wrote most of this book. At a key juncture, I received anonymous reader reports of the best sort—encouraging yet challenging. Their suggestions, along with those of the Cornell University Press editors, especially Jim Lance, helped me greatly strengthen the book. So, I'd like to thank them as well. Jim has been steadfast in his support of this project and encouraged me to write the book I wanted to write, one that uses creative nonfiction literary strategies to tell a story, challenge a myth, and still grapple with theoretical issues in a clear and engaging public anthropology manner.

During the writing process, my family has provided help in many ways, including talking about the ideas as they formed and reading over drafts. My thanks and love go to my wife Nicole and daughters Meridian and Arcadia, each of whom has read through a draft of the manuscript at different stages. Nicole, an accomplished poet and creative writing professor, did so shortly before it went to press. And it is to her that I owe thanks for encouraging me to experiment with creative writing strategies, an endeavor that has perhaps led to a "voice" of sorts that traverses *Man or Monster?*, *It Can Happen Here*, *The Anthropological Witness*, and a coauthored book, *Perpetrators*.

Thanks also go to my other family members who supported the project, including my father, Ladson, and late mother, Darlene, both of whom stayed up late into the night to watch my testimony at the Khmer Rouge Tribunal as it was taking place on the other side of the world. I'd like to acknowledge my brothers, Ladson and Devon, and their families (Susan, Carolee, Kendra, Dev, Carina, and Mika), as well as my in-laws, Peter (also a poet), Alissa, Josh, and my late mother-in-law, Jacki.

I'd also like to recognize my colleagues at the Rutgers Center for the Study of Genocide and Human Rights (CGHR) and UNESCO Chair on Genocide Prevention, Nela Navarro and Stephen Eric Bronner. Nela and Steve, as well as

Tom LaPointe, have been great colleagues for many years and helped create a vibrant intellectual atmosphere in which to consider issues related to the concerns of this book.

Most recently, the center has launched a Global Consortium on Bigotry and Hate with partners around the world. I'm grateful for the conversations and opportunity to discuss and present on issues raised in this book. The center also cohosted the Critical Transitional Justice Project, which also took up related issues. My thanks to the partners in this initiative, Jens Meierhenrich (LSE) and Lawrence Douglas (Amherst), and participants in different workshops.

Many thanks to Youk Chhang and his staff at the Documentation Center of Cambodia (DC-Cam). As I note in this book, Youk and DC-Cam have been continually supportive of my research, including this project. I'd also like to thank Youk for permission to include a number of images from the DC-Cam/Sleuk Rith Institute archive in this book.

I have also had the opportunity to give talks related to this book at various conferences and workshops and would like to acknowledge the feedback I received. Of particular note was the Second Annual Natalie Mayer Holocaust and Genocide Studies Lecture I gave at Pacific Lutheran University and presentations at Boston University, Japan International Christian University, Kean University, the New School for Analytical Psychology (NSAP) in Seattle, and New York University. My thanks to go Joyce Apsel, Kirsten Christensen, Timothy Longman, Lane Gerber, Giorgio Shani, and the members of NSAP for providing me with the opportunity to speak.

Thank you to my many other colleagues and students at Rutgers, including the Department of Sociology and Anthropology and Division of Global Affairs. Various offices at Rutgers, including the Office of the Chancellor, the Faculty of Arts and Sciences, RU Global, and the Research Council also provided sabbatical time and grants to help support this research. The ideas expressed in this book are, of course, my own and do not necessarily reflect the view of these institutions. My thanks also go to my departmental chair, Chris Duncan, and administrator, Dawn Wilson. I greatly appreciate their assistance during this project.

Once written, a book needs to find a home. In this regard, and as I noted before, I very much appreciate all that my editor, Jim Lance, has done to support the publication of this book. Different staff members at Cornell University Press have also provided critical assistance, including Clare Jones and the editorial, marketing, and production team in addition to Michelle Witkowski.

Finally, I'd like to thank the individuals in Cambodia who spoke to me, often for hours at a time, during interviews and conversations—including Bill Smith who agreed to speak with me the day after the verdict, when he no doubt was exhausted. The late Reach Sambath and his colleagues Sovannarom Dim,

Pheaktra Neth, Sok Heng, and Lars Olsen from the ECCC Public Affairs Office also greatly facilitated my research at different points, including granting permission to use some of the images in this book.

I'd also like to thank Victoria Sanford and Cathy Schlund-Vials for their comments on parts of the manuscript. My gratitude also goes to others who have contributed to my ECCC research or thinking about the issues in this book in different ways, including Joyce Apsel, Kurt Bredenberg, David Chandler, Lawrence Douglas, Khamboly Dy, Kok-Thay Eng, Craig Etcheson, Louis Harrison, Samphors Huy, Vannak Huy, Helen Jarvis, Sophat Morm, Charles Nuckolls, Robert Paul, Robert Ruffini, Sirik Savina, Bradd Shore, Greg Stanton, Mark Urken, Ernesto Verdeja, Richard Wilson, Andrew Woolford, and Carol Worthman. I also want to thank Rob, Adele, and the staff at Local Coffee, whose espresso helped energize my writing during the pandemic. My apologies to the many other deserving people I have inadvertently left off this brief list of acknowledgments.

Parts of a section in chapter 1 appeared in Alexander Laban Hinton, "What Makes a Man Start Fires?," in *Pre-Genocide: Warnings and Readiness to Protect*, edited by Anders Jerichow and Cecilie Felicia Stokholm Banke, 83–93 (Copenhagen: Humanity in Action, 2018).

ANTHROPOLOGICAL WITNESS

Introduction

LAW, ANTHROPOLOGY, AND EXPERT WITNESS

Tuesday, September 22, 2015 (Newark, New Jersey, USA)

As I sit at my desk, finishing a book manuscript on an international criminal tribunal being held in Cambodia, I receive a surprise e-mail from that very court. The message confronts me with a dilemma. It also raises questions about my role as an anthropologist and my responsibility to bring scholarly insights into the public sphere.

"I would like to inform you that your name has been put before the Trial Chamber of the ECCC on a confidential and provisional Expert Witness list,"[1] reads the message from an official at the Extraordinary Chambers in the Courts of Cambodia (ECCC). This UN-backed international hybrid tribunal was established to try former leaders of the Khmer Rouge for genocide and atrocity crimes that took place in Cambodia while they held power from 1975 to 1979.

The book I am completing, *Man or Monster? The Trial of a Khmer Rouge Torturer*, focuses on the first person to be tried at the court, Duch, the head of a Khmer Rouge security center where over twelve thousand people were killed, many after being tortured and forced to confess. Even as I read the e-mail, my desk is covered with piles of prisoner confessions and other documentation used as evidence in his trial. Duch was convicted and sentenced to life imprisonment in Case 001. The second case is now underway at the ECCC.

"The Trial Chamber has requested that I make contact with you," the message continues, "to determine your willingness and availability to travel to

Phnom Penh, Cambodia to testify before them as an Expert Witness" in the trial of the Case 002 defendants, Nuon Chea and Khieu Samphan.

Khieu Samphan held the largely ceremonial title of head of state during Democratic Kampuchea (DK), the period of Khmer Rouge rule in Cambodia. Nuon Chea is more notorious. Some call him a monster. He claims to be a champion of Cambodia's poor. He is known for his devotion to cause and willingness to do whatever was necessary to ensure the success of the revolution he and his Khmer Rouge comrades undertook when they seized power in Cambodia on April 17, 1975, following seven years of civil war.[2]

Although he served as "Brother Number Two," Nuon Chea emphasizes that he and "Brother Number One," Pol Pot, worked hand in hand, more or less as equals, while they attempted to completely transform Cambodian society. They sought to bring about a "Super Great Leap Forward" that would outdo even Mao by catapulting Cambodia, renamed Democratic Kampuchea (DK), toward communist utopia.

Pol Pot held the title of prime minister. Nuon Chea served as deputy secretary of the Communist Party of Kampuchea (CPK). Together, they led the brutal DK regime until January 6, 1979, when they were toppled by another group of Cambodians, some former Khmer Rouge who had fled purges, with the help of massive Vietnamese military support. By this time, the DK regime had implemented policies resulting in the deaths of around a quarter of Cambodia's eight million inhabitants.

Pol Pot died in 1998. Nuon Chea is the most senior leader left alive to stand trial for the group's crimes. Due to geopolitics, it has taken over thirty years for Nuon Chea to face justice.

Many scholars would leap at the chance to be a part of his trial at the ECCC, one of the most significant international criminal trials since the Nuremberg Tribunal's prosecution of Nazi leaders. My initial response is ambivalence and apprehension. I have reservations—and questions.

The Cons of Expert Witness

There are two reasons for my hesitation. The first involves a risk, the second a major quandary that is a focus of this book.

The risk is professional. I have been conducting research on the Cambodian genocide since the 1990s, and I have spent the last half dozen years undertaking research on the court. I am well aware that expert witnesses put their reputations on the line. During my research, I have observed firsthand how their testimonies

FIGURE I.1. Pol Pot (aka "Brother Number One"), prime minister of DK and the leader of the Khmer Rouge.

Photo courtesy of the Documentation Center of Cambodia (DC-Cam) / Sleuk Rith Institute (SRI).

FIGURE I.2. Nuon Chea (aka "Brother Number Two"), deputy secretary of the Communist Party of Cambodia.

Photo courtesy of DC-Cam/SRI.

are picked apart and their methods, analyses, and research impugned. I know I will become a target if I agree to testify.

The quandary is epistemological, a philosophical concept that refers to our ways of knowing and making truth claims about the world. Anthropology, like other academic disciplines, is based on epistemological assumptions reflected

FIGURE I.3. Khieu Samphan, DK head of state, in late May 1975.

Photo courtesy of DC-Cam/SRI.

in its methods, practices, concepts, facts, and validation procedures. So, too, is law as practiced at courts like the ECCC.

These epistemological assumptions may vary. They can also clash, sometimes dramatically. And I am well aware that they often do during academic expert testimony on the courtroom floor, since there is an underlying tension between scholarly research that prioritizes context, theory, and explanation (answering the question *why?*) and the legal need for cut-and-dried answers and facts that provide the basis for determining the guilt or innocence of the accused (answering the question *guilty?*). The academic mantra "it's complicated" doesn't play well in court, where time is precious and the goal is a verdict delivered in an efficient manner.

And indeed, some people claim that academic explanation doesn't belong in the courtroom. Such skeptics argue for legal minimalism, contending that law has important but strictly limited goals—determining guilt and rendering a verdict—that are accomplished by specific legal procedures and forms of reasoning.[3] This perspective was perhaps most famously pronounced by Hannah Arendt, who proclaimed that the purpose of a trial "is to render justice and nothing else."[4]

Others have articulated minimalism in terms of disciplinary epistemologies, including historian Henry Rousso, who refused to testify in a Holocaust-related trial because he believed that the historian's enterprise diverges too greatly from that of law. Rousso feared the "judicialization of the past" and a situation in which the historian would be "hostage" to legal procedure and the courtroom "line of questioning."[5]

My situation is even more complicated because I have been conducting long-term research on the very institution of which I am now being asked to become a part. Participant observation is a key anthropological method. But, if I testify, I will engage in a form of participant observation that not only is extreme but also raises ethical issues related to anthropological research.

In my e-mail reply to the court, I express these concerns. "There are a couple of factors that might make providing such testimony difficult," I write. "First, as you may be aware, I have been conducting ongoing research on the ECCC since 2008. I have completed one book . . . and am working on a second one on transitional justice and the ECCC more broadly."

"In carrying out this research," I continue, "I have interviewed hundreds of people, including court personnel. I worry that testifying could create difficulties in this regard, including making it harder for me to continue carrying out my research and interviewing people, especially at the ECCC."

"And second," I go on, "all of my research, dating back to my research in Cambodia in the 1990s . . . was done in accordance with university human subjects protocols. Many of the interviews were off the record and many of my interviewees asked that they not be identified. I expect that this situation might also cause some problems and restrict what I could say."[6]

These issues, I realize, may lead the court to rescind their invitation and therefore make it unnecessary for me to decide whether to testify. Either way, while awaiting a response I will have more time to consider the pros and cons of academic expert witness. Justice moves slowly. And it will be months until the court replies. As a result, I have plenty of time to ponder my dilemma. Testifying poses significant challenges. But there are also reasons to agree. Two loom large: explanation and obligation.

The Pros of Expert Witness

The first reason to testify is to offer academic explanation—helping to answer the question *why?*—in a public forum.

Some people, for example, argue that the legal minimalist position is overstated and overlooks the ability of international justice to fulfill goals beyond just rendering a verdict. Many of the most ardent advocates of this expansive vision of law come from the field of transitional justice, which situates international courts within the larger project of helping postconflict societies transition to peace and democracy, with redress serving as the bridge to this better future.

From this maximalist vantage, legal accountability is important but bound up with larger goods, including peace, truth, memory, justice, prevention, and reconciliation. As is the case with other post–Cold War international tribunals, these sorts of goals were written into the law establishing the ECCC. For such legal maximalists, law can deliver accountability and more, including truth and answers to the question *why?* Expert witness testimony, in this view, helps further broader transitional justice goals.

Others occupy a middle ground between legal minimalism and maximalism.[7] While underscoring the limitations of law, legal scholars like Lawrence Douglas and Mark Osiel contend that law can serve didactic purposes by creating dramatic and narrative understandings of the past. With regard to expert witness testimony specifically, anthropologist Richard Wilson has also charted out a middle ground, arguing that despite the differences between law and history, tribunals can contribute to understanding the past, and academic expert witness testimony has a potentially important role to play in this regard.

Similarly, my years of conducting ethnographic research on the Khmer Rouge Tribunal and studying genocide and transitional justice more broadly suggest that while there are courtroom constraints on what expert witnesses can say, they also have latitude when making their scholarly claims. In academia, we sometimes describe this situation in terms of structure and agency. Some legal scholars have drawn on Pierre Bourdieu's practice theory to describe law as a contextual "field" governed by rules and procedures that establish the grounds within which actors negotiate their actions—somewhat akin to people playing within the rules and parameters of a game or competition that is itself situated in a broader historical and institutional context.[8]

There are limitations to Bourdieu's metaphor, not the least of which is the fact that it ignores the multiple fields at play in a given context, but it usefully illustrates the complex situation expert witnesses face when giving testimony. Having studied the tribunal, I have perhaps a better understanding than many expert witnesses of the legal rules and procedures I will face—and how to negotiate them—if I testify.

Doing so, I know, is not easy. It's one thing to write about a topic, with ample time for reflection and careful prose; it's another to give answers in the rapid fire of courtroom questioning with truth at stake. And, in the ECCC trial in which they want me to testify, the defense is engaged in genocide denial.

Despite such difficulties, there is a second key reason for me to testify—obligation, in the sense of both ethical commitments and gratitude. These are sticky issues for scholars, who are often uncomfortable with situations in which questions of personal ethics and normative concerns are front and center. They usually prefer to study such issues at a distance. And indeed, morality itself is currently a topic of anthropological attention.[9]

Such scholars, and I count myself among them, tend to be more comfortable analyzing morality or truth as discourse than becoming directly enmeshed in the moral economies of institutions that produce these discourses—even as they are already intertwined with such moral economies including academia itself.[10] For this reason, I understand why scholars like Rousso refuse to testify out of concern that they will become exposed on the courtroom floor, where the epistemological assumptions of law hold sway. Clearly, there are trade-offs to expert witness.[11]

Yet, my perspective diverges from those who prefer a position of distanced critical theory. It aligns more closely with a tradition dating back to the Frankfurt school of critical theory. Although I don't share some of the Frankfurt school's stronger Marxist leanings—and as a scholar of genocide, I remain wary of totalizing visions, left and right—I have always been drawn to their view of critical inquiry, which allows space for ethics and public issues, including the Nazi atrocities with which they were very much concerned.

In this regard, members of the Frankfurt school were public intellectuals of their time. When teaching about genocide and mass violence, for example, I often assign Theodor Adorno's "Education after Auschwitz," which was first presented on radio in 1966 and later published as an essay. This public address draws in part on his earlier theoretical works written in the shadow of the Nazis, ranging from *Dialectic of Enlightenment* to *The Authoritarian Personality*, which Adorno recasts in more accessible form.

His essay begins with an ethical imperative ("never again") and public policy goal (education for prevention) as he states, "The premier demand upon all education is that Auschwitz not happen again."[12] Adorno proposes that education serve as an early intervention, teaching students to critically self-reflect on the ways in which their subjectivity is produced by larger social forces of domination such as those that gave rise to Auschwitz. In this regard, self-determination and resistance are linked to awareness of how instrumental reason—a key dynamic underlying capitalism, bureaucracy, science, and popular culture—fosters alienation, indifference, standardized and stereotypical ways of thinking, emotional "coldness," identification with the collective, and destructiveness.

Here we find Adorno bringing the insights of critical theory, including answers to the question *why?*, into the public domain as part of a normative and ethical pedagogical project promoting autonomy and prevention. This model of engaged critical theory will inform a book I later write that is narratively set in the classroom as it examines white power and the rising threat of atrocity crimes in the United States during the Trump presidency.[13] Indeed, even as I wait for the Trial Chamber's reply in the fall of 2015, Trump is emerging as the front-runner to gain the Republican nomination for president. This book is in a sense that book's companion volume; both were originally part of a combined project and therefore have echoes, including discussion of the Frankfurt school as well as Nuon Chea's life and trial.

In my primary discipline, these sorts of projects that link critique with engagement fall with the purview of public anthropology. The term "public anthropology" refers most basically to scholarship that uses anthropological insight to shed light on issues of public concern in a manner that reaches a broader readership, a goal furthered by the use of accessible writing.

There is a long history of anthropological engagement of this sort, dating back to the early work of Franz Boas and Margaret Mead and perhaps most visibly continued today by scholars like Mahmood Mamdani and Paul Farmer.[14] They are among those contemporary anthropologists who have public commitments that inform their research and writing and can be placed under the umbrella of public anthropology.

Partly in response to postmodernism and globalization, this term began to gain currency in the late 1990s, just as I was finishing my doctoral fieldwork in Cambodia. It is a perspective that has informed my work ever since. And it is a reason to consider serving as an expert witness. Doing so would dovetail with this tradition of public anthropology engagement and my long-standing commitment to address the issue of genocide as a step toward prevention, an ethical concern and approach resonating with that of Adorno and the Frankfurt school.

There is still another reason to consider testifying: my obligation as an anthropologist to make a small return to the many Cambodians who have helped me with my fieldwork research. This is a long-standing anthropological tradition. At the end of my dissertation fieldwork, for example, I had helped rebuild the dirt road that runs through the village where I conducted much of my research. I later contributed to the construction of a small structure where the village elders hold Buddhist ceremonies and pray. I have also advised and taught Cambodian graduate students after helping arrange for them to come study at my university.

These efforts are a modest return to the Cambodian communities who have welcomed me into their homes and patiently answered my questions, which often touched on the suffering of the Khmer Rouge past. Over my years of research in Cambodia, first as a graduate student and later as an anthropologist and professor, hundreds of Cambodians have told me, sometimes in tears, about their experiences during the Khmer Rouge genocide. Many still ask, *why?*

By testifying, I would have the chance to make another return to these communities, an opportunity that is a strong counterweight to the professional risks and epistemological challenges I would face as an expert witness.

Thursday, January 28, 2016 (Newark, New Jersey, USA)

These are the pros and cons I am considering when, four months later, I receive the ECCC's reply. "The Trial Chamber," the ECCC official's e-mail begins, "are very much hoping to hear you in the courtroom, perhaps as early as the last week of February or the first week of March."[15] A first issue is clarified. They still want me to testify, so I will need to make a decision.

"Concerning the scope of his testimony," the message continues, "please stress to Mr. Hinton that the ECCC operations are not a matter on which he is expected to testify, the main focus will be on genocide issues." They have, to draw on Bourdieu's metaphor, laid out parameters that will guide and constrain the actors, including me, in the courtroom "field" if I testify. The parties would be broadly expected to focus on my pre-ECCC scholarship and the issue of genocide.

"Concerning the fact that some of his sources are anonymous," the e-mail goes on, "if this was part of the protocol for his academic research and if anonymity was a condition requested by the interviewees to make statements, then he will not be forced to give the Chamber the identity of these individuals. This issue will be evaluated when the Chamber will assess the weight that can be given to the expert testimony/opinion."

The court agrees to respect my university's human subject protocols even as they suggest this means that they would likely give lesser weight to any related testimony I provide. Some of the tensions between anthropological and legal epistemologies are already in view: the methods of data collection, status of sources, and means of weighing facts and evidence. The Trial Chamber's decision presages the sorts of epistemological clashes that will likely arise if I agree to serve as an expert witness.

The time for a decision has arrived. In the end, the choice is clear. The pros, especially the sense of obligation, outweigh the cons. And so, unlike Henry Rousso and other academics who have declined to serve as expert witnesses, I agree to testify—in Cambodia, in public, and recorded and livestreamed in real time—to help answer the question *why?* The date is quickly set for the week of March 14, 2016.

Little do I know that while testifying, I will provoke the ire of "Brother Number Two." Breaking his unofficial boycott of the proceedings, Nuon Chea will ask to address me directly in court. When I was a graduate student doing research in Cambodia in the mid-1990s, the idea that I might testify at an international tribunal—let alone have a direct exchange with a Khmer Rouge mastermind—seemed out of the realm of possibility. As I drove a moped on dirt roads in the countryside interviewing perpetrators and survivors, nothing along these lines ever crossed my mind.

My exchange with Nuon Chea, which will center on issues of truth, history, denial, and explanation, provides a dramatic moment that underscores the argument of this book. In it, I tell the story of how I navigated the structures and constraints of law as I sought to make a pedagogical contribution to the process of justice by helping answer the question *why?*

My experience raises important questions about whether and to what extent there is a place for the public scholar and anthropological witness in the courtroom. Can scholars who serve as expert witnesses, the book asks, effectively contribute to tribunals for international atrocity crimes, where the focus is on legal guilt as opposed to such academic explanation? In other words, did Rousso get it right or wrong?

Writing the Story

Explaining *why?* and considering the possibilities of academic scholarship in the courtroom are two key threads that weave together the chapters of this book; a third is its public anthropology narrative style. While writing in the public anthropology vein varies depending on the person and forum, it typically involves an attempt to convey critically and ethnographically informed insights in legible prose. To do so, a public anthropologist may seek, as a university press editor once advised, to "craft a compelling story, build suspense through plot or questions, avoid paralysis by nuance, connect heart and head (connect viscerally with readers), and allow bold assertions and a clear takeaway message."[16]

Like its companion volume, *It Can Happen Here: White Power and the Rising Threat of Genocide in the US*, this book draws on these sorts of literary strategies, ones also used in experimental ethnographic writing.[17] And like *Man or Monster?*, the book I was finishing when the 2015 ECCC summons arrived, this book is written in an ethnodramatic form. It tells a story with a plot, suspense, and chronology (my experience testifying at the ECCC and courtroom encounter with Nuon Chea) while using setting and stage (the ECCC courtroom), dialogue (courtroom exchanges), voice (first-person and present tense), and conflict and tension (both between courtroom participants and in my endeavor to provide expert testimony).[18] In this story, I seek not just to "tell," as traditional expository academic writing does, but also to "show," as the creative writing "show, don't tell" injunction urges.

This book also uses character development, providing background on and giving a sense of Nuon Chea, key courtroom legal personnel, and the expert witness—me. Indeed, I discuss my academic training and research at length, not just to position myself in the narrative but because my testimony is at the center of the story. This background will also be a focus of courtroom debate and is important to understand the anthropological ways of knowing, or epistemological assumptions, that inform my attempt to provide anthropological witness in a court of law.

Finally, in keeping with its public anthropology orientation, this book is also written with an eye to audience. I seek to write this book in a clear and engaging manner that will be of interest to a broader readership, not just specialists and those already familiar with the Cambodian genocide and international justice. To this end, I have included basic background on Cambodian history, the genocide, transitional justice, and anthropology.

And, given that my testimony involves extensive discussion of my previous research, I have included discussion of it in the pages that follow because many readers won't be familiar with my earlier work. By writing clearly, using literary strategies, and providing background information, my aim is to make this book accessible to a wider audience and students in a range of courses—even in introductory classes, since, in a sense, the text introduces the reader to anthropology and its practice, relevance to public issues, and epistemological ways of knowing.

These aims and writing strategies inform the structure of the book, which is narratively centered around my testimony. Those readers who wish to follow the narrative may choose to now skip ahead to chapter 1. In many ways, this reading strategy is most in keeping with the writing style. For others who prefer a more traditional description of what is to come, in the remainder of this introduction I provide a brief, chapter summary glimpse of the story I tell.

A Glimpse Ahead

Chapter 1, "Truth, Politics, and the Accused," centers on the issue of truth and denial. It begins at the Tuol Sleng Genocide Museum—located on the site of S-21, the prison run by Duch, the first person to be tried at the ECCC—before considering how, after DK, the Khmer Rouge and the Peoples Republic of Kampuchea (PRK) regime produced different historical narratives about DK and the events that followed. Whereas the PRK regime's narrative framed DK in terms of Nazi-like atrocities, the Khmer Rouge denied the mass deaths while blaming Vietnam for the deaths that did occur and also claiming that Vietnam was committing genocide in Cambodia. The chapter turns to look at the life of Nuon Chea and how he engaged in denial, including in his defense at the ECCC. Along the way, the chapter provides contextual background that is necessary to understand both my experience of serving as an expert witness and the larger stakes involved in genocide denial.

In chapter 2, "Anthropological Witness," I describe my path to the ECCC and the anthropological research that was the focus of both my expert witness testimony and my book that was discussed extensively at the trial, *Why Did They Kill? Cambodia in the Shadow of Genocide*. Most of the chapter centers around my initial questioning by the Trial Chamber president, who asked questions about my background, research, and reasons for writing *Why Did They Kill?* His questions raised important issues about anthropological epistemology—and how it differs from that of law—which I sought to clarify in court.

Chapter 3, "The Genocidal Process," is focused on prosecution questioning and locates my testimony in the larger context of the trial and the battle over truth and history. If the prosecution was like a construction crew building a legal edifice proving that Nuon Chea belonged to a highly centralized and top-down joint criminal enterprise, the defense acted like a demolition crew, seeking to tear down the argument. I stepped into the middle of this battle.

After this initial contextualization of the case, chapter 3 discusses how the prosecutor sought to highlight my credentials before asking me to answer the *why?* of genocide. My testimony explained how genocide comes to take place, how this genocidal process unfolded in Cambodia under the Khmer Rouge, how the Khmer Rouge targeted specific groups for destruction, and how the Khmer Rouge leaders organized and incited violence.

In my testimony, I revisited the anthropological dissertation research I conducted in a village in Cambodia in the 1990s. Indeed, my expertise as an anthropologist and genocide studies scholar was center stage. This chapter raises important questions about the nature of fieldwork research, how it can contribute to major public issues, and the complexities that emerge—ranging from the use of the comparative method to human subjects protections.

One of the hallmarks of the ECCC is its extensive victim participation, including the direct involvement of civil parties. Chapter 4, "Lived Experience," centers on my questioning by civil party lawyers, who asked about the radical transformation of Cambodian life under the Khmer Rouge, including the regime's splintering of family, community, social networks, and religion.

These questions raised issues about the broader goals of the court in terms of providing redress—having not just a minimalist focus on legal accountability but also a more maximalist emphasis on collective reparation and healing, which spoke to the wider transitional justice goals of the court. The civil party questions also directly referred to my earlier anthropological research on the experience of living under the Khmer Rouge (the focus of *Why Did They Kill?*) and indirectly related to my ongoing research on local understandings of the ECCC, which are often mediated by Buddhism. My courtroom discussion of this lived experience and local knowledge constituted a second key way in which I was able to bring the insights of anthropology into the courtroom.

The next chapter, "Rupture," focuses on defense questioning. On the one hand, the defense tried to discredit my testimony and anthropological research insofar as it implicated Nuon Chea in genocide. On the other hand, they sought to assert an alternative narrative that placed Vietnam at the center of the violence—instead of Nuon Chea and the Khmer Rouge leadership. In making these arguments, Nuon Chea's defense lawyers used a legal strategy of "rupture," which had been popularized by the ECCC defense lawyer Jacques Vergès. Vergès, nicknamed "the Devil's Advocate" for his work defending notorious clients ranging from terrorist Carlos the Jackal to the Nazi Klaus Barbie, pioneered this legal strategy of reframing and politicizing trials to cast doubt on their legitimacy. The highly politicized ECCC was particularly vulnerable due to allegations of corruption, political interference, and a lack of judicial independence on the part of the Cambodian judges and legal personnel.

Chapter 6, "Denial," discusses my direct exchange with Nuon Chea, which took place at the end of my three and a half days of testimony. Nuon Chea finished his remarks by posing two questions to me about the role of foreign powers in the Cambodian genocide and the violence wrought by US carpet-bombing. Suddenly, this genocidaire became my accuser. His arguments were a form of genocide denial, at odds with existing scholarship as well as my own findings about the Cambodian genocide—a point I would make in my reply, which emphasized that it was the Khmer Rouge leadership, not foreign actors, who held control over the security apparatus, gave the orders, and were the ones directly responsible for genocide.

The book's penultimate chapter, "Judgment," is narratively framed around the November 2018 verdict in Nuon Chea's trial, which I attended and where he was convicted. The first section discusses the Trial Chamber's ruling. I then turn to an analysis of how my testimony informed the verdict, while noting how the use of my testimony was impacted by prosecution and defense contestations over my methods, sources, and objectivity.

The day after the verdict, I met the prosecutor who had questioned me. Following up on an academic article he had written that discussed my testimony, we talked about its broader significance. Beginning with this interview, the conclusion, "The Public Scholar," revisits the theoretical issues raised in the book's introduction through a contrast of the methods and epistemology of social science/anthropology and those of law, looking in particular at the synergies and discordances between the juridical production of a verdict and my disciplinary focus on explanation, context, and analysis. I finish by reconsidering the question that frames this book—whether public scholars have a place in the courtroom and can contribute to international justice in a manner that can, even within the strict confines of legal procedure, provide important insights about major public issues like truth, justice, genocide, and the question *why?*

1

TRUTH, POLITICS, AND THE ACCUSED

Monday, March 7, 2016 (Phnom Penh, Cambodia)

A month and a half after agreeing to testify, I study a black-and-white photograph of Nuon Chea at the Tuol Sleng Museum of Genocidal Crimes in Cambodia. He stands next to Pol Pot and other Khmer Rouge leaders as they await a Chinese delegation at the Phnom Penh airport, the same one at which I arrived last night after a twenty-four-hour journey. Their Mao caps indicate China's influence, including the Great Leap Forward and Cultural Revolution, two spectacular initiatives that, like the Khmer Rouge revolution, led to mass suffering and death. Nuon Chea's codefendant at the ECCC, Khieu Samphan, is nowhere to be seen, a suggestion of his lower status during Democratic Kampuchea (DK).

The Khmer Rouge dress in revolutionary attire: black trousers and long-sleeved shirts, traditional scarves, and black sandals. During DK, everyone in Cambodia was expected to dress in this manner, their individuality erased for the sake of the larger socialist good. Several leaders smile at the camera. Not Nuon Chea.

I have no idea that, at the end of my three and half days of testimony next week, Nuon Chea will break a long silence to confront me in court. In a gravel voice, "Brother Number Two" will claim that my expert witness testimony has been flawed and—the accused turned accuser—demand I answer his questions, including one suggesting that I, as a US citizen, am implicated in atrocity crimes.

During this startling turn of events in the last minutes of my expert witness testimony, I will confront genocidal denial directly and will need to quickly for-

FIGURE 1.1. Tuol Sleng Compound.

Photo courtesy of DC-Cam/SRI.

mulate a reply. In a sense, this moment is not completely surprising. Nuon Chea and the Khmer Rouge have been denying their crimes for years, just as he now denies his role in overseeing S-21, the torture and extermination center that was transformed into the Tuol Sleng genocide museum months after the DK regime was toppled in January 1979.

Nuon Chea has good reason to dissociate himself from S-21. Established shortly after the Khmer Rouge took power in April 1975, the security center was an engine of the DK violence, which unfolded in phases and was reflected in S-21's prisoner population.[1] The first wave began immediately, as the Khmer Rouge targeted former leaders, soldiers, police, and government officials from the Khmer Republic regime they had defeated after a violent, seven-year civil war. Ethnic Vietnamese also began to come under attack. Many were forced into Vietnam; most of those who remained were killed. Nuon Chea stands charged with their genocide.

FIGURE 1.2. DK leaders and members of the Standing Committee of the Central Committee of the Communist Party of Kampuchea (CPK) awaiting a Chinese delegation (c. 1975–78). From left: Pol Pot (general secretary of the party and prime minister), Nuon Chea ("Brother Number Two" and deputy party secretary), Ieng Sary (foreign minister), Son Sen (minister of defense), and Vorn Vet (deputy prime minister and minister of economics). Second and third from right, front row: Cheng An (minister of industry) and Koy Thuon (minister of commerce). Other people in this photograph are unidentified Khmer Rouge guards.

Photo courtesy of DC-Cam/SRI.

Duch, the first defendant to be tried at the ECCC, took charge of S-21 in March 1976 as a second wave of violence was getting underway, in part due to perceived plots against the government. At this time, the DK regime sought to eliminate "hidden enemies burrowing from within"—not just those believed to be counterrevolutionaries or have sympathies with the previous regime, but also traitors within their ranks. Muslim Chams, the second group against whom Nuon Chea is accused of committing genocide, also began to be targeted.

Thousands of Cambodians, many of them Khmer Rouge cadre suspected of treason, started arriving at S-21 as purges, which would continue throughout DK, swept the country. Some were killed immediately. Others were shackled in cells, enduring inhumane conditions until it was their turn to "confess" and name their alleged co-conspirators. Many refused to do so and were tortured, a process sometimes chronicled in interrogator notes.

One such record, regarding the interrogation of Ke Kim Huot, a longtime revolutionary, states: "On the morning of July 21, 1977, we pounded him another round. Electrical wire and feces. This time he cursed those who hit him very much, [and said] Go ahead and beat me to death. Had him eat two or three spoonfuls of feces."[2]

"By nightfall," the interrogator note continues, "we went at him again with electric wires, this time pretty seriously. He became delirious. He was all right. Later he confessed a bit." The interrogator then seeks instruction: "My operative line is to continue torture with mastery, because the enemy is breaking emotionally and is at a dead end. Along with this, I ask for opinion and guidance from Angkar ['the Organization'] in carrying out this task."

This request for instructions was sent to Duch, the S-21 commandant. During his ECCC trial, Duch claimed that he, in turn, sought guidance about such interrogations from his direct superior, with whom he was in regular contact.[3] From March 1976 until August 17, 1977, this superior was Son Sen, the DK minister of defense. Son Sen told Duch that he answered to Nuon Chea. After Son Sen was transferred to the battlefield as border tensions with Vietnam were intensifying, Duch said that he reported directly to Nuon Chea. Tensions with Vietnam soon escalated into war, which ended with a massive Vietnamese invasion that toppled the DK regime.

While Nuon Chea was already implicated in a host of atrocity crimes, his oversight role at S-21 meant that he was not just a leader who gave orders from afar, but an actor directly involved in the daily operation of the violence. His instructions had direct consequences for prisoners like Ke Kim Huot, who continued to be tortured and interrogated after Duch began reporting to Nuon Chea.

According to Duch, Nuon Chea was embroiled in the violence at S-21 in a number of ways.[4] He helped decide whom to arrest and execute. He read confessions and monitored interrogations. On occasion, Duch stated, Nuon even ordered that the bodies of prisoners be exhumed and photographed to prove they were dead. And, Duch claimed, Nuon Chea was involved in the medical experiments at S-21 as well as the deaths of prisoners who died after the extraction of their blood. Such acts are among the charges Nuon Chea now faces.

A mountain of evidence implicates Nuon Chea in these crimes. Much of this S-21 documentation was left behind when Vietnamese forces suddenly took Phnom Penh on January 7, 1979. Shortly afterward, a Vietnamese film unit was dispatched to the barbed-wired S-21 compound, from which a stench was emanating. The entrance was marked by a Khmer Rouge slogan: "Fortify the spirit of the revolution! Be on your guard against the strategy and tactics of the enemy so as to defend the country, the people and the Party."[5]

In April 2009, I interviewed Dinh Phong, a member of the Vietnamese crew. Dinh Phong said that his team put towels, scented with hand oil, over their mouths to cut the stench. They didn't know what to expect, but decided "we would film whatever we found."[6] Inside the gates of S-21, they discovered what looked like an old school, comprising four three-story concrete buildings, in the center of which stood a smaller wooden structure.

The crew soon found the source of the smell: the decomposing bodies of the last prisoners killed at S-21. Duch testified that in the final days of the regime, Nuon Chea ordered the execution of the remaining prisoners at S-21.[7] The corpses were inside one of the classroom buildings where, Dinh Phong recalled, "our team found maybe ten rooms with dead, maggot-filled corpses lying in pools of blood."

Some of the people had been executed on beds to which they had been chained. The rooms contained objects like hatchets, hoes, and iron bars, which Dinh Phong surmised must have been used to beat or kill the prisoners. Amid the stench, Dinh Phong's team filmed the rooms one by one, moving from the smaller cells on the bottom floor to larger ones on the second floor.

Dinh Phong and his team traversed the site but did not find anyone else, dead or alive. Churned earth marked the spot of what appeared to be mass graves. Inside other buildings, they found dozens of small cells as well as larger rooms where detainees were shackled. They also discovered a photography room filled with prisoner mug shots. Another room contained busts of Pol Pot.[8] Much of what they found would become part of the Tuol Sleng museum. Due to time constraints, the team had to work quickly. "We didn't have time to take in what we had seen," Dinh Phong told me. "I could barely eat that night."[9]

In the days that followed, a massive amount of documentation was discovered on the site, including memos, mug shots, prisoner information, charts, cadre notebooks, propaganda tracts, execution logs, and piles of confessions that included interrogator notes like the one describing Ke Kim Huot's torture. Given that this material directly implicated him, as well as the DK leadership, Nuon Chea was furious that Duch failed to destroy the S-21 documentation. Duch told a journalist that when the two met again in 1983, Nuon Chea said, "All the papers from the party were burned except yours. You are stupid." Duch added, "I was like a water boy for Nuon Chea. He didn't tell me that the Vietnamese were invading so I had no time to burn the documents."[10]

Faced with this overwhelming documentation and Duch's testimony about Nuon Chea's deep involvement in the workings of S-21, Nuon Chea turned to denial. "I would like to inform the Cambodian people that I have never at any time been responsible for the operation of S-21," Nuon Chea told the court on April 18, 2012, following testimony Duch had given. "I never gave orders to or received any documents from Duch. And I was never Duch's superior."[11] Nuon Chea's claim was immediately thrown into doubt by his former bodyguard, who testified the same day that "I used to take [Nuon Chea's] letters to Grandfather Duch at Tuol Sleng."[12]

The Khmer Rouge Politics of Memory

The strategy of denial is nothing new for the Khmer Rouge. They have been using it since they were toppled in January 1979 by a small force of Cambodians—many of whom were former Khmer Rouge who had fled to Vietnam during the purges—backed by over one hundred thousand Vietnamese soldiers.

The speed of the Vietnamese victory surprised the Khmer Rouge leaders. Pol Pot and Nuon Chea traveled separately to northwest Cambodia, where they would regroup and once again wage civil war—this time against the Vietnam-backed Peoples Republic of Kampuchea (PRK). The new government included many former Khmer Rouge, including the young minister of foreign affairs, Hun Sen, who became the country's leader in 1985 and remains prime minster today.

At a post-DK gathering of Khmer Rouge military officers and cadre, Nuon Chea acknowledged the troops were exhausted but stressed the importance of battling the PRK regime, which he said was controlled by Vietnam. If they didn't, he warned, invoking a Cambodian saying, "We are like sugar canes in an elephant's mouth."[13] Khmer Rouge diplomats and propaganda harped on the theme of Vietnamese aggression, accusing Vietnam of committing genocide in Cambodia while the PRK regime served as its puppet.

For the next decade, Cambodia remained caught up in Cold War politics, with Vietnam and its Soviet Bloc allies backing the socialist PRK regime, while the Khmer Rouge were supported not just by their longtime ally China, but also by the USSR's Cold War enemies, including the United States and Thailand. The Khmer Rouge were even given Cambodia's seat at the United Nations, a position it shared with other resistance factions.

They used this diplomatic platform to push denial. While the PRK regime was condemning the genocidal actions of the "Pol Pot–Ieng Sary clique," the Khmer Rouge claimed that it was the "Vietnamese Le Duan clique" that was carrying out a "war of genocide" against Cambodians. Echoing DK narratives about Vietnam, the Khmer Rouge argued that the "Vietnamese aggressors, expansionists, annexationists and exterminators" were engaging in mass slaughter, toxic warfare, looting and destruction, and starvation in "a war more ferocious and savage than Hitler's war of genocide."[14]

As a result of this "criminal policy of genocide," the Vietnamese had already "killed over 2 million Kampucheans" even as "the entire Kampuchean race [was] on the verge of extinction." Playing on geopolitical fears, the Khmer Rouge warned that this campaign was but one step in a war that threatened to spread "to Southeast Asia, Asia, and the Pacific region" and was a part of "the global strategy of Soviet international expansionism."[15]

The Khmer Rouge claimed they simply wanted to defend Cambodia's sovereignty and lay the basis for a "free, direct and secret-ballot election under the direct supervision of the UN secretary general or his representative," following a Vietnamese withdrawal.[16] In this narrative, the Khmer Rouge played the part of victim (having been deposed by an illegal invasion), hero (fighting the occupier), and defender of freedom and human rights. It is a line Nuon Chea continues to assert in court.

Like much of the international community, the Khmer Rouge avoided mention of their atrocity crimes, which didn't fit with their new narrative—an elision all the more glaring given that they now accused Vietnam of genocide. When questioned by the media about increasing reports of mass human rights violations during DK, the Khmer Rouge took things one step further, denying what had taken place. While admitting that local authorities had committed excesses, they claimed that "not many" had been killed, "in all of Cambodia perhaps some thousands."[17]

In a November 1980 interview, Khieu Samphan used two large maps to highlight how the Vietnamese invasion had proceeded. When asked about DK, he acknowledged "some errors" while suggesting they were insignificant compared to the abuses being perpetrated by Vietnam in Cambodia. As for Tuol Sleng, Khieu Samphan suggests it was part of a Vietnamese "propaganda campaign. . . . We all know how easy it is to create photographic 'montages' and spread false information. Well, this is what they have done."[18]

These denials continued even as the geopolitical situation changed with the end of the Cold War. In 1989, Vietnam withdrew from Cambodia, paving the way for the 1991 Paris Peace Accords that laid the groundwork for UN-backed elections in 1993. The Khmer Rouge pulled out of the peace process and resumed their armed struggle even as Cambodia was welcomed back to the international community, now as a transitioning democratic country with a market-based economy.

Toward the end of the 1990s, the Khmer Rouge movement began to implode, in part due to a Cambodian government defection program that split off Khmer Rouge factions, including, in 1996, a key one led by Ieng Sary, the former DK minister of foreign affairs who died while on trial at the ECCC. Nuon Chea told a journalist that it was at this time that the Khmer Rouge leaders increasingly began to distrust each other and that he and Pol Pot grew distant.[19]

By then, younger Khmer Rouge cadre were playing an important role in the group and Nuon Chea saw signs of moral decline, in part due to the circulation of money and wealth that came from the sale of gems and timber.[20] Small-scale capitalism and private property were permitted; the long-standing practice of criticism and self-criticism sessions ceased.

Pol Pot later ordered the execution of Duch's first superior, former DK defense minister Son Sen—and fourteen members of his family—who Pol Pot suspected of betrayal. This action further exacerbated tensions within the group. In 1997, a Khmer Rouge faction led by Pol Pot's former general, Ta Mok, arrested Pol Pot and held a kangaroo court that sentenced Pol Pot to house arrest, where he would die the next year and be cremated on a pyre of tires. "When Ta Mok arrested Pol Pot," Nuon Chea said, "I saw that we had finally lost. They had attacked the head of the machine so the people will be split."[21]

At the end of 1998, Nuon Chea and Khieu Samphan defected, a move that effectively ended the Khmer Rouge movement after decades of struggle. The Cambodian government celebrated the moment. Prime Minister Hun Sen told the country that the two men should be welcomed "with bouquets of flowers, not with prisons and handcuffs. . . . We should dig a hole and bury the past and look ahead to the 21st century with a clean slate."[22]

During a press conference at the time, Khieu Samphan stated that people should "let bygones be bygones" and "forget the past." Nuon Chea, in turn, offered a sardonic half-apology, saying, "Naturally, we are sorry not only for the lives of the people of Cambodia, but even for the lives of all the animals that suffered because of the war."[23] Soon, Nuon Chea and Khieu Samphan were living freely in a former Khmer Rouge zone, even as negotiations to hold a tribunal

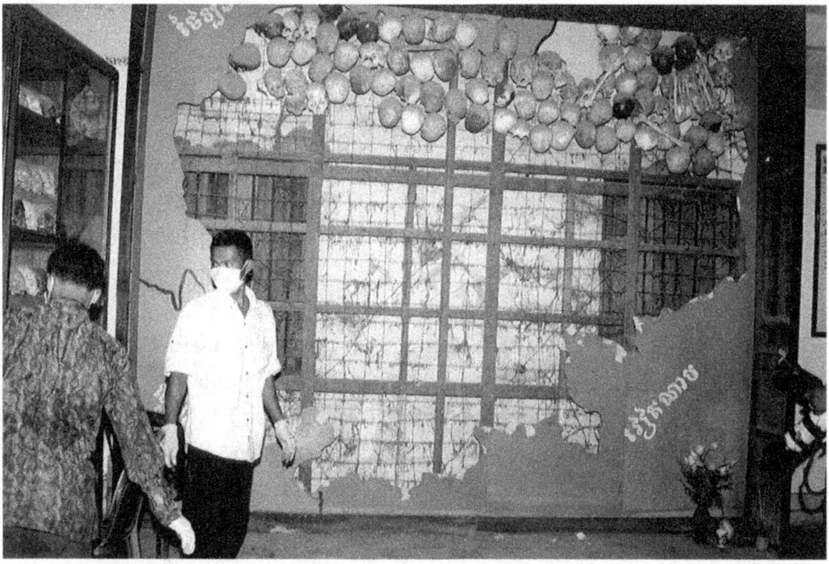

FIGURE 1.3. Construction of the Map of Skulls, Tuol Sleng Museum of Genocidal Crimes.

Photo courtesy of DC-Cam/SRI.

were proceeding. It wasn't until 2007, a year after the ECCC had commenced operations, that they were arrested.

Throughout this period, the Khmer Rouge continued their denials. They often centered on Tuol Sleng. One of the most powerful exhibits at Tuol Sleng, for example, is a map of Cambodia covered with skulls, its waterways painted blood red. Staff at Tuol Sleng apparently had to drink rice wine while building the map, which required removing bits of hair and scalp from the skulls.[24] It is the final exhibition that Tuol Sleng visitors see, one that reiterates the museum's message that the Khmer Rouge committed genocide in Cambodia.

Not surprisingly, the Khmer Rouge claimed it was a Vietnamese fabrication. A 1994 Khmer Rouge radio broadcast asserted that the Vietnamese had gathered the "skulls and bones from graveyards all over north and south Vietnam, brought them by trucks to Cambodia, and displayed them in an exhibition at Tuol Sleng as part of a propaganda campaign to legalize their aggression against and occupation of Cambodia."[25]

Similarly, when asked about Tuol Sleng in 1997, Pol Pot told a journalist, "Tuol Sleng was a Vietnamese exhibition." The skulls in the map, he added, "are smaller than the skull[s] of the Khmer people." As if to prove his denialist claims, Pol Pot said, "look at me, am I a savage person?"[26]

Tuol Sleng and the PRK Politics of Memory

Like many forms of genocide denial, the Khmer Rouge assertions mixed lies with partial truths. The Vietnamese had been directly involved in the creation of the museum and broader PRK propaganda efforts, as illustrated by the work of Dinh Phong's team. In the days that followed their discovery of Tuol Sleng, his unit traveled to other locations in Cambodia to document DK crimes. They filmed mass graves, met with victims, and produced stories.[27] By April, the Vietnamese army film studio had created a documentary on "the genocidal crimes perpetrated by the Pol Pot–Ieng Sary gang under Beijing's guidance" that included "scenes of large piles of human bones and mass graves of Pol Pot's victims."[28]

It was in this highly politicized context that Tuol Sleng was created from the ruins of S-21. First and foremost, Tuol Sleng was portrayed as a crime scene, providing evidence of the brutality of the "Pol Pot–Ieng Sary clique." Tuol Sleng would quickly come to serve as the preeminent symbol of Khmer Rouge atrocities.

By February or March 1979, a Vietnamese adviser, Colonel Mai Lam, began overseeing the transformation of the grounds of S-21 into a museum documenting the genocidal crimes of the Pol Pot clique. Mai Lam was well suited to the task. He had a law degree with a specialization in war crimes and had overseen the creation of a museum documenting US war crimes in Vietnam.[29] One of many Vietnamese experts who were sent to assist the PRK regime, Mai Lam advised Ung Pech, the first Cambodian director of the Tuol Sleng Museum and himself a survivor of S-21. Mai Lam would remain there for almost a decade.

Ong Thoeung Hoeung, a Cambodian intellectual who had been sent for reeducation during DK and who later worked briefly at Tuol Sleng, recalled his first meeting with Mai Lam. One day in July 1979, he stopped at a market stall to purchase some fried bananas, which were served to him in a paper wrapping.[30] The paper was covered in handwriting that he recognized as that of a person with whom he had studied in France.[31] The stall seller told Ong that her son had gathered the paper from Tuol Sleng, adding that many vendors in the market were using paper from the site to wrap food.

Ong went to Tuol Sleng, where he found documents and mug shots still scattered about, in search of more information. A former colleague who now worked at Tuol Sleng asked if Ong would like to join them, since they needed help organizing and translating documents. He was sent for an interview with "Brother" Mai Lam, whose office was adorned with "a large map of Indochina and a photograph of Ho Chi Minh."[32]

Mai Lam, "a greying fifty-year-old with a rather pleasant face," interviewed him in French, speaking a bit about his own travels to France and involvement in the anti-French resistance before concluding by "urging [Ong] to work for the fraternal solidarity amongst the peoples of Indochina" by making "a violent attack on China. . . . That was the watchword at the time: combat the expansionist ambitions of the Chinese, who had always wanted to annex Southeast Asia."[33]

Over the next few months, Ong worked as an archivist at Tuol Sleng, where he read, classified, and translated confessions.[34] Mai Lam, Ong said, "was really quite pleasant and tolerant, and left us to work in peace. Although he never missed an opportunity to inform us that he was an anti-Chinese communist and a nationalist, he didn't try to convert us. We had mutual respect for each other."[35] In contrast, a Vietnamese adviser attached to the Ministry of Information referred to himself as a "spiritual engineer" and repeatedly lectured Ong about communism, telling him about the need to let the "sleeping" documents at Tuol Sleng "speak out so that international opinion could distinguish between true and false communists."[36]

The importance of letting the "sleeping" documents speak to an international audience directly informed the museum's creation. Ong recalled that the Vietnamese brought in East German advisers to help organize the museum, modeling it on camps like Dachau to assert a parallel between the "Pol Pot clique" and the Nazis.[37] Mam Lai's team worked quickly, turning the grounds of S-21 into an "exhibition" just months after DK.

As the speed with which Tuol Sleng was created suggests, the PRK regime felt pressured to demonstrate the "genocidal crimes" of the Pol Pot clique. Already, Cambodia was caught up in a geopolitical maelstrom. While in control of the country, the new government, with massive Vietnamese support, continued to battle the remnants of the DK army, which began to regroup with international assistance. Large numbers of Cambodians had fled to the border, taking refuge in camps where hundreds of thousands of Cambodians would reside, some for more than a decade.

All this took place amid Cold War geopolitics, which often led to the obfuscation, minimization, and denial of the atrocities that had taken place in Cambodia during DK. On an international level, the United States and its Cold War allies viewed Vietnam's invasion of Cambodia as a further Soviet bloc expansion into Southeast Asia, one that also violated the principle of state sovereignty. This alarmed Association of Southeast Asian Nations (ASEAN) countries as well, particularly Thailand, which confronted a massive influx of Cambodian refugees and Vietnamese troops on its border. China, the longtime supporter of the Khmer Rouge, also regarded Vietnam's invasion as a threat, particularly given China's historical tensions with Vietnam and frosty relationship with the Soviet Union.

Cambodia became a key proxy site in which all of these tensions would play out. The United States, China, Thailand, and a number of western powers joined together not just to rearm and revitalize the Khmer Rouge, who had been soundly defeated by the Vietnamese troops, but to provide them with international legitimacy. At the United Nations, discussions about the "Kampuchea question" centered on the issue of Vietnamese withdrawal from Cambodia and who should be given Cambodia's seat at the UN—the deposed DK regime or the new PRK regime.

Legitimacy was the issue at the heart of this debate. On June 1, 1979, as debate about Cambodia's seat at the UN was intensifying, the PRK Foreign Ministry issued a long statement defending its legitimacy by noting all of the crimes and abuses perpetrated by the Pol Pot clique, which had created "the most savage gigantic slaughterhouse of our century. It was hell on earth."[38]

This PRK legitimacy narrative was closely bound to a framing of the violence as genocidal. On the one hand, Pol Pot's group was a "fascistic dictatorship . . . whose barbarism was unmatched in history" as they systematically violated "the most basic human rights" and "pushed the Kampuchean people to the brink of extermination."[39] On the other hand, the PRK regime and its "fraternal" Vietnamese comrades had liberated Cambodia from this genocidal scourge, an action that gave it legitimacy, both as a liberator and as a protector who could prevent the genocide regime from returning.

The geopolitical stakes became even more salient after the September 21, 1979, UN vote allowing Democratic Kampuchea to retain Cambodia's seat at the UN.[40] Two months later, the UN General Assembly passed a resolution calling for states not to intervene in Cambodian affairs and for all "foreign forces" to withdraw from Cambodia. These countries faced a quandary, as they effectively were granting international legitimacy to a genocidal regime, whose mass human rights violations were often hidden by euphemisms masking what had transpired. This practice continued until the 1991 Paris Peace Accords, which referred vaguely to preventing a recurrence of the "politics and practices of the past."[41]

With the "Kampuchea issue" firmly situated in a Cold War framework, the PRK regime would continue to use Tuol Sleng to highlight the genocidal acts committed by the Pol Pot faction. The Khmer Rouge, in turn, continued to deny these crimes by demonizing Vietnam and questioning the legitimacy of Tuol Sleng, including the evidence stored in the archive where Ong had worked.

Power, Silence, and Making History

While battles over historical truth take place in all countries, they are particularly fraught in postconflict situations where mass human rights violations have taken place. This is especially true when those violations are overtly minimized or denied by the perpetrators, as has been the case with former Khmer Rouge like Pol Pot and Nuon Chea in post-DK Cambodia.

The question of historical truth, as noted in the introduction, is directly linked to epistemology, an issue that anthropologist Michel-Rolph Trouillot discusses in his book *Silencing the Past*. Trouillot argues that silence and power enter into the production of history at four interrelated points: "The moment of fact creation (the making of *sources*) . . . fact assembly (the making of *archives*) . . . fact retrieval (the making of *narratives*) . . . [and] retrospective significance (the making of *history* in the final instance)."[42] At each of these points, certain things are foregrounded and others backgrounded in the narratives and histories that are being created.

The Tuol Sleng photo of Nuon Chea and other Khmer Rouge leaders at the airport illustrates these different moments. On the one hand, the photograph was created at a particular time during DK. One the other, it was incorporated into an archive, set in a narrative (a captioned photo at the museum), and placed in a historical narrative at Tuol Sleng (reflecting the larger PRK atrocity frame that structures the museum).

Power and silence inform these different moments. The Khmer Rouge delegation photograph was taken as part of a DK propaganda effort to assert the glory and success of the revolution, an image suggested by the smiles, the Mercedes limousine next to which the leaders are standing, and the fact that they are awaiting a foreign delegation from China, one of the most powerful countries in the world. This depiction erases the reality of the conditions on the ground during DK, which were far from glorious and remembered by survivors as a "prison without walls."

Some Tuol Sleng exhibition rooms feature checkerboards of black-and-white photographs of Khmer Rouge prisoners, many taken when they were registered on arrival at S-21. As Michelle Caswell has noted, silence and power operate in these photographs in ways ranging from the "mug shot" inscription of alleged criminality to the erasure of the many other prisoners who weren't photographed.[43] Caswell adapts Trouillot's framework to look at how the S-21 photographs have been created, archived, narrated, and historicized, a process that varies depending on the time, place, and actors involved.

Though only implicit in the first (Building A) exhibition of the cells where Dinh Phong and his team found the last prisoners executed at S-21, the PRK atrocity frame is visually asserted in the room where I am standing, the first in Building B. The exhibition panel in which the airport photo with Nuon Chea appears is labeled "Leaders of Democratic Kampuchea" and includes photos of Pol Pot and Duch, the head of S-21. Other panels focus on the 1975 Khmer Rouge takeover, collectivization and forced work, and death.

The key elements of the PRK atrocity frame are already in place: the genocidal and Nazi-like violence and suffering inflicted on the Cambodian population by Pol Pot and his allies during DK. There are many silences in the historical frame, which doesn't mention what transpired before Pol Pot and his allies arrived in Phnom Penh; the fact that many PRK leaders and current government officials, including Prime Minister Hun Sen, are former Khmer Rouge who fled the DK purges; and the reasons and paths that led Pol Pot and Nuon Chea to foment revolution. Instead, they are simply depicted as merciless perpetrators, in keeping with the politics of memory and legitimacy asserted by the PRK regime at the time of Tuol Sleng's construction. Nuon Chea's defense now focuses on such silences.

Many of the materials used to assert the PRK atrocity frame are stored in the Tuol Sleng archive, located on the second floor of Building B, almost directly above the room where I now stand looking at the photo of Nuon Chea and the other Khmer Rouge leaders. I spent much of the last month of my doctoral research there examining prisoner photos, cadre notebooks, and confessions.

I was especially interested in documentation related to Khmer Rouge cadre from the area where I conducted my fieldwork, "Banyan" village and districts near Kompong Cham city, which were part of Region 41 of the Northern (later reorganized into the Central) Zone during DK. One such cadre, Reap, was sent to S-21 and tortured after staging a failed rebellion amid the broader Khmer Rouge purges. There was little supervision in the archive as I flipped through piles of dust-covered confessions looking for related files, which I found and discuss in the book that is the focus of my ECCC testimony, *Why Did They Kill?*

My book on Duch's trial, *Man or Monster?*, also extensively draws on such Khmer Rouge documentation and takes up the issue of the silence and the production of history by examining the interrelationship of "articulation" and the redactions or silencings that inevitably ensue. The book describes how, during the process of interrogation and torture, the S-21 prisoners whom Nuon Chea helped oversee were forced to write confessions that accorded with the larger historical narrative the DK regime was asserting about a revolution threatened by Vietnam and a range of "hidden enemies burrowing from within." Silence and power operated to erase the complex biographies of the prisoners as their lives were transformed into standardized stories of revolutionary betrayal, which stood at the center of the DK historical narrative. This narrative is also being invoked by Nuon Chea's defense.

"Searching for the Truth"

My research for my book *Man or Monster?* drew, in turn, on archival materials gathered by the Documentation Center of Cambodia (DC-Cam), a local nongovernmental organization whose origins date back to the US 1994 Cambodian Genocide Justice Act, which provided funds to gather documentation that could be used in trials. Over time, DC-Cam discovered additional troves of documentation, including confessions, correspondence, meeting minutes, and photographs—as well as the photograph of Nuon Chea and the Khmer Rouge leaders at the airport, which had been part of a photo album belonging to a former DK official.[44] DC-Cam also mapped mass killing sites and interviewed former witnesses, perpetrators, and victims. As the ECCC began operation, DC-Cam transferred half a million pages of its archival documentation to the ECCC, which incorporated much of it into the court's database.[45] Given the scope and incriminating nature of this material, it has become a target for ECCC defense lawyers.

Although DC-Cam's work initially focused on gathering documentation, it quickly began undertaking related memory, justice, peace-building, and educational initiatives. In 2002, I became an academic adviser to DC-Cam and subsequently observed many of these initiatives firsthand, which included everything from artistic performances to mental health programs. DC-Cam also brought people from all over Cambodia to Phnom Penh, where they visited Tuol Sleng. Some, like Ong, found photos of their friends and relatives there.

As suggested by the center's magazine, named for its informal motto, "Searching for the Truth," a number of DC-Cam projects are aimed at helping people reclaim the stories of their family, relatives, and friends—or, to use Trouillot's language, to rupture the silences of the past.[46] For example, whereas previously the stories of S-21 prisoners—as materialized in their mug shots and interrogation records—had been framed in terms of first the DK counterrevolutionary narrative and then the PRK atrocity (and implicitly by post-DK Khmer Rouge denialist) narratives, they were now reappropriated by friends and relatives who provided context about the prisoners who had been previously erased. DC-Cam recorded these stories, which they sometimes published in *Searching for the Truth*.

DC-Cam has also worked with Tuol Sleng to provide some of the context that is stripped away by the original Tuol Sleng / PRK atrocity frame, in part by holding temporary exhibitions. A long-running DC-Cam–sponsored exhibition at Tuol Sleng, *Genocide: The Importance of Case 002*, provides basic background information about the Khmer Rouge leaders and the crimes of which they stand accused.[47]

An introductory message from Youk Chhang, the director of DC-Cam, emphasizes the importance of Case 002 because it is trying the most senior Khmer Rouge still living. "Many questions about [DK]," Chhang states, "have not been answered. These leaders have not admitted any responsibility for the crimes of that period but instead blame the lower cadre and others. Their trial offers an important chance to show that the DK regime made decisions that caused the deaths of nearly 2 million Cambodians." Chhang continues, "This case could provide answers to many questions that Cambodians have about the Democratic Kampuchea era, as well as an opportunity to bring some justice to the Cambodian people by punishing those responsible for their suffering and for the deaths of their loved ones."

A mulitpanel placard focuses on Nuon Chea. The first panel features a recent photograph of Nuon Chea, who stares back at the camera, head tilted with an eye half shut. Nuon Chea's facial expression is flat, as befits a man who prioritized rationality over emotion in the name of revolution—even if it meant suspect comrades and even family would be killed. And indeed, two of Nuon Chea's nieces and their husbands were sent to S-21 while Nuon Chea was supervising Duch.[48]

Another panel features an interrogation note about Ya, a longtime revolutionary and comrade of Nuon Chea. Because Ya "continues hiding his enemy lines and traitorous acts," Duch authorizes the interrogator "to employ hot torture methods for long periods of time . . . even if it may cause death." Along with the interrogation note, the panel includes a photo of Nuon Chea at court and pictures of a monk and a pagoda. During DK, a caption states, monks from the pagoda were forced to defrock and do manual labor as part of the larger Khmer Rouge assault on Buddhism, which was all the more striking since many Khmer Rouge, including Nuon Chea, had been Buddhists and lived in pagodas during their youths.

Another panel provides basic background on Nuon Chea and his alleged crimes. 'Nuon Chea was born on July 7, 1926 in . . . Battambang province," the panel begins. "He went to high school and took law classes in Bangkok, where he joined the Communist Party of Thailand. When he returned to Cambodia in 1950, he joined the local Communist Party and by 1960 he was a senior member." Nuon Chea, the panel continues, "held important positions including Chairman of the People's Assembly and Acting Prime Minister. He was the second most powerful member of the DK regime, after Pol Pot. It is believed that Nuon Chea was in charge of the DK regime's prisons, including S-21 (Tuol Sleng)."

Besides genocide, the panel states, Nuon Chea is charged with "'crimes against humanity' (murder, torture, imprisonment, persecution, extermination, deportation, forcible transfer, enslavement, and other inhumane acts) and 'war crimes' (willful killing, torture, inhumane acts, willfully causing great suffering or serious injury to body or health, willful deprivation of rights to a fair trial, unlawful confinement and unlawful deportation or transfer)." In addition, the text notes, Nuon Chea is "charged with homicide, torture, and religious persecution under the 1956 Cambodian Penal Code. He was arrested in 2007 and has been held in detention since then." The panel ends by naming Nuon Chea's lawyers, "Mr. Son Arun, who has experience defending Cambodians charged with serious crimes . . . and Mr. Victor Koppe," his Dutch international lawyer.

Son Arun defends a man accused of responsibility for the death of more than thirty of his family members.[49] "I became Nuon Chea's lawyer because I want to know the truth," Arun explained. "I want to know why so many people died."[50] Some Cambodians hate him for defending Nuon Chea. But he says he does so in the name of the law, even as he is careful not to publicly criticize the Cambodian government, fearful of retribution.

Victor Koppe has no hesitation. Nuon Chea's slender Dutch lawyer openly calls the ECCC a farce. While strained relations are common in international courtrooms, tensions are usually pushed behind the mantle of professional decorum. That veil has long since been lifted in this court.

Just this morning, before heading to Tuol Sleng, I read a magazine interview in which Koppe states he almost resigned because he was "close to a breakdown" and is extraordinarily frustrated with the court. Koppe singles out the Trial Chamber's French judge, who Koppe says is "on an active path to try to prevent

[Nuon Chea's] story being told." Ultimately, Koppe says, he decided to remain on the defense team after Nuon Chea pleaded with him to do so. Koppe also wants to "use the ECCC proceedings to tell [Nuon Chea's] story."[51]

Nuon Chea's History

It is a story Nuon Chea has been telling for years, one that mixes truth, lies, and denial. In it, he stands as a tragic hero, a man pursuing a righteous cause—liberating the poor and creating an egalitarian socialist state—that ultimately failed because of treachery and betrayal. He told parts of this narrative on the stand, and he had recounted it to a Cambodian journalist and genocide survivor, Thet Sambath, who established a relationship with Nuon Chea and interviewed him for over a decade, generating material that eventually resulted in a book and a film.[52]

Here as elsewhere, Nuon Chea frames his life story as a path toward enlightenment and Marxist-Leninist truth. It begins in 1926, when he was born into poverty in rural Battambang province. Nuon Chea was his mother's favorite and not particularly close to his siblings. A strong student, he was allowed to focus on his studies instead of working in the rice fields. He had few friends.

Nuon Chea said his ideological perspective was influenced by his childhood observations of French colonial oppression, ranging from taxation to corvée labor, as well as the devastation caused by moneylenders and his family's related massive debt. "The French treated Cambodians very badly," Nuon Chea claimed, "so [my] feelings of hatred and revenge started then."[53] He witnessed the arrogance of the rich and maltreatment of Cambodia's poor. He had firsthand experience as students from town looked down on him and even beat him.

His life took many twists and turns, especially with the onset of World War II and Thailand's seizure of Battambang province. This event opened a new path for Nuon Chea: he was able to finish high school in Bangkok, where he lived with monks, listening to sermons as time allowed. He took a new name to match his new Thai life, becoming "Rong Loeut."

Nuon Chea told Thet that he avoided girls and studied hard. After passing his exams, Nuon Chea gained admission to the University of Moral Science and Politics, later renamed Thammasat University, where he planned to study law. Thammasat was a center of activism, and Nuon Chea became embroiled in politics. He read Thai communist newspapers and participated in political meetings, sometimes giving speeches on French colonial oppression. He soon was just a step away from communism, even as he worked for the Thai Ministry of Finance and still was considering a career in law.

In 1950, Nuon Chea made his decision. With two paths before him, he chose revolution. He joined the Thai Communist Party and began formal political education. It was a moment filled with revolutionary possibility amid the rise of Mao and Ho Chi Minh in China and Vietnam. Cambodia's nationalist movement was growing and would lead to independence in 1953, though not by revolution. The country's communist struggle had barely begun.

Nuon Chea returned to Cambodia in 1950. He received political training in Vietnam even as he built networks and raised money to support the Cambodian revolutionary movement. To this end, Nuon Chea worked for a Chinese businessman before quitting after witnessing the immorality of bribery, drinking, and womanizing firsthand. The corruption he observed was widespread and included his relatives.

Nuon Chea, in contrast, wore old clothes and had few possessions—a symbol of his purity and revolutionary devotion. Like his childhood experiences of class inequality, Nuon Chea's observations of such moral decadence directly informed his later views about revolution and the need to create a "pure" society liberated from the temptations and immorality of capitalist materialism.

These views, which eventually coalesced in the DK party line, developed over time and in dialogue with other revolutionaries, including Pol Pot. So, too, did a third theme in Nuon Chea's account: suspicions about Vietnam, which grew into outright antipathy during DK. A key moment in this regard was the 1954 Geneva agreement signed in the wake of French colonial defeats in Indochina. The Vietnamese communists were granted control over the northern half of Vietnam, while Nuon Chea and other revolutionaries, who controlled significant portions of Cambodian territory, received nothing at the bargaining table.[54]

In addition to feeling betrayed, Cambodian revolutionaries worried that their Vietnamese counterparts primarily wanted to dominate a future communist Indochina at Cambodians' expense, instead of promoting solidarity among equals. The map of Indochina that Ong observed in Mai Lam's office suggests that Vietnam had long wanted to be first among equals, even if Nuon Chea mixed this partial truth with the lie that Vietnam wanted complete domination. Regardless, during the years to come, including the civil war that preceded DK, North Vietnamese forces played a key role in helping the Khmer Rouge seize power.

After 1954, the Cambodian revolutionaries sought to regroup amid a crackdown by Prince Sihanouk's new government. It was during this period, in 1955, that Nuon Chea first met Pol Pot. They grew close as they worked together, despite their somewhat different backgrounds and pathways to revolution. Born in 1925 to a moderately wealthy family in the countryside, Pol Pot had also observed the oppression of the poor.[55] In 1949, as Nuon Chea was undergoing his political awakening in Thailand, Pol Pot received a scholarship to study in Paris, where he learned about Marxism-Leninism and Stalinism, met friends who would become follow revolutionaries, and joined the Communist Party.

In early 1953, Pol Pot returned to Cambodia just as independence from France was achieved. He began to teach and foment revolution. He soon met Nuon Chea, and together with others, including Tou Samouth, a leading revolutionary who would later mysteriously disappear, they sought to chart a new path to revolution, one that would decrease their dependence on Vietnam.

And so, in the late 1950s the Cambodian revolutionaries sought to "analyze . . . the real nature of Kampuchea society" and formulate a set of guiding principles for the moment.[56] According to Nuon Chea, Pol Pot was tasked with analysis of the Cambodian political situation, while Nuon Chea examined the plight of the poor. They studied history and gathered information.

From September 28 to 30, 1960, the revolutionaries held a party congress at the Phnom Penh railroad station to formally promulgate the party line. On September 29, 1977, Pol Pot gave a speech commemorating this meeting, during which the revolutionaries established their political platform and leadership headed by Tou Samouth, Pol Pot, and Nuon Chea (Pol Pot would take over after Tou Samouth disappeared in late 1962).[57]

Only after extensive "scientific analysis," Pol Pot proclaimed to the nation, did the revolutionaries see that there were two main "contradictions" in Cambodian society. The first contradiction involved foreign imperialism, including Cambodia's state of military, economic, cultural, and social "semi-colonialism," especially in relationship to US imperialism. Partly in response to such foreign influences, the party line emphasized "independence, sovereignty, and self-reliance, in order to be masters of our own destiny, applying Marxism-Leninism to the concrete realities of Kampuchea."[58]

The second and more primary "antagonistic contradiction" was class based, involving the oppression of the poor by the rich and powerful. Though there were five classes (feudalists, bourgeoisie, petty bourgeoisie, workers, and peasants, who were further subdivided on a spectrum from rich to poor peasants), the main contradiction was between the exploitative capitalists and landlords and the peasants, who comprised 85 percent of the population.

This "life and death" contradiction generated hatred that historically had been "buried," in part due to Buddhist doctrine, which suggested that one's present life was the result of one's past actions. To rectify this situation, the revolutionaries needed "to arouse the peasants," especially the lower-middle and poor peasants, "so that they saw [the contradictions], burned with class hatred and took up the struggle."[59]

Khmer Rouge cadre began to build their base of support, especially in the countryside, where they lived with the poor as they "carried out agitation and propaganda among them about feudal and semi-feudal exploitation, and the exploitation by the merchants and the capitalists."[60]

More broadly, the Khmer Rouge often described the party line in terms of politics, organization, and consciousness. *Politics* referred to revolutionary ideology and corresponding propaganda ranging from slogans to formal education (for example, political tracts or stories that explained class oppression and contradictions and proper revolutionary stance).

These ideas were operationalized through proper *organization*, including management structure, following the chain of command, institutional practices (such as participating in criticism and self-criticism sessions), and the revolutionary transformation of the means, relations, and forces of production from capitalist to socialist, including collectivization and the elimination of private property.

Consciousness, in turn, involved the constant struggle to "forge" a proper revolutionary subjectivity, often expressed through the metaphor of "stance." Pol Pot's speech emphasized that "contradictions" remained "among the people because we all carry vestiges of our old class character, deep-rooted for generations." To "resolve" these reactionary traits, each person needed to continuously "struggle" to temper their consciousness through organizational practices such as "education, study, criticism and self-criticism, and periodic self-examination of our own revolutionary lifestyle."[61]

"Our line was right," Pol Pot stated in his 1977 speech, "and we applied it correctly" as they began to foment revolution following the 1960 meeting. As a result, by 1967, when the first armed insurrection took place, the "situation in the countryside had reached a new height, like dry straw in the rice fields" needing only "a small spark to set it on fire."[62]

If it offers insight into the Khmer Rouge rise to power, Pol Pot's speech provides only a partial account, a teleological narrative painting a picture of inevitable success, a revolution guaranteed to be victorious given the "all-seeing" party line.

The reality was more complicated, foregrounding certain historical moments while silencing others, to return to Trouillot's framework. For example, Pol Pot's history erased an alternative genealogy that linked the party's origins to the Kampuchean People's Revolutionary Party, which was founded in 1951 with the assistance of Vietnamese revolutionaries—an association that Pol Pot and his allies wanted to obscure as tensions with Vietnam had escalated and the two countries were on the brink of war.[63]

Pol Pot's speech also masked the group's much more circuitous path to power. At first, the revolutionaries had modest success in building their revolutionary forces.[64] A more immediate spark was provided by the Vietnam War, including carpet-bombing that devastated parts of the countryside, the arrival of foreign troops on Cambodian soil, and the degradation of the Cambodian economy.

The 1970 coup that led to the overthrow of Prince Sihanouk also galvanized their movement. Sihanouk responded by joining the Khmer Rouge in a united front, which greatly increased the revolutionary ranks after Sihanouk called for his rural "children" to fight the new Khmer Republic (1970–75), headed by his former general turned traitor, Lon Nol.

In 1970 and 1971, North Vietnamese troops took the lead in destroying the best units of the Cambodian army. By 1973, the Khmer Rouge controlled almost all the country with the exception of the urban centers, which were filled with refugees fleeing civil war violence and US bombing. The Lon Nol government was able to remain in power with US support until the Khmer Rouge took over on April 17, 1975, two weeks before the fall of Saigon.

They immediately launched one of the most ambitious projects of social engineering in history. Thet's film, *Enemies of the People*, captures this ambition in a segment that begins with a Khmer Rouge–era propaganda video depicting Cambodians, dressed in black, doing construction at a collective labor site as triumphant music plays in the background.

"Our project was to transform the nature of society," Nuon Chea explains in the segment, his voice nostalgic. "We did not allow private ownership of anything: land or factories or rice. All this came under collective control." His voice hardens as he complains, "But those who did not want change became set against us. Ours was a clean regime. A clear-sighted regime. A peaceful regime. That was our aim, but we failed because the enemy's spies attacked and sabotaged us from the start."[65]

In Nuon Chea's telling, this story of a glorious revolution achieved against the odds has a tragic end: a collapse caused by "hidden enemies burrowing from within" and the malicious machinations of "the crocodile," Vietnam. It dovetails with the historical truth the Khmer Rouge asserted even as their regime began to collapse. And it is a history premised on genocide denial, which Nuon Chea now places at the center of his ECCC defense.

Such forms of denial represent one of the most extreme forms of, to use Trouillot's phrase, "silencing the past." The victims of genocide are silenced in the first instance by their murders. This erasure is then doubled by the denial of their deaths and suffering. The Khmer Rouge, including Nuon Chea, have been engaged in this silencing for years. It began during DK, when the victims were taken away, killed, and buried in mass graves. Their relatives were often forbidden to mourn or even talk about the disappeared. Those who did risked their lives. After DK, the Khmer Rouge denied their mass murder by minimizing the numbers, blaming others, and claiming that torture and execution sites like Tuol Sleng were fabrications created with the help of the Vietnamese.

This is what Nuon Chea now argues in court. As I prepare to testify, the stakes are high because the court seeks to parse the truth and lies that underpin such denials. I will confront denial first during questioning by Nuon Chea's defense lawyer and then, in the dramatic conclusion to my testimony, during the face-to-face exchange with Brother Number Two.

2

ANTHROPOLOGICAL WITNESS

8:30 a.m., Thursday morning, March 17, 2016
(ECCC grounds, Phnom Penh, Cambodia)

"I swear to only tell the truth."

Palms pressed and raised in respect, I face the ECCC's tutelary spirit, the Lord of the Iron Staff, who stands above me on a pedestal. A court clerk has just enjoined him to preside over my oath ceremony. True to the spirit's name, the mustached and muscular figure raises a bludgeon in his right hand, ready to strike, while pointing an index finger at me with his left in warning. His eyes blaze blue, the color of the UN and a symbol of the court's hybridity. I hold three lit sticks of incense as an offering and sign of respect.

Most courts in Cambodia have a tutelary spirit before which witnesses swear oaths. Apparently, I am the first foreign witness to ask to do so at the ECCC, an anthropologist respecting a local practice. My request had resulted in some back and forth, after which it was decided I would both take a secular oath in court and swear an oath before the Lord of the Iron Staff before my testimony, which I am doing now.

I stand in the middle of a fenced courtyard where the greenish-gold statue of the spirit stands under a roofed enclosure, around which his energies are said to circulate. The detention center where Nuon Chea and the other defendants are jailed is just a dozen yards behind me. Opposite me stands the pale-yellow courtroom and, in the distance, the ECCC administrative building.

FIGURE 2.1. The Lord of the Iron Staff.

Photo courtesy of the ECCC.

The ECCC complex is located on a Cambodian military base, a choice that, though it provides security, immediately raised concerns about political interference.[1] Some also worried that the court would be distant from the population since the site is located on the outskirts of Phnom Penh, a forty-five-minute drive that can take twice that time during rush hour.

To beat the morning traffic, the ECCC sent a white SUV adorned with the ECCC logo to transport me to the court two hours before the 9 a.m. start of the day's proceedings. Before entering the ECCC compound, security officials inspected our vehicle, even checking the undercarriage for weapons or a bomb. After parking, I was led to a small witness support room on the bottom level of the court, which has mint-green walls and a cushioned bamboo couch and chairs. On one wall there is a diagram of a man in shorts, arrows pointing to different parts of his body to indicate where people experience psychosomatic distress.

Each morning before testifying, during lunch, and at the end of the day, I will sit in this room. When I asked what the rooms on the other side of the corridor are used for, a ECCC staffer paused, then replied, "holding cells." I wondered if Nuon Chea had already been transported to one of the rooms, where he spends his trial days as part of his unofficial boycott of the court. During the breaks I spend in the witness support room, I will often ponder what is going through his mind in the nearby cell.

Now, as I recite the oath before the Lord of the Iron Staff, the sun beats down on me. Though it is not even nine o'clock, the temperature rises rapidly, the air hot and humid, and I feel it more since I wear a dark suit. The stakes of the oath ceremony are high. It obligates me to tell the truth in "accordance with what I have personally seen, heard, know, and remember." The consequences of lying are dire. "If I answer falsely on any issue," I swear, "may all the guardian angels, forest guardians and powerful sacred spirits destroy me, may my material possessions be destroyed, and may I die a miserable and violent death."

The oath ends with an incentive. "But, if I answer truthfully," I finish, "may the sacred spirits assist me in having abundant material possessions and living in peace and happiness along with my family and relatives forever, in all my reincarnations." After finishing, I place the incense in a gold lotus-shaped vessel inside the enclosure. I will think of Lord of the Iron Staff often while testifying.

9:30 a.m., Monday morning, March 14, 2016, ECCC courtroom
(Trial Chamber questioning)

"It's time."

A court clerk pokes his head into the antechamber just outside the courtroom, where I had been led minutes before. I follow him through a side door and into the court. Bright lights and a blast of cold air hit me.

From the five-hundred-seat public gallery, I have observed many people enter the court. Now I am the object of the gaze. I glance at the cameras mounted high up on the courtroom walls, wondering which is streaming my entrance, recording my every move.

The parties are positioned in horseshoe form, the Trial Chamber judges on a raised dais at the front, defense to their left, civil parties and prosecutors to their right. Three enormous banners hang on the wall behind the judges: the Cambodian flag, the UN flag, and between them the court emblem, an ancient Angkorean figure holding a sword surrounded by olive branches, the UN symbol of peace.

The witness stand, which I will come to think of as "the hot seat," is situated in the back heel of the court near the public gallery, which is separated from the courtroom by a thick glass wall said to be bulletproof. Each day, the five hundred seats—upholstered, like everything associated with the tribunal, in UN blue—are filled mostly with Cambodians ranging from monks in saffron robes to villagers who have been bussed in.

Today, high school students from the countryside are also attending, white dress shirts striped by bright green ties. They sit chatting and laughing, relaxed and ready for today's courtroom show.

The seven Cambodian civil parties in the courtroom, in contrast, sit silently behind their lawyers. Their folding chairs are pressed against the court's black-tinted AV booth, which controls everything from the microphones to the four cameras mounted on the courtroom walls.

At the ECCC, civil parties participate directly in the proceedings, supporting the prosecution, testifying about their victimization, and seeking collective and moral reparations as they await judgment of the defendants accused of being responsible for their suffering.

And they have been waiting for years. Sometimes justice comes quickly, like the Nuremberg trials set up immediately to try Nazi leaders after the Holocaust or the international tribunals established to try crimes committed in Rwanda and the former Yugoslavia in the mid-1990s. But more often justice arrives late and is plodding.

This was certainly the case in Cambodia. As noted in chapter 1, geopolitics trumped justice during the 1980s. After a peace agreement and UN-backed election in 1993, prospects for a tribunal began to improve even as Hun Sen's government launched a national reconciliation campaign, including amnesties, to encourage Khmer Rouge to defect. Meanwhile, DC-Cam began gathering documentation that could be used in a trial.

It was only in the late 1990s, as the Khmer Rouge movement imploded and different factions and leaders defected, including Nuon Chea and Khieu Samphan in late 1998, that the possibility of a trial began to gain traction. Negotiations

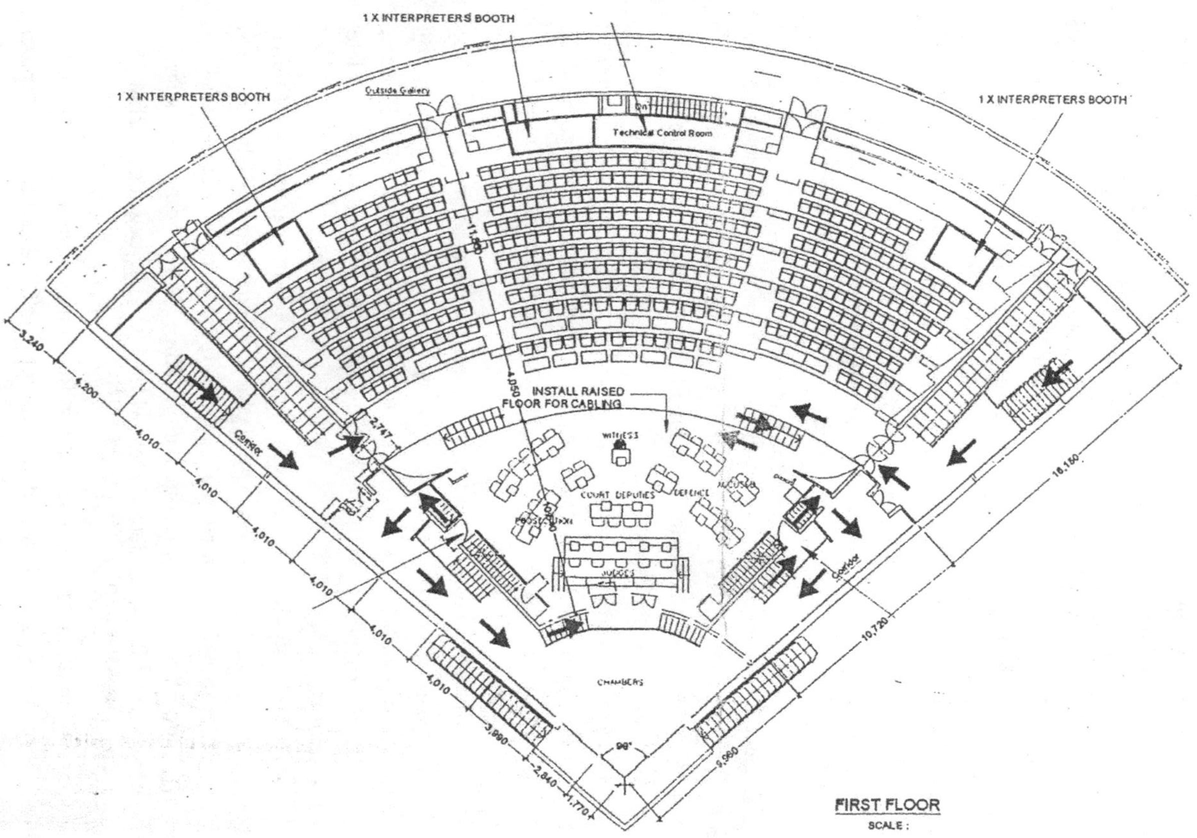

FIGURE 2.2. Diagram of the ECCC courtroom.

Source: ECCC Court Report, August 2008. Image courtesy of DC-Cam/SRI.

FIGURE 2.3. Judges of the Trial Chamber (back row, left to right): You Ottara, Ya Sokhan, Silva Cartwright, Nil Nonn (president), Thou Mony, Jean-Marc Lavergne, and Claudia Fenz.

Photo courtesy of the ECCC.

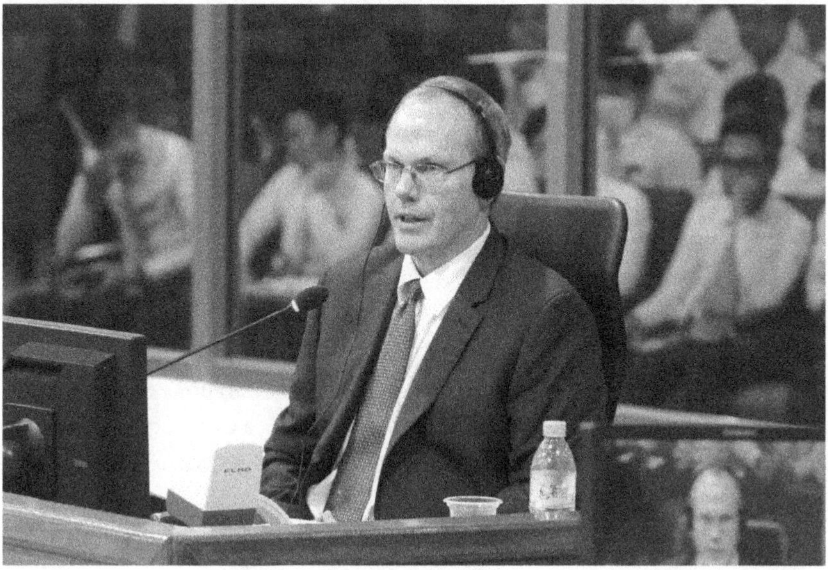

FIGURE 2.4. Expert witness Alex Hinton testifying at the ECCC, March 16, 2016.

Photo courtesy of the ECCC.

between the United Nations and Cambodia commenced but were slow and repeatedly verged on collapse. It was during this period that Sambath began his almost decade-long process of interviewing Nuon Chea.

In 2003, the Cambodian government and the United Nations finally reached a deal to establish the ECCC, an international hybrid tribunal.[2] This new model of global justice, mixing international and national personnel, was meant to address issues that had plagued the international tribunals set up in the mid-1990s. Hybrid courts were supposed to be cheaper and faster—and more directly involve victim populations. With them came a new set of problems, including accusations of inferior justice, political interference, and corruption. The ECCC was no exception.

The court's mandate is to try "senior leaders" and "those most responsible" for crimes committed during Democratic Kampuchea. Nuon Chea and Khieu Samphan were arrested in 2007 along with DK minister of foreign affairs Ieng Sary and his wife and DK minister of social affairs Ieng Thirith. Duch, who had been arrested in 1999, was also charged in 2007. His trial (Case 001) was held in 2009 and culminated in a life sentence.

Nuon Chea and the three other defendants were tried jointly in the court's second case, which was split into two parts. The first trial (Case 002/01), which focused on the Khmer Rouge evacuation of Cambodia's cities at the start of DK and subsequent forced relocations, began in late 2011. Ieng Sary died during the trial; his wife, Ieng Thirith, was declared mentally unfit to stand trial, then died in 2015.

Throughout the time I have been on the stand, the other surviving defendant in Case 002, Khieu Samphan, has sat so silently that I forget he is there until he rises for a bathroom break. Like Nuon Chea, Khieu Samphan, who served as DK head of state and studied in France prior to joining the revolution, is in his eighties. Both men could die at any moment. In the 2014 judgment in Case 002/01, these two former Khmer Rouge leaders were convicted of crimes against humanity. Now the second half of their trial (Case 002/02) is underway.

I look at the defense section and see the bespectacled Khieu Samphan sitting with his lawyers. Nuon Chea is nowhere to be seen.

As I approach the witness stand, I pause before the public gallery, press my palms and slightly bend my head, respectfully greeting the audience. The Cambodian students smile back at the odd foreigner observing a Cambodian practice.

The clerk helps me into my seat and slips headphones over my head.

Before the Law

"Good morning, Mr. Witness," the Trial Chamber president Nonn Nil begins. "Can you state your name?"

I gaze across the open well of the court at the judge.

Before I can begin, he holds up his hand, pauses me. Already, I have forgotten the clerk's instruction to wait until the red light on my microphone is illuminated before speaking.

President Nil asks some biographical questions: birthdate, nationality, address. "And what is your current occupation?" he continues. I reply that I am a professor at Rutgers University.

"The greffier reports that you took a Buddhist oath before the Lord of the Iron Staff," President Nil says, a bit surprised. "However, the Chamber is informed that you wish to take a secular oath as well." President Nil instructs a court clerk to administer it. I stand and repeat after her, "I solemnly swear that I will assist the Trial Chamber honestly, confidentially, and to the best of my ability." The oath feels perfunctory in comparison to the one I swore before the Lord of the Iron Staff.

"Mr. Expert," President Nil goes on, "the Chamber would like to thank you for the very long journey you have made to help this Court in its journey to ascertain the truth in this case in relation to matters of importance to this trial as well as to the Cambodian people."[3] There it is: the Truth. Immediately front and center at this international trial. Something contested. Something critical at stake.

President's Nil's brief remark speaks to profound issues at the core of the proceedings and my place within them. On the one hand, he is referencing the truth in relation to both the trial and the Cambodian people, a differentiation suggesting that while the court seeks truth as evidence of criminality, there is also explanatory truth seeking on behalf of the Cambodian people. My testimony speaks to both these goals.

On the other hand, ascertaining the truth is premised on epistemological assumptions, or claims about knowledge, including the reality that it reflects (the worlds examined and "known"), concepts through which it is filtered (analytical categories), and the ways it is accessed and assessed (methods).[4] In law, this epistemology is centered around alleged crimes that are assessed on the basis of rules of procedure and evidence. Depending on whether the "facts" that emerge during a trial fulfill the elements of the crime in question, the court renders a verdict, its determination of whether guilt has been proven.

Trouillot's model provides one way to think about these epistemological assumptions.[5] Whereas, as Trouillot argues, historical truth is produced through the making of sources, archives, narratives, and history, legal truth is produced through the making of sources, facts, narratives, and judgments. In law, data (information collected) is classified and organized into evidence (data supportive of facts or proposed to be true). This evidence is then tested in courtroom proceedings and, if verified, is deemed factual (units of verified data that have truth status).

These facts are then pieced together into legal narratives regarding the alleged crimes and incorporated into a judgment, the larger truth claim about innocence or guilt that can be considered the analogue of Trouillet's "making of history." Just as power and silence enter into the production of history, so, too, do they infuse the production of the judgment in similar ways. Some data is collected while other data is not. The organization of this data into evidence likewise involves making choices, as does the courtroom testing that establishes the facts that are selectively woven into the judgment. And, of course, the entire process is mediated by the epistemological assumptions of law (as noted above, the worlds examined, analytical categories, and methods) that generate truth claims.

Through his questioning, President Nil now seeks to draw out the epistemological assumptions that undergird my anthropological research, an issue that the prosecution and defense questioning will no doubt also explore as they examine, to adapt Trouillot's framework once again, my anthropological making of sources, facts, narratives, and ethnography. They will test the data, concepts, and methods that I used to produce ethnographic truth (researching and writing *Why Did They Kill?*) and that underpin my expert witness testimony—even as the Trial Chamber is the ultimate arbiter of any evidence I give and decision maker about how it bears on the legal truth they will produce in the judgment.

Anthropological Witness

"Mr. Hinton," President Nil asks, "please inform the Chamber of your academic background."

"I'm an anthropologist," I reply, knowing my disciplinary identity will be a target for the defense.

Anthropology. In the imagination of my students in the United States, it often conjures images of Indiana Jones and Lara Croft. When I walk into the first day of class, some half-expect me to be wearing an Indiana Jones fedora, satchel, and lumber up boots, and to tell stories about my digs in exotic places and dangerous encounters with remote "primitives." To overcome such misconceptions, I often provide a brief primer on what exactly the students will be studying and what cultural anthropologists do.

If anthropology can be loosely defined as the study of what it means to be human, I explain to my students, the discipline centers on knowledge-seeking about humanity across time and place. It does so with an array of analytical categories (culture, society, language, economy, social structure, evolution, biology, material artifacts, power, nature, and so forth) and methods, most of which are centered around fieldwork, or long-term, immersive, and onsite data collection.

Just as I do in class, I need to give a brief overview of anthropology and its epistemology here in court. Describing anthropology will not be easy to do. In addition to the time constraints, conceptual specificities, and preconceptions, there is also the issue of translation. Everything said in the court is translated into Khmer (the Cambodian language), English, and French—and many people involved in the proceedings speak other languages as well.

After discussion with colleagues, I have decided to give my testimony primarily in English, switching to Khmer if necessary, since English is my first language, the one in which I can be most precise, and also the one in which I anticipate the majority of my questioning will take place in this international hybrid court. I am also less familiar with Khmer legal vernaculars. Nevertheless, I pull one side of the headphones slightly to the side to monitor the Khmer, a language I have long spoken, in addition to French when used.

This strategy will prove important at points, particularly when we discuss a derogatory term used to refer to Vietnamese. But whichever language a speaker decides to use in court, there are translation challenges that all tribunals face. And indeed, I am currently working on a second book on the ECCC that has the running title "Justice in Translation" (it will become *The Justice Facade*) and discusses precisely this issue.

The word "anthropology" translates differently across linguistic and cultural contexts, including Cambodia. Indeed, the ECCC interpreter now translates my English "anthropology" with a gloss (*noreavitya*) that is unfamiliar to many Cambodians—including, most likely, the students and villagers in the public gallery—and doesn't convey the full sense of anthropology as practiced as an academic discipline in the United States. With these challenges in mind, I provide a quick overview of anthropology and its epistemology in court.

"As an anthropologist," I begin, "my concerns are somewhat different than those, for example, of a historian."[6] Historians, I explain to the court, are predominantly concerned with the study of the past, whereas anthropology involves the study of what it means to be human both in the past and the present and across time and space. The "four fields" of anthropology include archaeology, linguistic and biological anthropology, and my subfield, cultural anthropology, which explores lived experience and practice across time and place as well as the sociocultural views that inform them.

Anthropology, in turn, is holistic, seeking to approach a phenomenon from multiple angles ranging from history to cosmology and biology. To do so, most anthropologists undergo extensive language training, as I had done prior to going to the field. Another anthropological principle is cultural relativism, which involves trying, as much as possible, to suspend your own judgments while seeking to understand things as they exist in local terms. Anthropology is also comparative, seeking broader insights from what is discovered from in-depth and on-the-ground fieldwork research. To this end, part of my research focuses on comparative genocide studies, including the dynamics of mass violence and extremism.

Epistemology of an Ethnography

"Can you tell the court why you are interested in writing about the events that happened in Cambodia," President Nil asks, "particularly in relation to genocide?" Once again, his question opens larger issues about disciplinary epistemology—in this case, the formulation of research questions that inform data collection and analysis.

"Thank you, Mr. President," I begin. "You know, when I first came to Cambodia in 1992 as a graduate student, I thought that I would study a different set of issues. . . . [including] Cambodian conceptions of psychology," trauma, and emotion, all of which link back to the larger anthropological question of what it means to be human.

Indeed, I decided to attend Emory University's anthropology doctoral program in part because it focused on one of the less explored disciplinary interfaces that takes up this question, the intersection of cultural and biological anthropology. My decision was also informed by my interest in psychological anthropology, a subdiscipline of cultural anthropology that, like another subdiscipline I was also interested in, medical anthropology, explores issues of mind, self, body, society, and culture.

These interests informed my initial desire to center my doctoral research on conceptions of self and emotion in a country where Buddhism, which has elaborate theories of mind, is widespread. I had narrowed my choices to Tibet and Cambodia before choosing the latter country because of its history and greater accessibility, since Cambodia was just opening up as the Cold War ended and the peace process was underway, with UN-sponsored elections to be held in 1993.

In 1992, I went to Cambodia to conduct preliminary research and continue my language training in Khmer, building on two summers of Khmer language study at the Southeast Asian Summer Studies Institute. Another key part of anthropological fieldwork is gaining the ability to conduct research in the local language as part of an attempt to, as the early anthropologist Bronislaw Malinowski famously put it, "grasp the native's point of view, his relation to life, to realize *his* vision of *his* world."[7]

Of course, doing so is difficult, and over time, people increasingly came to question the extent to which this endeavor is possible and how best to conduct research given the challenges involved. The issue appeared repeatedly in the graduate classes I took prior to my initial 1992 visit to Cambodia. Postmodern, poststructuralist, and postcolonial studies were on the rise, leading to critiques of anthropological categories, epistemologies, and lack of reflexivity and attention to power and history. Bourdieu's practice theory was one attempt to create a middle road between these critical approaches and the more empirically oriented anthropological research advocated by Malinowski.

Although it was critiqued for not attending to issues like power and agency, symbolic anthropology was still strong in anthropology in the early 1990s, and it approached the attempt to "grasp the native's point of view" from a different direction. In a well-known article, Clifford Geertz sought to recast this anthropological endeavor as an interpretative act that tacked between "experience-near" local knowledge and the more "experience-distant" analytical concepts of the social scientist.[8]

If it was not possible to enter another person's subjectivity, then, it was possible to do an experience-near "reading" of culture through symbolic forms ranging from words to behaviors. Geertz illustrated this point in discussing how the experience-distant concept of the person differed across cultural contexts by analyzing the experience-near conceptions of the person in Java, Bali, and Morocco—which served as a point of contrast with the "Western conception of the person as a bounded unique, more or less integrated motivational and cognitive universe."[9] Along these lines, I initially planned to undertake an experience-near analysis of person, self, and emotion in Cambodia, including examination of trauma and the psychosocial impact of mass violence.

While these interests did inform some of my subsequent scholarship, the three months I spent in Cambodia in 1992 altered the focus of my doctoral research. The shift began the week I arrived in Cambodia. As I traveled to my Khmer language lessons at the university, I passed by the body of a woman lying dead in the road. She had been shot in the head. Guns were everywhere, and I saw or heard shots fired on a number of occasions. Later I noticed more subtle signs of violence, such as the bullet holes in the walls of the classroom where I was doing language training, a remnant of the Cambodian civil war.

But perhaps the most significant thing that shifted my research focus were the stories that people told me about their suffering under the Khmer Rouge. One of the most vivid was told over a meal. To further my language skills, I lived with a Cambodian family in the center of Phnom Penh. Power was erratic and the lights often went out at night, as happened one evening while I sat eating dinner with the family. It was pitch black and all I could hear was the clink of silverware as everyone continued eating their meal in the dark.

Suddenly, the father, who had been a Khmer Republic pilot, began recounting his experiences during DK. In the dark, I couldn't see him. I just heard his voice as he told me about his family members who had died or been killed and how he had suffered after his identity was revealed. He was interrogated and sent to a reeducation camp where many people perished.

Such experiences led me to shift the focus of my research to center on the sociocultural dimensions of the Cambodian genocide. On the one hand, the Khmer Rouge drew on Marxism-Leninism and Maoism, transnational ideological strands that deeply informed their policies, including their targeting of perceived "enemies burrowing from within." On the other hand, such ideologies are recast in terms of local knowledge and practices in particular localities. The Khmer Rouge use of Buddhist concepts to translate Marxism-Leninism provides one illustration of this point. My research sought to unpack such "ideological palimpsests" and other forms of knowledge through which violence on the ground was mediated.[10] The goal was not to reductively argue that "Cambodian culture" caused genocide, but to examine how local understandings and practices helped give violence, like all human behavior, shape and form in given contexts.

My project was influenced by three theoretical strands. The first was symbolic anthropology, with its interpretive and dialectical approach that tacked between, as Geertz had put it, experience-distant concepts (violence, genocide, ideology) and their experience-near glosses (local knowledge and practice). Second, my project was informed by cultural models theory, which sought to unpack the knowledge structures mediating human thought and behavior.[11] This perspective, which my adviser, the University of Chicago–trained anthropologist Bradd Shore, was teaching in Emory's doctoral program at the time, converged with other theoretical strands, including practice and structuration theory, that sought to account for, as Anthony Giddens put it, "the duality of structure."[12]

Finally, my research was influenced by Fredrik Barth's generative anthropology of knowledge. Barth taught the Emory doctoral methods class that informed my project and had recently published a related book, *Cosmologies in the Making*. In the course, we examined long-standing anthropological methods related to fieldwork, ranging from participant-observation to interviewing, and Barth spoke at length about how he examined local knowledge through a process of epistemic model construction and testing to validate his findings. This method provided a granular complement to cultural models theory, which is often undertaken at the level of discourse analysis.[13]

These different currents informed the epistemological assumptions of my project, which, in seeking to answer a research question about the sociocultural dimensions of genocide, made knowledge claims about a reality (for example, Cambodian society and the DK past) using a set of analytical categories (for example, genocide, cultural models, local knowledge, ideology, structure) and methods (for example, fieldwork, participant observation, discourse analysis, model testing, etc.)—all of which informed the ethnography I wrote with related truth claims based on this anthropological epistemology.

Methods

"Thank you," President Nil says after I describe my path to studying the Cambodian genocide and writing *Why Did They Kill?* "When did you start writing that book and what were the main issues? Could you tell the court about your research methodology and the sources upon which it is based?"

Sources and methods. I have observed ECCC defense lawyers repeatedly attack expert witnesses on this point. I start by providing more backstory to my book. After preliminary fieldwork in Cambodia in 1992, I begin, I returned to live in Cambodia from 1994 to 1995. The doctoral research I undertook served as the basis for my dissertation and its revised iteration as *Why Did They Kill?* This book, I tell the court, centers on two questions: "How does genocide come to take place . . . [and] what motivates someone to kill another human being?"[14]

I turn to methods. "I conducted [what] anthropologists call a multisited ethnography," I explain. I lived with a family in a provincial town while doing research, often commuting by moped to my rural village fieldsite, "Banyan," located in Kompong Siem district, which is part of Kompong Cham province. I selected Banyan in part because it was near a massive execution center where over twelve thousand people had been killed. When the Banyan villagers returned home after DK, they found mass graves in their fields and corpses stuffed in their wells.

As I would discover, many people from the area had been killed, especially in 1977 when the Khmer Rouge carried out a massive purge overseen by cadre from the Southwest Zone who had replaced local officials. These new cadre included Grandfather An—another ECCC suspect who was the head of Kompong Siem district when much of the killing took place—and Grandmother Yit, who was said to have been so ruthless and committed to the Khmer Rouge that she killed her husband to demonstrate her loyalty to the regime.

In my research, I continue, I used traditional ethnographic methods. I undertook an initial survey, visiting every household in Banyan and collecting data that included information about their DK experiences. I also conducted numerous interviews, including repeated in-depth interviews with a handful of key informants from Banyan who would be featured in my book. To further understand lived experience and practice, I go on, anthropologists engage in participant observation, a method that involves observing and being part of everyday life in a fieldsite to discover what happens outside the context of a formal interview or survey.

And, of course, I note to the court, I carried out research according to university human subject protocols meant "to protect the human rights and confidentiality of our sources." In the United States and other countries, universities like Rutgers have elaborate research requirements, including a review process that must be completed prior to doing field research. These requirements include being transparent, informing interviewees about the focus of a research study, offering the option of anonymity, and obtaining consent.

There are a variety of factors behind the emergence of human subject protections, including the Nazi medical experiments that led to the Nuremberg Codes, institutionalizing the principle of research subject consent.[15] In the United States, outrage over the 1932 to 1972 Tuskegee Study of Untreated Syphilis in the Negro Male was a key factor in the promulgation of the 1974 National Research Act, which laid the groundwork for contemporary human subject protocols, including confidentiality codes requiring consent before revealing a source. It was for this reason that, when the court first approached me about testifying, I replied that I would be unable to reveal most of my sources, especially former cadre and perpetrators.

I know the defense will use this constraint to their advantage, seeking to undermine my testimony by arguing that my sources are unverifiable. Controversy will emerge, in particular, over a cadre I interviewed who had worked at a subdistrict office and been privy to orders targeting, among others, Muslim Chams and ethnic Vietnamese. My interview with this person was among a range of research data I gathered during my doctoral fieldwork that supported the charge of genocide.

"Epistemological Hypochondria" and Public Anthropology

"Thank you," President Nil tells me when I have finished. "And perhaps this is my last question. Can you tell you tell the Court why you decided to choose the title of your book, *Why Did They Kill?*"[16]

"I selected the title because it addresses directly the concerns of the book," I reply. But it was also a question, I go on, that I have heard Cambodians ask, "many, many times." Their question became my question. *Why?*

On first glance, the sort of explanation I offered in *Why Did They Kill?* would seem like a straightforward exercise in bringing the insights of anthropological research to bear on major public issues like genocide. At the time, however, the epistemological foundations of anthropology were being interrogated from a number of directions, including the aforementioned critiques from scholars with postmodern, poststructuralist, and postcolonial orientations. Some critics questioned the correspondence between anthropological findings and objects of study. Others lambasted the field's enmeshments with power and neocolonialism. Still others disavowed the concept of culture and attacked analytical essentialism.

Other scholars pushed back on the growing epistemological skepticism, particularly given the conflicts that broke out after the Cold War, including mass violence in Rwanda and the former Yugoslavia. In an article titled "The Trouble with Truth," for example, Richard Wilson inveighed against the widespread "epistemological hypochondria" of anthropology, which had too often led to silence on such topics of urgent public concern and, in the extreme, can paralyze the ability of scholars to respond to issues like Holocaust denial.[17]

Wilson argued that although critique was important, it was nevertheless possible to test and assess the validity of anthropological truth claims and thereby bring the knowledge gleaned through fieldwork research to bear on urgent public topics, including international justice. Coming from a political and legal anthropology perspective, Wilson's argument converged with a growing call for anthropologists to grapple more directly with public issues, an endeavor referred to as "engaged anthropology," "public ethnography," or most often, "public anthropology."[18]

Public anthropology, as I discuss in this book's introduction, is more of an orientation than a discipline, though there are books, conferences, degrees, literatures reviews, and now even a journal focused on it. When I was a graduate student at Emory, several scholars had this public anthropology orientation and sought to bring critical anthropological insights to bear on major public issues in ways that reached audiences beyond academic anthropology. The biological anthropologist and doctor Mel Konner, for example, was recognized for this sort of work as he wrote and spoke about the human condition. Fredrik Barth and his spouse, the anthropologist Unni Wikan, could likewise be placed under this umbrella and were recognized as major public thinkers in their home country, Norway.

Indeed, they might be characterized by the broader term "public intellectuals," which refers to scholars who are more widely recognized voices on topics of public concern, as reflected by their writing of books, essays, and now social media posts that are widely read and provide related commentary in the media. But only a small number of public anthropologists reach the point of being recognized as major public intellectuals.

There are a variety of scales for public anthropology, then, and such engagements are undertaken in ways large and small. In a sense, teaching and mentorship are acts of public anthropology. So, too, is work done with institutions, such as nongovernmental organizations, which seek to address social problems. Paul

Farmer's nonprofit organization, Partners in Health, is exemplary in this regard, but there are many other examples—even if public anthropology is more recognizably carried out in broader public modalities such as op-eds, blogs, media interviews, essays, and books.

I have also sought to undertake public anthropology in a variety of related ways. Beyond writing and speaking in the public domain, I continue to serve as an academic adviser to the Documentation Center of Cambodia (DC-Cam) and to direct the Center for the Study of Genocide and Human Rights. *Why Did They Kill?* was also written in part as a work of public anthropology and appeared in Robert Borofsky's new University of California Press book series on public anthropology.

My subsequent research has been informed by additional conceptual approaches (for example, Holocaust and genocide studies, law and society, political and legal anthropology, global studies, transitional justice, literary anthropology, race studies, and even graphic narratives), and it has also been increasingly influenced by critical theory. In this regard, and as I note in the introduction, Adorno's "Education after Auschwitz" always serves as a reminder of the centrality of ethics and public engagement to even highly theoretical scholarship such as that of the Frankfurt school.

Finally, and as I also underscore in the introduction, my testimony at the ECCC is another example of anthropological engagement, reflecting my commitment to contribute to the process of justice and explain the origins and dynamics of genocide in a very public forum. For me, the "public" of public anthropology suggests a movement from an insular position ("private" in the sense of singular or restricted, including something restricted to an insular academic community of anthropologists) to one that is open and expansive (in the sense of moving beyond the restricted community boundaries).

In this regard, I am influenced by Hannah Arendt, who critiqued philosophers, including her mentor Martin Heidegger, for retreating from the public sphere, a move that helped pave the way for totalitarian states to atomize society. For Arendt, scholars have an obligation to express their ideas in public, where they can be tested, challenged, and contribute to the vitality of the public sphere. Such engagement is also an essential part of being a thoughtful person, a quality that she spent years ruminating on after attending the trial of the infamous Nazi bureaucrat Adolf Eichmann, who, she argues, epitomized the "thoughtlessness" that enables totalitarianism.[19]

Such dynamic notions of "public" contrast with the more static stereotype of "public" as a national community including those who are active in the public sphere or who watch television and read books, newspapers, and social media posts related to issues of public concern.[20] A more productive way to think of "public" is in terms of different audiences and scales. In this sense, my testimony is addressed to a variety of publics, including international (such as legal personnel, scholars, and members of the international community invested in the tribunal) and domestic communities (ranging from the Cambodian students and survivors observing my testimony in the public gallery to the Banyan villagers and others whose stories inform my research and remarks in court).

If President Nil's question about my reasons for titling my book *Why Did They Kill?* speaks directly to my public anthropology concerns with providing explanation, then, it also raises issues related to the larger scholarly context in which my book was written, including my academic training and related debates in anthropology about epistemology and explanation. The questioning that follows will echo these debates.

The prosecution and civil parties seek anthropological insights about the genocidal process and how Khmer Rouge policy impacted Cambodian society and everyday life. The defense, in turn, challenges my truth claims and the validity of my anthropological findings, methods, and sources—even as these debates are informed by legal epistemology and logics that diverge from those of anthropology and the explanatory epistemology of my book. The first round of debate begins as President Nil now gives the floor to the ECCC's deputy international co-prosecutor, William (Bill) Smith.

3

THE GENOCIDAL PROCESS

Monday mid-morning, March 14, 2019, ECCC courtroom

Bill Smith slowly rises, then jokes, "Professor Hinton, again, thank you for coming so far and not going back to America when you saw the binders of material that Prosecution and defense counsel and civil parties asked you to review."

Whereas Victor Koppe, Nuon Chea's international defense lawyer, is quick and agile, speaking rapidly to make his point, Smith is tall and thick-framed, soft-spoken even as he presses his arguments with the patience of a police investigator, his first career in Australia. Later, he turned to work on international human rights and justice, spending a decade at the International Criminal Tribunal for the former Yugoslavia and working in East Timor.

"You're going to be in this Court for quite a while," he adds. "I think for about three, three and a quarter days." Noting that I had told the Trial Chamber that *Why Did They Kill?* takes up the frequently asked question about why Khmer killed Khmer, he asks if it also considers why "Khmer killed Cham or Khmer killed Vietnamese?"[1]

He cuts straight to the heart of the trial's most symbolically loaded component: the genocide charge. The court, of course, is using the UN legal definition of genocide, which is restricted to certain sorts of destructive acts, ranging from killings to child removals, perpetrated against specific groups of people ("a national, ethnical, racial or religious group, as such").

There is a glaring absence: political groups. And indeed, "political and other groups" had been included in an initial 1946 UN resolution before being dropped in the final 1948 UN Genocide Convention. Raphael Lemkin, the person who coined the term "genocide" in 1944, likewise included political groups in the purview of his definition of the word. The same is true of lay understandings of genocide, which usually view it as the mass murder of a group.

The majority of people the DK regime killed were political and class enemies. Thus, there is no easy path to a genocide conviction for these deaths, even if a Cambodian judge will later make the case in a dissent.[2] It can come vicariously from the charge that the Khmer Rouge targeted ethnic Vietnamese and Muslim Chams, protected ethnic and religious groups under the UN convention. Of course, the defense contests this allegation. To explain my use of "genocide" in *Why Did They Kill?*, then, I need to tell this backstory about the origin of the term.

"Thank you," I begin. "It's a big question." My book does take up the targeting of ethnic Vietnamese and Chams, I explain, groups that were clearly targeted in the region around Banyan village as well. Nevertheless, in genocide studies and colloquial speech, I note, genocide is defined more broadly to refer to the destruction of "a group because of who they are."[3]

"As I'm sure you know," I continue, "the term 'genocide' was coined by Raphael Lemkin in 1944 . . ."

"Please hold on, Mr. Expert," President Nil stops me. Koppe, Nuon Chea's defense lawyer, is on his feet. It is the first of many interruptions, a key tactic of the defense. "You have the floor now, Victor Koppe."

"Already quite quickly," Koppe complains, "we are entering the debate as to what defines genocide. As we are all aware . . . 'genocide' is, at least in this courtroom, primarily a legal term." My comments, he adds, raise "what possibly could be the most contentious legal dispute within the realm of the second trial."[4] This is not a classroom, Koppe adds. "We are in a court of law. And there the word 'genocide' has a specific meaning."[5] Can we have some guidelines about the use of the term?, Koppe implores.

There are more exchanges. Smith has his say. Then the judges rule. Judge Claudia Fenz, from Austria, suggests that a "middle way" forward is to focus on whether certain facts "might or might not constitute genocide." By focusing on the facts, she suggests, "you should be able to avoid the word 'genocide.'"

Already, a legal epistemology very different from anthropology is on display, one that filters facts through the analytical categories of law and assesses their evidentiary weight in making a determination of criminality. In this juridical context, I am being asked to speak in a manner that accords with these logics by not using the term for a crime in question. From my vantage, it seems like censorship.

This courtroom moment is a first glimpse of the juridical logics that shape and constrain what I am able to say, even as I also have agency and latitude to make my points and offer explanation within these parameters. The degree of latitude is informed by a number of factors, including the court rules, individuals involved in the proceedings, and relationships that develop between these actors on the courtroom floor. And it was concern about issues like the extent of this latitude that led historian Henry Rousso to refuse to testify.

The Construction Team versus the Wrecking Crew

Smith and Koppe began arguing about my testimony before I even took the stand. The first battle was over my expertise, and it started with early skirmishes carried out through initial motions. In some respects, the prosecution and defense are like a construction team and a wrecking crew. Following a carefully engineered plan to prove criminality, the prosecution builds its case, piece by piece, linking facts to charges. The job of the defense, in contrast, is to punch holes in this edifice by presenting alternative interpretations, deploying the strategy of "rupture," and challenging evidence, including that given by witnesses like me.[6]

In Case 002/02, the prosecution argues that Nuon Chea and Khieu Samphan were part of a Khmer Rouge joint criminal enterprise that committed a host of crimes while implementing five policies: forced population transfers; coerced labor and enslavement in cooperatives and worksites; the operation of security and execution centers; forced marriage and rape; and the targeting of specific groups including those subject to genocide—Vietnamese and Muslim Chams.[7]

To prove their case, the prosecution draws on a wide range of evidence. Much of it is documentary. I know this all too well from the tens of thousands of pages of documentation I had been given on a thumb drive a week before I took the stand, with the explanation that the documents might be brought up in court. Faced with an impossible task, I hurriedly reviewed the materials: DK telegrams, reports, speeches, meeting minutes, radio broadcasts, and publications like the party magazine *Revolutionary Flag*, which included ideological tracts Nuon Chea likely penned.

Certain documents are critical to the prosecution's attempt to prove that, while carrying out their joint criminal enterprise, the Khmer Rouge leadership exercised highly centralized, top-down control.[8] The Communist Party of Kampuchea (CPK) party statutes, for example, both highlighted key ideological principles and stipulated a strict, hierarchical decision-making and reporting structure. A March 30, 1976, Central Committee memo, in turn, invests four groups with "the right to smash [enemies] inside and outside the ranks." Still other documents are more granular, such as confessions and prisoner lists.

FIGURE 3.1. Cambodians working on an irrigation project, the "January 1" Dam, Chinith River, Kompong Thom province, 1976. This image is thought to have been taken by a Chinese photographer during a visit by DK minister of social affairs Ieng Thirith, who died while on trial at the ECCC.

Photo courtesy of DC-Cam/SRI.

FIGURE 3.2. A Khmer Rouge wedding.

Photo courtesy of the DC-Cam Archives/SRI.

Witness testimony provides another key source of evidence. In Case 002/02, 185 people will take the stand, including 114 witnesses, 63 civil parties, and 8 experts. Many witnesses are former Khmer Rouge, including some who worked directly under the Khmer Rouge leadership. Some of the most emotional moments in the trial have been when victims testified.

I have known some of the civil parties for years, including Bou Meng, the S-21 survivor whose Case 001 testimony I observed firsthand. At one point, Bou Meng had pleaded with Duch, the head of S-21 prison, to tell him where his wife had been killed; Bou Meng wanted to perform a ceremony for the spirit of his wife, who haunted his dreams. As Bou Meng made this plea, he and Duch broke down in tears. Other moments were more stark, such as when Bou Meng described how Duch's interrogators beat, whipped, and tortured him until he confessed.

Expert witness testimony is more distanced. The court specifies, "The role of expert witnesses is to enlighten the Chamber on specific issues of a technical nature, requiring special knowledge in a specific field."[9] In my initial correspondence with the court, I was told my testimony might touch on anything from "the history of the CPK; the origins and evolution of CPK policies towards the Vietnamese and Buddhists; the implementation and evolution of these policies during the DK period; use of CPK and DK propaganda and language generally in the context of genocidal violence; perpetrator motivations; and the Operation of S-21 Security Centre."[10]

Smith and Koppe will debate issues large and small related to my testimony, and four subjects loom large: my expertise, especially as it bears on the centralization of DK control; incriminating evidence that emerged during my anthropological research; the concept of genocide and the genocidal process; and DK hate speech and incitement. The first dish to be served up is my academic reputation, a shining star for the prosecution, a target for the defense's wrecking ball.

The Bedrock of Expertise

Smith knows that the defense will be on the attack, questioning my expertise, undermining my research, and challenging my sources. His questions, he tells me, will touch on three areas: perpetrator motivation, "universal factors" and the local dynamics of mass killings, and the targeting of ethnic Vietnamese.

But first, Smith says, nonplussed by Koppe's interruption, which is nothing new, he wants to discuss my "experience in genocide studies."[11] He needs to build a bedrock of expertise to help ward off the defense team's battering ram.

"When did you start to focus on the area?" he asks.

"Thank you, Mr. Lawyer," I reply. "When I began my doctoral studies, I don't think I even knew there was a field called 'genocide studies.' . . . But I soon came to realize that, to understood what took place in Cambodia . . . it was necessary to gain a broader knowledge of the dynamics of these processes of genocide and mass violence," which were also evident in Rwanda and the former Yugoslavia at the time.

Around 1996, as I was finishing my dissertation, I note, I joined the International Association of Genocide Scholars, and since that time I have been "quite immersed in genocide studies," even if I am often "the only anthropologist sitting in the room" at related events. Indeed, although anthropologists had carried out important work on the genocide of indigenous peoples, they had largely ignored the topic of genocide, including the Holocaust. I sought to help bridge this gap through my work and the publication of an edited collection and reader on the anthropology of genocide.[12]

Although Lemkin had long ago conducted genocide studies research, the field only began to emerge in the late 1970s and early 1980s. The origins of the field were partly intertwined with Holocaust studies, which had begun to coalesce a decade earlier—in part linked to the influence of the Eichmann trial and new interest in trauma and memory—and which some scholars felt was too narrow and needed to be studied in conversation with a broader range of cases, including contemporary and future ones.[13] In this sense, and echoing its "founding father" Lemkin, the field has long had a concern with prevention and activism, though this latter current would recede as the field matured through the 2000s.[14]

The field is highly interdisciplinary, including scholars from the humanities and social sciences who bring different disciplinary methods to bear on their shared analytical categories (genocide and associated concepts like state, identity groups, perpetrator, victim, intent, the Holocaust, and atrocity crimes) and the violent realities falling under this conceptual umbrella. While epistemological methods vary, much genocide studies research is undertaken directly or indirectly with an eye on comparison.

This concern dovetails with the comparative concerns of anthropology even if anthropologists often tack between, as Geertz put it, the experience-near focus of ethnography and the experience-distant purview of comparison. Smith is well aware that the defense will focus on the former, seeking to dismiss my findings as those of "just an anthropologist," so Smith wants to also emphasize the latter—the comparative and interdisciplinary genocide studies aspects of my research, including the explanatory framework I offer in *Why Did They Kill?* that is a key focus of his questioning.

Smith's inquiry about my genocide studies background is part of his larger effort to highlight my academic expertise. Brick by brick he does this credentializing.

My degrees. My positions held. Keynotes given. Positions on boards. Number of books and publications. And especially my work in comparative genocide studies: former president of the International Association of Genocide Scholars, director of the Rutgers Center for the Study of Genocide and Human Rights, position as UNESCO Chair on Genocide Prevention. And so forth.

But the stage is set: "Expert anthropologist and comparative genocide scholar" or "just an anthropologist" who worked in a remote village and was unable to see the big picture. Koppe will hammer my credentials. Nuon Chea will try to finish the job.

Monday, late morning, March 16, 2017, ECCC Courtroom (prosecution questioning)

"You state in your book that there are common universal macro factors that often appear in countries where there's systematic mass violence and killings," Smith begins, opening his main line of questioning for the day. To prove the charges, the prosecution needs to demonstrate that the DK violence was centralized and systemic, echoing dynamics manifest in other cases of genocide and mass violence. Smith wants to draw on my expertise in anthropology and comparative genocide studies to make the connection—and to provide an answer to the question Cambodians like civil party and S-21 survivor Bou Meng still ask today: *why?*

"Can you summarize [your] thesis?" he goes on.[15]

The Genocidal Process

"It's a big question," I begin, glancing down at several images I brought and have spread out on the small desk in the witness stand. A copy of the DK national emblem signifies the regime's grand designs and centralized control. To remind myself of the suffering these designs caused, I have a copy of Bou Meng's portrait of himself and his wife standing blindfolded before the gates of S-21. The third image is the cover of a S-21 prisoner confession annotated by top Khmer Rouge leaders. It highlights that there was a chain of command and criminal responsibility.

I provide a first quick summary, which Smith will seek to clarify throughout the day. The genocidal process varies, I explain, but if we look at cases like the Holocaust, the Armenian genocide, Rwanda, and Cambodia, ones that have a strong ideological element, a cluster of shared dynamics is evident.

The first is political and socioeconomic upheaval, usually linked to domestic strife or open war. World War I in Ottoman Turkey. World War II for the Nazis.

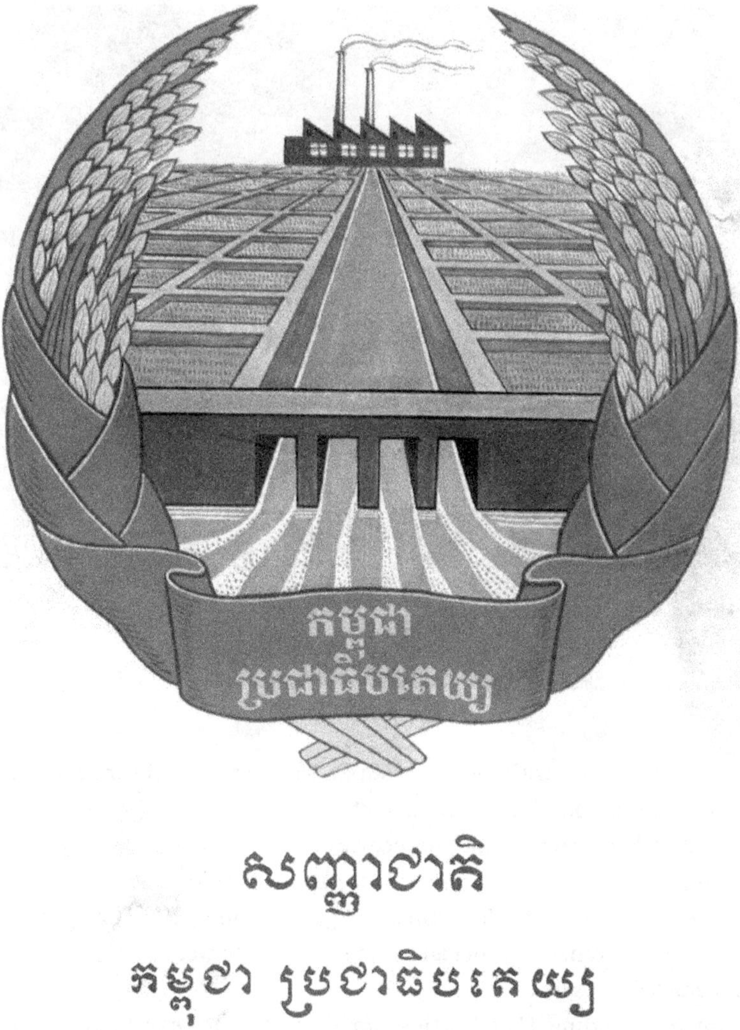

FIGURE 3.3. "The national emblem consists of a network of dikes and canals, which symbolizes modern agriculture, and factories, which symbolize industry. These are framed by an oval garland of rice ears, with the inscription 'Democratic Kampuchea' at the bottom" (DK Constitution, Article 17).

Image courtesy of DC-Cam/SRI.

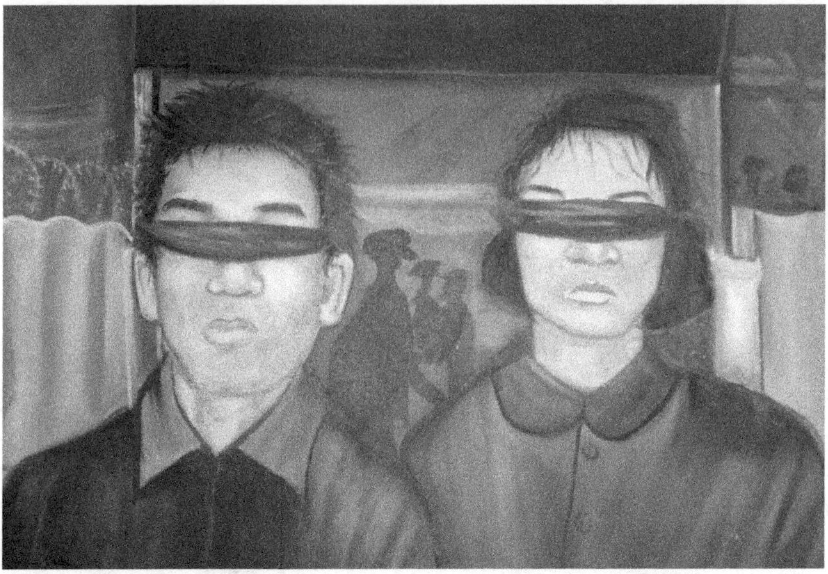

FIGURE 3.4. Bou Meng and his wife blindfolded before the gates of S-21, in a painting by Bou Meng.

Image courtesy of DC-Cam/SRI.

Simmering tensions with the Rwandan Patriotic Front in Rwanda. In Cambodia, civil war, US bombing, and the Vietnam War.

Amid such upheaval, I continue, people become more receptive to propaganda that promises a simple and clear vision for a better world, ranging from the German *volk* community to the Khmer Rouge party line. This "blueprint" is the second prime. "When a genocidal regime comes to power . . . ," I continue. Then President Nil stops me.

Koppe is standing. He takes the floor, disrupting my explanation, as he will do the rest of the day. "Thank you, Mr. President." He starts. "Slowly but steadily we are slipping into the—I believe a very careless use of the word 'genocide,' 'genocidal regime.'"

Then, suddenly, he announces, a first warning, "my client downstairs [is] quite upset with things he heard from his holding cell—as a matter of fact, he wanted to come up." The possibility Nuon Chea might actually appear never crosses my mind.

"'Genocide,'" Koppe argues, should only be used in a "very restrictive" legal sense, and a broader analysis of genocide is "way outside the scope of the expertise [of] this expert."[16]

"Perhaps we can talk about 'mass violence' or 'systematic killings aimed at particular groups?'" Smith offers in turn.

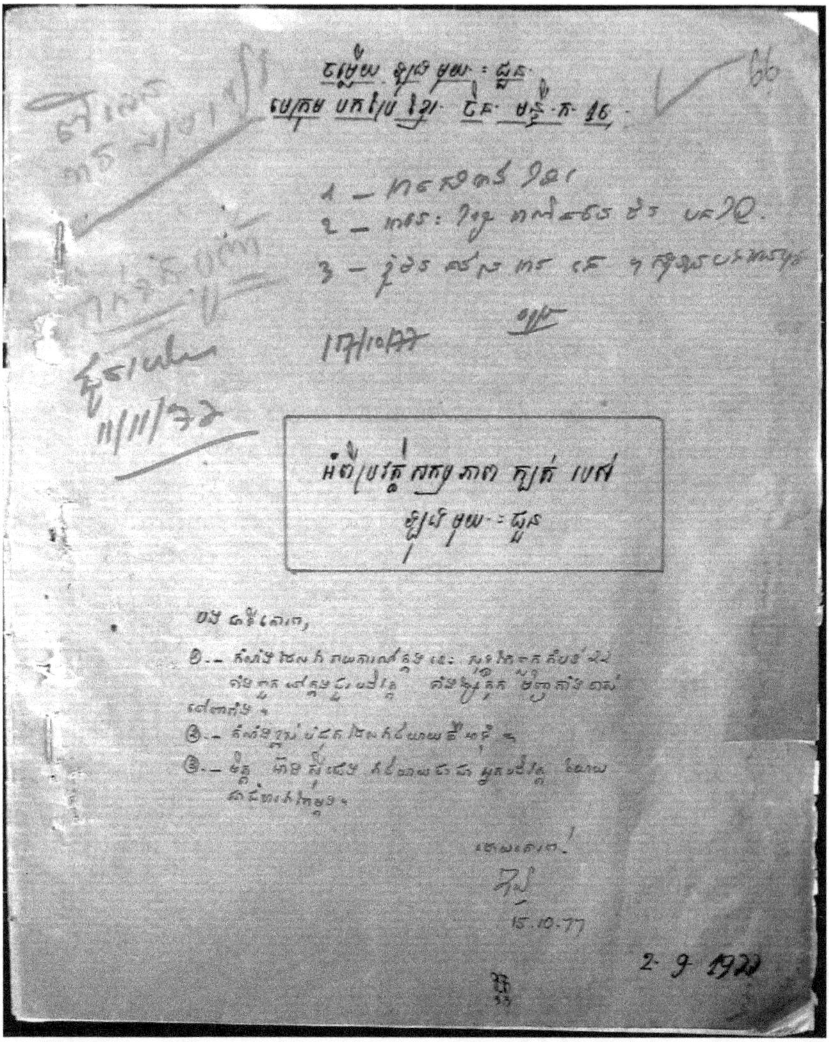

FIGURE 3.5. The annotated cover sheet of Long Muy's forced S-21 confession, one of many used as evidence at the ECCC. This one demonstrates the chain of command and centralized control of the DK regime and, according to Duch, the commandant of S-21, includes annotations by himself, his superior Son Sen, and Pol Pot (the checkmark at the top).

Image courtesy of DC-Cam/SRI.

"It's somewhat difficult," I reply, "if I'm referring to a process of genocidal priming, not to use . . . the word 'genocide.'" Not doing so, I add, would also be a form of self-censorship.[17] And indeed, this is the sort of restriction that Rousso feared would make it impossible for him as an academic to participate in this sort of courtroom proceeding.

There's silence, then Smith resumes, reading an excerpt from my book: "While each genocide has a distinct etiology that resists reduction to a uniform pattern, many are broadly characterized by a set of primes and make the social context in question increasingly hot."[18]

These include, Smith continues to read, "socioeconomic upheaval, deep structural divisions and an identifiable target group, structural change, effective ideological manipulation, a breakdown in moral restraints, discriminatory policy changes, and an apathetic response from the international community." He finishes, "As these and other facilitating processes unfold, genocide becomes increasingly possible."[19] How does the genocidal process proceed? I'm read an answer I already penned.

Vernaculars of Genocide

Smith turns to local factors, another piece of my book's argument that ideology has to be translated into terms that resonate for a movement's followers. I caution the court that it is important to avoid culturally determinist arguments, even as all ideologies must be translated in ways that resonate with everyday life and practice.

I offer an example. Abstract Marxist-Leninist theory alone made little sense to a rural Cambodian population. Accordingly, Pol Pot and Nuon Chea spent several years studying conditions in Cambodia before forming a party line that would resonate with peasants. Using familiar idioms and sometimes Buddhist language, Khmer Rouge political education focused on how the poor were exploited and oppressed by the wealthy and the capitalist system that sustained their power. The poor, they told their followers, had a "class grudge" against the rich, who deserved their hatred and revenge.[20]

On the other hand, there is also dissonance between ideological ideals and the realities of lived experience. I think of the copy of the national emblem on my desk. The national emblem, I note to the court, epitomizes the regime's grand vision for the revolutionary society. It features a factory, representing industry and the working class, and water flowing through a grid of paddy fields, representing the peasantry. Everything, I note, "looks perfect, [as if the country is] moving toward industry or a prosperous future."[21] The lived reality of DK, however, was quite different. And despite evidence that there were serious flaws in their revolutionary vision, the DK regime continued to "stick with [their] blueprint, with the [party] line . . ."

Abruptly, I am cut off. Koppe is standing. "Mr. President, an observation in relation to the last answer given by the expert," Koppe begins. "We, the defense, completely disagree," he continues. "The expert, who is an anthropologist . . . [is making] all kinds of far-reaching conclusions . . . going beyond his expertise . . . [and] should confine himself to what he can say from an anthropological standpoint. . . . Mr. Hinton is an anthropologist: he is not a political scientist [or] historian."[22]

The cycle continues. "Mr. President," Smith begins his rebuttal, "Mr. Hinton is an expert on mass violence . . . [and] human behavior. He's studied propaganda in different genocides around the world. . . . He's the very person who that should be able to respond to these questions."[23] The judges confer, then rule against Koppe.

Judge Fenz offers an aside. "Mr. Expert," she says to me, "perhaps avoid words in German or Latin where you can. Because I'm not sure I want to know how this sounds in Khmer. And not only for the interpreters, but also for us, [please use] short sentences very much to the point."[24]

I receive a public anthropology lesson. There is a need to remain aware of not just translation, but also how abstract academic ideas can be clearly expressed in a public trial. I have always worked to communicate such ideas clearly, in keeping with my public anthropology orientation. Fenz reminds me how critical doing so is in a context like a court of law.

Manufacturing Difference

And so the proceedings go, as we discuss issues ranging from dehumanization to moral inhibition. Smith poses his questions. I answer. Koppe interrupts: "What are his sources?"; "I object for procedural reasons"; "I don't think Mr. Hinton is an expert in authoritarian regimes"; and, again and again, "He's just an anthropologist!" Each time, Smith patiently undercuts Koppe's objection. Most are overruled, and I resume answering. But the defense objective is to disturb the flow of my answers, to make my explanations less clear.

Familiar with Koppe's tactics after scores of court sessions, Smith patiently presses on. Much of the remainder of his questioning focuses on the dynamics of the genocidal process, including how victim groups are ideologically distinguished, marked, dehumanized, and disempowered—a process I refer to as "manufacturing difference" in *Why Did They Kill?*

Smith reads a related passage from my book: "Differences are manufactured as genocidal regimes construct, essentialize, and propagate sociopolitical categories of difference, crystallizing what are normally more fluid forms of identity (the 'crystallization of difference') [and] stigmatizing victim groups in accordance with the differences that are being crystalized (the 'marking of difference')." These dynamics, he continues, are accompanied by "institutional, legal, social, and political changes that transform the conditions under which the targeted victim groups live (the 'organization of difference')."[25]

Smith pauses. "Perhaps I'll leave it there."

Judge Lavergne advises, "Could you, maybe, put shorter questions? I'm afraid we might lose a lot in the interpretation." Too much academic Latin.

Smith takes up each dynamic in turn. First, the *crystallization of difference*. We live in a world of difference in which identities are more or less legible depending on the situation. During times of upheaval, these differences are accentuated, particularly when amplified by ideology and propaganda. I provide an example from the United States: the sudden foregrounding of Muslim and Arab identity immediately after 9/11. The events of a single day transformed the way in which identity was seen for years to come. The same was true of the visibility of Japanese Americans after Pearl Harbor.

In DK, the Khmer Rouge similarly crystalized difference. The Khmer Rouge party line made broad distinctions between the rich and the poor, as well as finer distinctions in terms of class composition, with fine gradations within each class category. These abstract categories provided the contours for the crystallization of difference during DK, and they were accentuated in various ways depending on the historical context and moment.

Smith next turns to *the marking of difference*, or how the targeted groups that are distinguished are marked as more or less pure through association with negative and even contaminating qualities. The Khmer Rouge, for example, stigmatized those with a capitalist or counterrevolutionary taint. Urban evacuees were labeled as (capitalist and oppressor) "new people," who were devalued and viewed as less pure than (the formerly oppressed peasant and worker poor) "old people" or "base people," who had supported the Khmer Rouge during the war. So, too, were former revolutionaries marked as traitors and targeted for elimination.

To highlight this point, Smith reads Khmer Rouge tracts emphasizing the need to eliminate "traitorous elements burrowing from within" and "subversive rats."[26] One is from a December 1976 to January 1977 issue of the DK magazine *Revolutionary Flag*, which Nuon Chea helped oversee. The piece focuses on enemies within the revolutionary ranks, who are likened to germs. "During 1976," Smith reads, "the disease within the Party . . . that could not be seen was exposed. . . . [Previously,] we could not see and locate the germs inside the Party.

They were able to embed. But when we carried out socialist revolution profoundly and strongly and broadly within the Party, the Army, and the people, we found the bad germs."[27]

Such language is part of larger effort of *moral restructuring* that perpetrator regimes use to legitimate violence against groups who have been dehumanized and to whom moral injunctions against killing are no longer said to apply.[28] The Khmer Rouge used a range of euphemisms to further facilitate violence, including the widespread use of "cleaning up" or "smashing enemies."[29] And, over time, perpetrators become *desensitized* to violence that has been normalized and is viewed as legitimate against "impure" target groups.

Such violence is also facilitated by the *organization of difference*. "Did the CPK leadership organize difference?" Smith asks. I explain that the DK regime had an elaborate security system running from the party center down to the districts, where spies crept about at night, listening for signs of subversion. People were disciplined through work regimes, cooperative living, and practices like writing life histories and engaging in criticism and self-criticism sessions. People were also categorized and monitored through classificatory practices, such as ledgers in which local officials recorded each person's former occupation and class background.[30]

Why? I provide some first explanations.

Tuesday morning, March 15, ECCC courtroom (prosecution questioning)

"Good morning, Professor," Smith starts the next morning. "Yesterday, we discussed a number of the causes for the mass killings in [DK], both large-scale universal factors and some local customs and practices that made killings more likely. Today, I'd like to move to the third part of the questions, and that's looking at, specifically, the treatment of the Vietnamese in [DK]." He poses his first question, "How were the Vietnamese portrayed historically in Cambodia?"[31] The cycle starts again. Smith questions. Koppe interventions.

"Thank you, Mr. Deputy Co-Prosecutor," I begin, noting that, while varying through time and place, there are long-standing currents of fear and animus directed at Vietnam and ethnic Vietnamese. This hostility is partly linked to the perception that Vietnam covets and steals Cambodian territory, a notion highlighted in a 1978 DK tract, *Black Paper: Facts and Evidences of the Acts of Aggression and Annexation of Vietnam against Kampuchea*, published as war with Vietnam was escalating.[32]

Black Paper is centered on a narrative of alleged Vietnamese perfidy, woven around historical events (Vietnam's alleged "Southern March" and "swallowing" of Cambodian territory) and stereotypes portraying the Vietnamese as immoral, thieving, deceitful, and evil, as opposed to an implied Khmer goodness and purity.[33] In colloquial use, I tell the court, the term *yuon* is used to refer to Vietnamese. While sometimes used in a more neutral sense, *yuon* is often almost spat out with vitriol to signal "hatred of the Vietnamese other."[34]

During my doctoral fieldwork, for example, this strong anti-Vietnamese sentiment was dramatically revealed during an interview when a highly intelligent and thoughtful informant suddenly went on a diatribe about the Vietnamese. "I hate them," the man told me. "I don't have words to tell you how much I hate them." When I asked why, he explained, "History and their actions clearly show that the Yuon have repeatedly done bad things in Cambodia. They learn the tricks of thieves. They steal from [our] economy. They start many fights. They have come to live in Cambodia, but they don't respect the rights of the Khmer. And their biggest professions are stealing and prostitution. Even the Yuon women are thieves."[35]

Such comments are not uncommon in Cambodia and are sometimes used by politicians to manipulate political affect and draw support. DK was no exception; indeed, its anti-Vietnamese animus was taken to an extreme. The foregrounding of the term *yuon* in Khmer Rouge propaganda, then, underscores how difference is crystalized, marked, and organized to facilitate mass murder.

Genocidal Targeting

Smith turns to the DK targeting of ethnic Vietnamese. Many were killed or expelled during the Khmer Republic, which also launched a campaign against Vietnamese "nonbelievers." Perhaps 150,000 or more ethnic Vietnamese were forced out of Cambodia at the start of DK. Almost all of the remaining 20,000 ethnic Vietnamese were later killed or died.[36]

These deaths, along with the targeting of Muslim Chams, are at the heart of the genocide charge. Smith zeroes in on this point. He cites an April 1976 Khmer Rouge tract that appears to refer to the attack on ethnic Vietnamese: "We've swept hundreds and thousands of these foreigners, cleaned and expelled them out of our country."[37]

I provide a note of caution I would repeat many times during my testimony. While there was preexisting animus against the Vietnamese, the genocidal process did not unfold in a straight line. In Holocaust historiography, a related debate emerged between "intentionalists" and "functionalists." While intentionalists (pushing a more "straight-line" explanation) argue that preexisting anti-Semitic intent—manifest in Hitler's rhetoric, including *Mein Kampf*—drove the Nazis, "functionalists" contend that the process was often disjointed, less top-down, and emerged in phases, a notion sometimes referred to as "cumulative radicalization."[38]

It may be useful, I suggest to the court, to consider the trajectory of the genocide against ethnic Vietnamese and Chams in similar terms. In both cases, it is useful to think of the violence as a process that emerged over time (cumulative radicalization). But there was strong racial animus against the Vietnamese from the start, even as it ebbed and flowed before spiking as tensions and then war with Vietnam commenced. Muslim Chams, in contrast, became suspect after early rebellions protesting DK policies that conflicted with their traditions. In neither case did the violence flow in a straight line; instead, it emerged as events unfolded.

Smith asks me for the basis of my conclusions—interviews, academic sources, documents, and anthropological research on the ground. "What I would like to do now," he continues, "is to discuss the interviews you had with people in Kompong Siem in relation to the fate and the treatment of the Vietnamese in that area."[39] He turns to *Why Did They Kill?* and cites a passage in which I discuss Teap, an interviewee who worked at a subdistrict office near Banyan during DK.

"You state that Teap told you that the subdistrict office received a letter . . . from Grandmother Yut's district headquarters in mid-1977," Smith begins. "Teap stated, 'The letter instructed us to smash internal enemies—Chams, Vietnamese, capitalists, former Lon Nol workers, intellectuals and CIA agents.'"[40] According to my Banyan informants, I tell the court, Muslim Cham families and most of the ethnic Vietnamese in the area were taken away around this time.

"I have an objection," Koppe intervenes, complaining that I'm "introducing magical Teap, who knows all kinds of things about the treatment of targeted groups in Kompong Siem. I think it's very important that we determine whether Teap is, indeed, the person that gave four statements to investigators."[41]

Koppe knows I can't divulge the identity of my informants due to university human subject protections, so he presses the point. "To shorten this, Professor," Judge Fenz intervenes, "please take a piece of paper and write the name on it. Do you know who Teap is?"[42]

"I know him because I met him," I reply. Teap is a pseudonym, I continue. I can't reveal his identity and would need to check with him and my university before doing so. Fenz accepts my answer. But I'm left to consider the sometimes double-sided nature of human subjects protocols, which are pressed to their limit in this sort of context, when informants have provided information that can serve as evidence of genocide and atrocity crimes in an international tribunal. Journalists sometimes face a similar dilemma and go to jail rather than reveal a source. I am glad I don't face that choice.

Smith resumes his questioning, focusing on the DK purges of the areas around Banyan. He discusses other interviews in the court record that recount the killings of Kompong Siem district's ethnic Vietnamese and Chams and asks if the pattern of targeting fits my model of the genocidal process. I reply that it does.

Smith concludes with genocidal incitement and intent. He reads a series of DK radio broadcasts and propaganda tracts. "We must wipe out the enemy . . . suppress all stripes of enem[ies] at all times," says the first, taken from a 1977 Khieu Samphan address. Such speech, I respond, "would increase the likelihood [of particular target groups being killed]. It would be, as well, an authorization and a moral legitimation of doing so. . . . It's general incitement. It doesn't seem to be explicit in the sense of being targeted at Chams or ethnic Vietnamese."[43]

Smith reads additional documents that are specific. In a 1978 speech, Smith notes, Pol Pot urged his forces to kill thirty Vietnamese for each DK soldier killed. Pol Pot stated that "the 'Yuon' have wanted to make Kampuchea their subject since 1930. . . . [Now] there are no Yuon in Kampuchean territory. Formerly there were nearly a million of them. Now there is not one seed of them to be found."[44]

"Would this type of statement have [increased] the likelihood to encourage or discourage the killing of Vietnamese civilians in [DK]?" Smith asks. "Clearly," I reply, before he reads another DK tract that speaks of the *Yuon* as "the most noxious and acute . . . life-and-death contradiction."[45] There's a Koppe intervention, then the prosecution's day and a half of questioning concludes.

"I have two last questions for you," Smith states. "The first one is, in your opinion, based on interviews you have had, the propaganda you have reviewed and the research you have done, were Vietnamese civilians living in Cambodia targeted for killing during the DK regime?"[46]

"Yes," I answer. "The case seems strong and compelling."

"Who was leading that campaign?" Smith finishes.

"The CPK Standing Committee," I reply, glancing at Nuon Chea's empty chair.

4

LIVED EXPERIENCE

Tuesday late morning, March 15, ECCC courtroom (civil party questioning)

"The Chamber gives the floor to the lead co-lawyer for civil parties," President Nil announces when Smith is finished.[1] One of the major accomplishments of the ECCC is its extensive victim participation, including the involvement of civil parties who sit in the court and have lawyers who, while arguing in support of the prosecution, represent their client's interests and seek reparations. Each day, as is the case today, up to a dozen civil parties sit behind their lawyers. Others sometimes watch the proceedings from the public gallery.

Given the scale of civil party participation in Case 002, legal representation is consolidated by civil party lead co-lawyers who coordinate the efforts of the individual lawyers representing the almost four thousand civil parties involved. To be a civil party, a person must have suffered a "physical, material, or psychological injury" as a result of an alleged crime committed during DK. Civil party lawyers seek to prove this injury and claim collective and moral reparations on their behalf. Like the other major legal units at this hybrid court, one lead co-lawyer is Cambodian and the other international—in this case, a French lawyer with thick-rimmed glasses who now stands, ready to question me.

"Good morning, expert, my name is Marie Guiraud," she begins, "I represent the consolidated group of civil parties in this trial."[2] Her questions, she continues, will center on the impact DK policies had on the population, ranging from their social institutions to their individual daily lives.

I glance at the seven civil parties sitting behind Guiraud. Like the Banyan villagers, they suffered greatly during DK. One had witnessed the execution of ethnic minorities and been forced to marry. Another was an ex-soldier who had been tortured by electric shock at a Khmer Rouge prison. I wonder what they think as they sit in court watching the trial of the accused masterminds of their suffering. It is remarkable they can do so.

Transitional Justice, Victim Participation, and the Right to Truth

In the early 1940s, as World War II was raging amid Nazi aggression and war crimes, such participation in an international criminal tribunal would have been close to impossible.[3] Efforts to try German and Turkish leaders after World War I had largely failed. Initial proposals for dealing with the Nazis included firing squads and mass executions. US public sentiment leaned in the same direction. It was only in 1944, when news broke that the US government was discussing "pastoralizing" Germany, that those advocating war crimes trials began to gain ground. If imperfect in a number of ways, the Nuremberg and Tokyo tribunals that were soon established represented a first key step toward global justice and courts like the ECCC.

From the start, questions were raised about goals, purview, and possibilities of tribunals devoted to trying war crimes and other mass human rights violations. In a letter to philosopher Karl Jaspers, Hannah Arendt famously questioned the ability of law to grapple with such atrocities. "The Nazi crimes," she wrote, "explode the limits of law; and that is precisely what constitutes their monstrousness. For these crimes, no punishment is severe enough. It may well be essential to hang Göring, but it is totally inadequate." She continued, "That is, this guilt, in contrast to all criminal guilt, oversteps and shatters any and all legal systems. We are simply not equipped to deal, on a human, political level, with a guilt that is beyond crime and an innocence that is beyond goodness or virtue."[4]

Though her statement didn't elaborate on how the Nazi atrocities exploded "the limits of law," her remarks pointed to the larger difficulty of grappling with the enormity of what we now call "atrocity crimes," a term that encompasses crimes against humanity, war crimes, and genocide.[5] Law, of course, is all about limits. It serves as an institutional mechanism to contain transgressive behaviors that unsettle and endanger a community or political order.

This containment is undertaken in at least five interrelated ways: through *narrative* (legal argumentation or arrangements of "the facts," including the culminating judgment), *procedure* (trial "proceedings" informed by legal rules, roles, conventions, and practices), *performance* (everyday enactments by parties strategically operating within the field of such affordances and constraints), *sanction* (the sentence as deterrent), and *restoration* (reparations and the sentence as retribution).[6] The narratives, procedures, and performances, in turn, drive a *truth-seeking* process that determines the facts and weighs the evidence leading to the judgment and, if the defendant is found guilty, sanction and recalibration (the reparative dimension may also play a role in truth seeking through, for example, civil party participation).

If atrocity crimes "explode the limits of law" by the magnitude of their transgressive excess, then, one's view of law's capacity to grapple with such massive transgression depends in part on the aspects of containment one prioritizes. Arendt's remark on the limits of law, for example, emphasizes sanction, or the inability of a sentence (hanging Göring) to contain extraordinary crimes (extreme and unprecedented Nazi transgressions).

Arendt's famous remark regarding the 1961 Israeli trial of the Nazi bureaucrat Adolf Eichmann, in turn, emphasizes procedure and sanction: "The purpose of a trial is to render justice, and nothing else. . . . Law's main business [is] to weigh the charges brought against the accused, to render judgment, and to mete out due punishment." Accordingly, for Arendt, larger questions related to the narrative, performative, and restorative aspects of law—including ones being asked by the Eichmann prosecutor about "Why did it happen?" and "Why the Jews?" needed to be "held in abeyance."[7] Otherwise, Arendt argued, the proceedings stood in danger of devolving into a show trial of mere theater, not justice.

In law, Arendt's arguments dovetailed with rule-based theories of "legalism" or "legal formalism," more minimalist approaches that emphasize procedure over narrative, performance, and historical explanation.[8] These issues were very much at stake during the Eichmann trial, which Arendt feared was being undermined by politics, attempted history lessons, and a strong victim focus including powerful testimonies.

While appreciating her insistence on legal process, some have critiqued Arendt for ignoring the other ways law seeks to contain atrocity crimes. Lawrence Douglas, for example, has argued that by disregarding the narrative and performative dimensions of law, Arendt missed important ways in which law can address radical transgression while extending the reach of its own constitutive "limits"—by creating, for example, a legal narrative of a traumatic past that otherwise seems beyond comprehension.[9]

This broadening of the purview of law greatly accelerated after the Cold War, culminating in the robust maximalism of transitional justice. Previously, the momentum for international justice had largely come to a standstill after Nuremberg and the Tokyo trials due to Cold War politics, even as domestic trials for atrocity crimes, like the Eichmann trial, continued to be held and the international human rights regime slowly expanded.[10]

While the genealogy of transitional justice is complicated, the field emerged in the late 1980s and early 1990s as a number of countries sought to deal with violent pasts and there was a post–Cold War optimism about the possibilities of peacebuilding and democratization in the "new world order."[11] The term "transitional justice" came to refer to a broad range of mechanisms—including criminal trials, truth and reconciliation commissions, memorialization efforts, and institutional reforms—claimed to facilitate transitions from troubled (violent or authoritarian) pasts to better (more democratic) futures.[12] These mechanisms were said to deliver a host of goods, including helping to prevent recurrence, educate affected communities, combat impunity, restore the rule of law, promote reconciliation, and reveal the truth about what had happened.

Criminal tribunals, which emerged as the preeminent modality of transitional justice, were no exception, as illustrated by a key 2004 UN report, *The Rule of Law and Transitional Justice in Conflict and Post-Conflict Societies.* By this time, special ad hoc tribunals were operating in Rwanda and the former Yugoslavia, the International Criminal Court (ICC) was getting off the ground, and mixed or hybrid courts had been or were close to being launched in Sierra Leone, Cambodia, Bosnia and Herzegovina, Timor Leste, and Kosovo.

By supporting such courts, the 2004 report states, the UN had sought to realize a number of ends. These included not just the (legal minimalist) objective of "bringing to justice those responsible for serious violations of human rights and humanitarian law," but also the (more legal maximalist) goals of "putting an end to such violations and preventing their recurrence, securing justice and dignity for victims, establishing a record of past events, promoting national reconciliation, re-establishing the rule of law and contributing to the restoration of peace."[13] Such objectives directly inform the Khmer Rouge Tribunal and were written into the 2003 agreement between the UN and the Cambodian government that established the ECCC, which states the proceedings are undertaken "in the pursuit of justice and national reconciliation, stability, peace and security."[14]

By including these sorts of goals within the purview of international justice, transitional justice asserts a much more robust and expansive vision of the limits of law and its capacity to contain the extreme transgression of atrocity crimes. In doing so, such maximalist approaches, while still prioritizing procedure and sanction, recognize and seek to accomplish this broader range of objectives through the narrative, performative, and reparative dimensions of law. The increasing emphasis on victim participation, including the extensive civil party participation of the ICC and ECCC, provide one illustration of how victim stories, testimony, and reparations are increasingly being incorporated into international justice.

Victim participation is also connected to the broadening truth-seeking aims of such courts. Over time, "the truth" has increasingly grown in stature and eventually become a legal right.[15] One key origin of this "right to truth" was Latin America, where in countries like Argentina, Chile, and Guatemala families fought to find out what had happened to "the disappeared" under militant and violent regimes.

This demand for the truth gained renown in the weekly marches of the Mothers of the Plaza de Mayo in Argentina, though struggles took place in several domains, including domestic courts. These legal efforts helped catalyze recognition of the right to truth by the Latin American Human Rights Court, building momentum for UN recognition and the 2012 creation of a UN Special Rapporteur on the Promotion of Truth, Justice, Reparation and Guarantees of Non-Recurrence. Related language about the right to truth now pervades transitional justice discourse. While more fully realized through truth commissions, a victim's right to truth also informs international justice, including assertions that courts need to unpack root causes and clarify the historical record.

At tribunals like the ECCC, then, truth seeking takes places on at least two levels. On the one hand, truth seeking takes place in a legalistic manner. In this legalistic truth-seeking frame, the narrative, performative, and restorative aspects of law are backgrounded in favor of procedure and sanction. Facts are meant to prove or disprove the charges, determine criminality, and deliver appropriate sentences for crimes—Arendt's vision of juridical logics.

While legalistic truth seeking still dominates in the courtroom, explanatory truth seeking now plays a more important role in international justice, even as the extent to which it does so varies from court to court. Dating back to Nuremberg, tribunals have claimed to help clarify the historical record, but this goal was minimized and subordinated to law. With the ascendancy of transitional justice discourses, however, the second track of explanatory truth seeking has increased in importance as courts try to address victim concerns and satisfy their right to truth.

While the ECCC has faced criticism for political interference and corruption, it has gained distinction for its civil party participation. Close to one hundred civil parties were involved in Duch's trial, with twenty-two giving powerful testimony. The same is true in Case 002, which has admitted 3,866 civil parties, including those now sitting in the court with me.[16]

As these civil parties formally support the prosecution and seek reparations, they are heavily invested in the truth-seeking process that emerges, to refer back to the five forms of legal containments discussed above, through juridical narrative, procedure, and performance. Civil parties are involved in this process in several ways. Not only do they observe and learn from truth as produced in the courtroom, but they also contribute to truth seeking by telling their stories.

Here civil parties play a crucial role in, to return to Trouillot, recovering narratives that have been erased from the historical record—even as these narratives are clipped and pruned in the context of courtroom procedures. In this regard, related efforts undertaken by NGOs like DC-Cam are critical to the larger process of truth seeking, especially since these initiatives are often framed, at least in part, in terms of local understanding and practices, including Buddhist rituals.[17]

Revolution and Social Transformation during DK

It was precisely this kind of practice that the Khmer Rouge sought to destroy—a process Guiraud will ask me about extensively during her questioning—as they began to "clean up" the country after the war.[18] Nuon Chea had been at the center of planning as the Khmer Rouge undertook one of the most radical projects of social engineering in history.

In keeping with the Marxist-Leninist philosophy informing the party line they formulated at the 1960 party congress after research and "scientific analysis," the Khmer Rouge set out to create a pure revolutionary society in which the means and relations of production would be completely transformed. Private property, market exchange, and currency were eliminated. The Khmer Rouge even blew up the central bank. Production was collectivized as people worked in teams and ate communally.

To achieve their Maoist-inspired goal of achieving a "Super Great Leap Forward," the Khmer Rouge moved more quickly than any other socialist regime in history. The rapid speed of the change and unrealistic quotas contributed to missteps and shortages, which sometimes translated to starvation on the ground and what many survivors describe as slave labor–like conditions.

DK transformations penetrated every aspect of society, including three key pillars in the everyday socioeconomic lives of most Cambodians: family, village, and religion.[19] The Khmer Rouge frequently separated family members and took over key familial responsibilities ranging from providing meals to arranging marriages, the focus of one of the key charges in Case 002/02 (forced marriage). Village life was reorganized in terms of cooperatives. And religious life, which Marx long ago referred to as the opiate of the masses, was effectively disbanded.

These radical revampings of social organization were paralleled by an attempt to transform the mind. Each person had to strive to refashion their ways of thinking and feeling, a process that was sometimes likened to hammering hot iron on an anvil. "Forging" a proper revolutionary stance required forgetting the corrupt habits learned in the capitalist-tainted past while embracing socialist ideology and related revolutionary transformations. This process was facilitated by hard work and constant indoctrination, including dreaded meetings held at the end of long workdays when people were exhausted.

Those who appeared to lack proper enthusiasm or showed signs of laziness were sometimes accused of having "memory sickness." The Khmer Rouge security apparatus extended to the ground level, where people were encouraged to report on each other, and spies crept about listening for signs of subversion and a regressive consciousness.

Ignoring the widespread and arbitrary killings of those who came under suspicion, Nuon Chea told journalist and film-maker Thet Sambath, "Our policy was first to re-educate them to stop. Then we gave them two or three warnings to stop their treacherous activities. Next we required them to present their revolutionary personal history and make a self-criticism."[20] Those who were incorrigible had to be dealt with to "stop the rot from spreading" and contaminating the pure new society in the making.

In this revolutionary order, everything needed to be purified, including the mind. Nuon Chea explained to Thet, "The old imperialist regime was corrupt. Prostitution and vagrancy were widespread. We needed to clean up society completely. This is the first step on the revolutionary path to prosperity." Accordingly, the regime eradicated "corruption, gambling, beating, stabbing, robbing and idleness," as well as the "financial exploitation of the poor by the rich." The old system was eliminated and replaced by "socialism and collectivism."[21] As part of this process, everyone was expected to eliminate their individualistic traits and transform themselves into pure new revolutionaries.

Khmer Rouge propaganda illustrated revolutionary ideals—like having a proper stance and revolutionary consciousness—using moral stories, a medium familiar to rural Cambodians who had grown up hearing parables and tales. One, "The Red Heart of Dam Pheng," was published in late 1973 in a Khmer Rouge magazine, *Revolutionary Youth*.[22] Thought to have been written by a Khmer Rouge leader—quite possibly Nuon Chea, and indeed, the narrative has echoes with Nuon Chea's early life—the story recounts how a poor peasant, whose family suffered under the oppression of colonialists, feudalists, and capitalists, joined the revolution in 1961.

Dam Pheng worked to hone his consciousness and eventually "started to have a clear vision" and understand "the reasons behind the suffering of his family and relatives." Dam Pheng "became a role model" because of his "gentle attitude, patriotism (particularly toward the poor), willingness to sacrifice his personal

FIGURE 4.1. Nuon Chea (right) giving a speech during DK.

Photo courtesy of DC-Cam/SRI.

FIGURE 4.2. Celebration after the completion of an irrigation project.

Photo courtesy of DC-Cam/SRI.

interest for the shared cause, and absolute stance against the Imperialists and the oppressors."[23]

These qualities were revealed by how he didn't talk when captured by the police, even after severe torture that ultimately killed him. Before he died, the Khmer Rouge tract recounts, Dam Pheng used his blood to write on the cell wall, "Red heart, I care for you and educate you every day for the valuable revolution, the poor, and the peasants."

The story of Dam Pheng appears to have been well known at the time and was incorporated into Khmer Rouge political education, including one version that was performed during DK.[24] During his Case 001 testimony, Duch, the head of S-21 prison, characterized the state of his revolutionary consciousness and passion by stating that he tried to struggle like Dam Pheng.[25]

Of course, many people were perceived to have fallen short of the ideal. When local leaders received warnings about "hidden enemies burrowing from within," they usually took people from suspect groups ranging from ethnic Vietnamese and Muslim Chams to the "new people" from urban areas. Many Banyan villagers, most of whom were labeled "old people," told me stories about the targeting of these groups, even as they noted that life for them, too, was precarious during DK. Khmer Rouge soldiers and cadre who had "pure" poor peasant backgrounds were also sometimes targeted, especially as purges got underway.

Civil Party and S-21 Survivor Bou Meng

Bou Meng, the S-21 survivor and civil party who had sobbed in court with Duch, is one such former cadre. From a rural peasant background, Bou Meng had joined the revolution during the civil war, before he and his wife were arrested and imprisoned at S-21.[26] He never saw her or their two children again. Bou Meng was shackled in a crammed communal jail cell, where the prisoners were given starvation rations and the hygiene was poor, leading to lice infestations and skin infections.

Eventually, Bou Meng was tortured, leaving scars that still cover his back today. After days of being beaten, whipped, and shocked, Bou Meng gave a forced confession. Normally he would have been executed at this point, like the other S-21 prisoners. Bou Meng was a rare exception. He survived because he could paint, a skill he had learned as a child at the pagoda. He spent the rest of DK creating propaganda art in the prison.

FIGURE 4.3. S-21 Survivor and ECCC civil party Bou Meng attending the Supreme Court Chamber's final decision in Case 001, when Duch was sentenced to life imprisonment, ECCC courtroom, February 3, 2012.

Photo courtesy of ECCC.

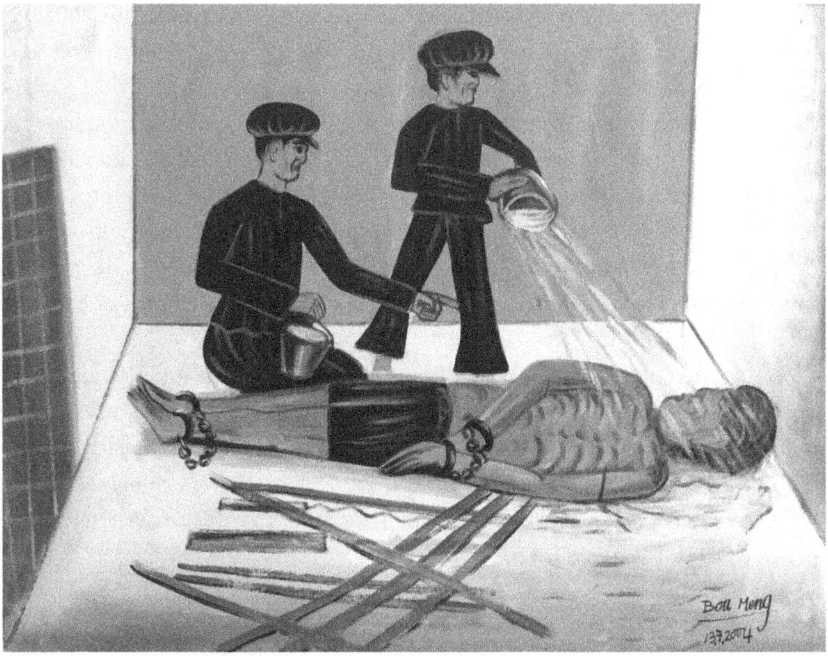

FIGURE 4.4. Civil party Bou Meng's portrait of his torture at S-21 prison that left his back covered in scars.

Image courtesy of DC-Cam/SRI.

Among the images I have brought to court is a reproduction of a Bou Meng painting depicting him and his wife standing blindfolded before the gates of S-21. Part of his reason for participating as a civil party was to find out what happened to her and where she died so that he could perform a Buddhist ceremony in her honor. Bou Meng still carries a photo of his wife, a reproduction of her S-21 prison mug shot. The first time he showed me the photo and spoke about his wife, Bou Meng began to quietly sob, a hand pressed across his forehead. I brought this image to court as a reminder of the lived experience of suffering that Cambodians endured during DK, how it continues to impact their lives, and the questions people like Bou Meng want answered by the ECCC, including the question *why?*

Given the enormity of the DK suffering, some Cambodians are bitter about the treatment Nuon Chea and the other former Khmer Rouge leaders receive at the court. In an international tribunal like the ECCC, defendants are afforded basic human rights, including a fair trial with representation before an impartial court. Their dignity is respected. They don't stand trial in metal cages. No one beats them or berates them with dehumanizing slurs. Their basic needs must be met in detention: a bed, meals, exercise, books, and medical care.

This bitterness was evident at the first ECCC hearing I attended, the 2008 pretrial detention hearing of the former DK minister of foreign affairs, Ieng Sary. During a break, I decided to sit in the front row of the gallery to get a closer look at the proceedings. Just as the proceedings were about to recommence, a small man with receding gray hair and droopy eyes sat down next to me. It was Bou Meng.

We sat together for much of the rest of the day, which took an odd turn. Ieng Sary's lawyer told the court that his client was not feeling well, and a debate broke out over whether or not his due process rights would be violated if the proceedings continued. Eventually a doctor from the detention center was called to evaluate his condition.

While the doctor was speaking, Bou Meng looked at me and nodded, smiling slightly, as if to acknowledge the irony of the situation. "It's not just," he told me. "Ieng Sary should not get off for health reasons. I have bad health because of what they did to me. I startle easily and shiver a lot. I have trouble seeing and my hearing is bad. And no one looks after me. He has a doctor. When I was in prison at S-21, I suffered [so much more]."

For Bou Meng and other Cambodians, the top-notch medical care they observed former Khmer Rouge receiving at the ECCC—far beyond what most Cambodians have today—was ironic given their suffering during DK. Some complain that the former Khmer Rouge leaders are jailed in relative comfort and afforded full due process rights while their victims starved, worked day and night, and were beaten and killed on a whim during DK.

Now, as I sit waiting for Guiraud to ask her first question, I wonder if some of the civil parties sitting in court are having similar thoughts about Nuon Chea, whose health is carefully monitored and who is resting on a cot in a holding cell below, listening to the proceedings.

Buddhism

"I would like to start my questioning with Buddhism," Guiraud says. "Your book *Why Did They Kill?* states that it was one of the three pillars of traditional Cambodian society and a locus of social, moral, and educational activity in everyday life."[27] She asks me to explain what I meant by this statement and how DK policy impacted this key social institution and everyday life for Cambodians. In contrast to Smith's questions, with their more experience-distant focus on the genocidal process, Guiraud's questions centered more directly on the sort of experience-near concerns that are a focus of anthropological research.

"Thank you, Ms. Civil Party Co-Lawyer," I begin. "Prior to Democratic Kampuchea, Buddhism, as is well known, was an absolutely central pillar of everyday

Cambodian life both in the cities and in the countryside—especially the countryside, because people lived in proximity to pagodas. Much of everyday life revolved around the pagoda," which served social, educative, and moral functions.[28] The pagoda was also a key locus of ritual life, including merit-related practices critical to karma, social balance, and relations with the spirits of the dead.

The Khmer Rouge attack on religion, I explain, therefore ruptured the fabric of social life for Cambodian Buddhists, just as it did for the much smaller numbers of Muslim Chams and other religious minorities in the country. Religious ceremonies were stopped, and religious statuary was destroyed or treated like rubbish. Monks were disrobed. Pagodas were destroyed and sometimes converted into security centers where people were imprisoned, tortured, and executed—as was the case with Wat Phnom Bros, the pagoda near Banyan village.

The effect on the populace was devastating, particularly when combined with the simultaneous Khmer Rouge transformations of familial, economic, and community life. Cambodians lost a key moral safeguard that Buddhism had provided through moral education, including sermons on the five moral precepts, the first of which was the prohibition on taking life. Not only did the elimination of Buddhism erode prosocial norms and moral restraints on violence, but the Khmer Rouge sought to replace religion with a revolutionary morality that glorified violence. Pol Pot noted this in his 1977 speech when he discussed the motif of blood, struggle, and "class and national hatred" in the national anthem.[29]

Another major impact of the attack on religion was the loss of rituals critical to social equilibrium. Buddhist meditation helped people to achieve the mindfulness and equanimity that both alleviates suffering and leads to a desired state of social balance. Buddhist healing rituals also served an important function in this regard. The loss of Buddhism also meant that it was no longer possible to mourn the dead, at least in a public manner, at a time when excess mortality was skyrocketing.

For Buddhists, death is not the end point of life but a bridge to rebirth. This passage may be smooth or more prolonged and disrupted, particularly when people have violent deaths of the sort that were common during DK. To facilitate this transition and soothe the spirits of the dead, the living may perform Buddhist rituals like the *bangsokol* ceremony, in which offerings are made and merit is transferred to the spirits through monks chanting scripture.[30] Otherwise, the spirits of the dead may appear in dreams and haunt the living, thereby disrupting social balance. Other ceremonies serve a similar function, including the lighting of incense at home.

As noted earlier, one of Bou Meng's reasons for participating as a civil party was to find out where his wife had been killed so he could gather soil from the location and perform a ceremony. He once told me that he had bad dreams about his wife, including one in which "my wife appeared leading a large group of prisoners who had been executed [at S-21]. They were dressed in black, and she led them in front of my house. . . . She said, 'Only Bou Meng can help us find justice.'" Bou Meng believed that "the spirit of my wife is not calm (*sngop*). Therefore, I want reparations to hold a big ceremony and send merit to [the spirit of] my wife."[31]

Sometimes these spirit beliefs intruded into the secular courtroom. During his 2009 testimony, for example, Case 001 civil party Neth Phally raised a photograph of his older brother, a former soldier who had been killed at S-21, and told the court, "It's like my elder brother is sitting here by me in this court watching as the accused is tried. His spirit can be calmed by the court." He then addressed his brother directly, asking him to remain in the photograph he was still holding since Neth had no remains and wanted to "pay my respect and perform ceremonies to send merit to you."[32]

When I interviewed Neth in 2015, he told me that his brother visited him in his dreams. At home, Neth had created a small memorial where the portrait of his brother—the same one he held up in court—hung near a painting of the Buddha and incense bowls.[33] Before testifying, Neth had lit incense and prayed that the spirit of his brother would enter the photograph when Neth raised it in court.[34] By doing so, Neth said in another interview, "I felt this would help release his soul from wandering and help him find peace so he could be reborn."[35]

Coping, Distress, and Equilibrium

"When does a genocide end?" I ask in court after mentioning Neth's invocation of the spirit of his dead brother during Duch's trial. "Well, in a sense, it goes on and on and on and the reverberations continue [into the present]."[36] This ongoing impact, I continue, extends to issues of psychological well-being, which is also often viewed through the prisms of bodily flow and equilibrium in Cambodia. Violence, social suffering, and trauma disrupt this ideal of balance and flow and can lead to unease ranging from "not feeling well" (*min sruol khluon*) to more severe forms of psychological distress and even mental illness.

Both Bou Meng and Neth Phally displayed signs of such distress, which are often expressed through somatic complaints. At Ieng Sary's 2008 pretrial detention hearing, for example, Bou Meng had noted some of his symptoms, including being easily startled, shivering, and headaches. When he testified at Duch's trial the following year, he said that he also had insomnia and "thought too much." Neth likewise suffered from somatic symptoms, including feelings of anger (when thinking about the past), difficulty sleeping, frequently needing to relieve himself at night, and the lack of "calm" (*sngeam*) sleep. Like Bou Meng,

Neth Phally also had a problem with "thinking too much," a Cambodian cultural idiom of distress.[37]

While Buddhism provides rituals to help with such psychosocial distress, Bou Meng and Neth Phally drew on a variety of traditional practices to deal with their symptoms. When I was sitting with Bou Meng at the Ieng Sary pretrial detention hearing, for example, he took out Tiger Balm, a traditional Cambodian remedy for somatic ailments, and began rubbing it on his neck and forehead while periodically placing his forefinger against his upper lip and inhaling deeply. Later he told me that the trial proceedings "reminded me of what had happened to me at S-21 [Tuol Sleng], how they beat me and tortured me with electric shocks. I also started thinking about my wife wondering how can it be that she was killed. My head began to ache as I listened. I stopped being able to hear and understand clearly. This is why I used the Tiger Balm."[38] Bou Meng had also sought psychological support through the court and began taking medication.

Neth similarly drew on a range of practices to cope with his distress, including distracting himself by thinking about other things or talking to neighbors, visiting a local healer (*krou khmaer*), taking traditional medicines, applying Tiger Balm to alter the disturbed humoral "wind" in his body, making offerings to monks, being sprinkled with holy water, lighting incense, and praying. Like Bou Meng, he had also sought treatment from a local Cambodian NGO affiliated with the court, the Transcultural Psychosocial Organization, which had given him medication and helped him learn to "lighten" (*tuu sral*) his tension, "ease" (*somruol*) his mind, and "kill"/control (*romnoap*) disruptive emotions.[39]

Cambodians were able to draw on a few of these emotion-management techniques during DK, but many, like Buddhist rituals, were banned or could be viewed as a sign of "memory sickness"—thereby impeding the ability of Cambodians to cope with the massive stress, upheaval, danger, and terror they were experiencing. The civil parties now sitting in court lived through this time of suffering and likely now use the same sorts of treatments as Bou Meng and Neth Phally to deal with their psychosocial distress.

Buddhist Vernaculars of DK Ideology

"In your book," Guiraud goes on, "you say that the Khmer Rouge drew upon Buddhist themes, despite the fact that Democratic Kampuchea had prohibited Buddhism. Can you explain the Buddhist themes that were used by Democratic Kampuchea to consolidate its doctrine?"[40]

"Yes, this is an interesting issue and a big, big topic," I reply. It is also one Smith had begun to question me about yesterday, when I discussed how the

Khmer Rouge had recast Marxist-Leninist ideology in terms that were familiar to poor rural Cambodians, many illiterate, who they viewed as more pure than the wealthy, educated, and urban. Buddhism provided a key bridge given how intertwined it was with village life, including its role in education.

I provide the court with examples, beginning with the story of Grandmother Yit, the Region 41 cadre who killed her husband after his loyalty to the DK regime had become suspect. This was an act of both renunciation and detachment, key Buddhist concepts that were reformulated by DK ideology to valorize a willingness to cut off one's attachment to achieve a proper revolutionary consciousness.

The term the Khmer Rouge used for consciousness, *sâtiaramma*, is also the Buddhist term for mindfulness. Just as one needed to focus one's *sâtiaramma* during meditation, so too did revolutionaries need to focus their revolutionary consciousness on the party line, honing their revolutionary "stance." As noted above, consciousness was a concept central to the party line and frequently discussed in propaganda, including the story of Dam Pheng.

Even as they attacked Buddhism and other forms of religious worship, the Khmer Rouge positioned "the Organization" (*Ângkar*) as a quasi-religious entity. The term was used in various ways, including as a metaphor for higher levels of authority or even the DK leadership, and *Ângkar* could also connote semi-divine presence. Haing Ngor explained, "Logically, Angka had to be a person or a group of people, but many found it easier to believe that Angka was an all-powerful entity, something like a god."[41] Its power and clairvoyance were epitomized by a common DK saying, which was also used as a warning: "*Ângkar* has the eyes of a pineapple." Like a deity, *Ângkar* was often described in exalted terms, including language adapted from Buddhism. *Ângkar* was "clear-sighted" and "enlightened" and therefore something to be "believed in" and worshiped. "The Organization" also sought to co-opt sentiments of personal dependency and protection related to family, village, and social life, the focus of Guiraud's next line of questioning.

Ontological Security

"I would like to put a series of questions to you on the impact of policies implemented in Democratic Kampuchea on the family and the individuals," Guiraud continues, "but I'd like to start by revisiting the issue of the need for protection, which you talk about in your book."[42] She had earlier asked how Buddhism served as one "protection mechanism," enhancing balance, bodily flow, energy, luck, and security in a world filled with disruptive and potentially malevolent forces like the spirits of the dead. If the *bangsokol* ceremony illustrates one way Buddhism offers protection, there are many other examples, ranging from the power of Buddha amulets, talismans, and tattoos to practices such as monks tying protective strings around the wrists of supplicants, recalling some of the multiple animating forces (*broleung*) that inhabit and sometimes flee the body, holding blessing ceremonies, and sprinkling holy water on congregants.[43] All these Buddhism mechanisms for supporting psychosocial well-being were eroded or lost due to the DK ban on religion, thereby greatly diminishing the ability of people to cope with their suffering.

Transactions with potentially dangerous forces take place in other domains as well, including on or across the boundary between the domesticated (*srok*) village environs and more liminal and uncultivated spaces of the wilderness (*prei*) where powerful spirits reside. Some of the most common are territorial spirits (*neak ta*), which inhabit mounds, trees, and wooden and stone objects. Some are relatively more domesticated, residing on the outskirts of a village or compound.

The Lord of the Iron Staff is one such tutelary spirit. Bou Meng actually invoked the Lord of the Iron Staff at one point during his testimony, saying "The *neak ta*, the Lord of the Iron Staff, if I'm not telling the truth may he let a car strike and kill me."[44] He pointed toward the *neak ta* as he spoke.

Banyan, the village where I did my doctoral fieldwork, similarly has two *neak ta*, said to be the sprits of the village founders. To prevent affliction and bad luck, Banyan villagers make offerings to these territorial spirits, entering into relationships of personal dependency with them. The ritual lay practitioner at Banyan explained, "People pay homage to *neak ta* so the *neak ta* will take care of their well-being. People know that the *neak ta* have supernatural potency, so they entreat the *neak ta*, saying, 'Please give me health and security. . . . Help protect me.' The people strongly believe this." At the same time, he noted, "*neak ta* can harm people as well. If we forget them or don't pay homage to them, the *neak ta* will come and afflict us. . . . So the people are really scared about what the *neak ta* might do to them."[45] Other *neak ta*, as well as various spirits and beings, reside in the wilderness and are viewed as more dangerous since villagers lack a relationship with them.

This idiom of personal dependency and protection extends to other domains ranging from the home to the workplace. In the home, relationships are often described using the language of care and protection, such as that provided by parents to their children, and older siblings to younger siblings. Like other civil parties who testified at the ECCC Neth Phally had used these idioms of dependency when talking about his older brother who was killed at S-21. The student-teacher relationship may similarly be viewed as one of beneficence, as the teacher does good deeds and takes care of a student who is expected to make a small return by expressing gratitude and addressing the teacher with honorifics. Such relations of personal dependency are also operative in the workplace and in politics, where patronage networks are sometimes described as "strings" (*khsae*).[46]

The Khmer Rouge ranks were also organized partly in terms of such patronage networks, which contributed to the purges as the regime eliminated the networks of cadre who had come under suspicion. The region in which Banyan was located provides an example of this dynamic, as Southwest Zone forces purged "strings" of cadre and soldiers in the Northern Zone who were connected to a longtime revolutionary leader, Koy Thuon, and his associates. The Southwest cadre who replaced them, in turn, were part of networks connected to General Ta Mok and Ao An, the suspect charged in Case 004 at the ECCC.

In terms of the everyday life, however, the DK sociopolitical transformations shattered such preexisting relations of personal dependency, from the home to the workplace, since the DK regime viewed them as possible sources of alternative loyalties. Even as it attacked these social structures, the Khmer Rouge sought to redirect sentiments of personalized dependency and patronage toward itself. Parents had previously provided for children and arranged marriages for them, but *Ângkar* now did so—just as it provided food for the masses who labored day and night to build the new revolutionary society. In return for this beneficence, people were expected to hone their revolutionary consciousness and enthusiastically "build and defend" the country.

Atomization

The result of this multipronged attack on the foundations of Cambodian social, family, economic, and political life was atomization. Perhaps more than any other regime in history, the DK regime came to resemble the sort of totalitarian system Hannah Arendt warned about in *The Origins of Totalitarianism*, in which thoughtful exchange in the public sphere was erased as everyone was expected to parrot back ideological doctrine.[47] North Korea might be the one exception, and it illustrates what the DK regime might have looked like had it lasted.

In the Khmer Rouge imagination, the new revolutionary society would be composed of atomized people bleached of their individuality and interpersonal connections beyond the socialist collective. People were stripped of their possessions and dressed alike, often in black. Men and women cut their hair short. The collective "we" was preferred over the pronoun "I," and everyone, even parents and children, were supposed to refer to each other as "comrade." The dissolution of personal traits and individuality was idealized in revolutionary propaganda and sayings, ranging from warnings about the "disease" of individualism to exhortations like "Destroy the garden of the individual; build up a united garden."[48]

For many Cambodians, the impact of these social transformations was devastating and greatly heightened their social and psychological suffering amid the atmosphere of fear, insecurity, and terror. Many people remained focused on procuring food and surviving for one more day. As Youk Chhang, the head of DC-Cam, put it, "Food became my god during the regime. I dreamed about all kinds of food all the time."[49]

These sentiments were sometimes referenced by a widespread saying, "Plant a kapok tree" (*dam daoem kor*). In Khmer, the term for kapok tree, *kor*, is a homophone of the word *ko*, the third consonant in the Khmer alphabet, which has a secondary meaning of "mute, muffled, and hollow."[50] A person who is mute is a *monuss ko*. The phrase "plant a kapok tree" therefore signified that one had to build a wall of silence to survive.

Sometimes, the injunction was whispered between family members and friends. In other situations, it might be invoked by a Khmer Rouge cadre to advise someone how to act. In response to this situation, many people shut down or became depressed, a state that could lead to accusations of "memory sickness" and then execution. It was, in other words, a time of profound imbalance, the effects of which continue into the present for Cambodians, including civil parties like Bou Meng.

As Guiraud's line of questioning highlights, prior to DK, Cambodians had a wide range of protection mechanisms and support structures to which to turn during times of psychosocial distress. During DK, however, it was no longer was possible to visit a monk at a pagoda or participate in rituals to appease the spirits of the dead, which were rapidly increasing in number. Friend, family, and community networks had been torn asunder. Everyday relations were pervaded by an undercurrent of fear and mistrust.

By directing my testimony to the impact of DK policies on the everyday lives of Cambodians and their lived experience of social suffering, Guiraud's questions focus on issues that more macrolevel analyses often miss, and about which anthropology has much to say. When the defense next takes the floor, Koppe, who has said almost nothing during the civil party questioning, will try to argue that this is more or less the only thing that anthropology, with its supposedly microlevel perspective and methodological flaws, has to contribute to a court of law.

5

RUPTURE

Tuesday late afternoon, March 15, ECCC courtroom
(Nuon Chea defense team questioning)

"Have you ever heard of a notion called the 'standard total academic view'?"[1]

I have been waiting for Koppe to ask this question. The idea is a key part of Nuon Chea's defense—and a fulcrum of his denials.

Koppe begins as expected, seeking to sledgehammer my testimony, credibility, and anthropological research. "I would like to start first with asking you some questions about your methodology," he states, "and the sources you have used both for your book and also for today's testimony."[2] These encompass, he goes on, my academic scholarship, interviews, and documentation. Koppe will repeatedly question my testimony, sources, interpretations, and data, including "magical Teap."

His invocation of the "standard total view" is meant to typologize my scholarship and reduce it to just another manifestation of what he argues is the dominant and biased state-centric genocide studies point of view. A key part of Nuon Chea's defense is based on critiquing this "consensus" perspective on DK and offering an alternative history—their wrecking ball for the prosecution's carefully constructed legal edifice that seeks to prove the DK leadership's highly centralized control.

"You just used the word 'consensus' within the scholarly community," Koppe continues, thinking he has me trapped. "Can you explain what your understanding of this notion of 'standard total view' is?"[3]

"The standard total view," I answer, is espoused by the scholar Michael Vickery, who critiques the assumption that events in DK unfolded in a singular manner by highlighting that "there was variation across [DK] zones, variation across time and place. And I think that's a very important point."[4] It is also a point made by Vickery in 1984, one long since acknowledged by historians and scholars, including me, even if Vickery has his own reductive point of view.[5]

Nevertheless, the notion of a "standard total view" serves the purposes of the defense well, suggesting there is a monolithic version of DK history—the atrocity frame manifest at Tuol Sleng and promoted by the Cambodian government since 1979 to assert its legitimacy—that needs to be critiqued because it obfuscates the very truths the court is supposed to reveal. Nuon Chea's defense team briefs argue this biased view is systemic at the ECCC, apparent in factors ranging from the composition of the justices ("nationals of France, the United States and their closest allies") to the expert witnesses selected—a "small circle of western academics," mostly from the United States and its allies, who are "least sympathetic to the CPK" and more broadly antisocialist.[6] Koppe seeks to place me on the list.

Instead of centralized control and planned crimes, his defense team argues, DK was characterized by fragmentation, variation, dispersed power, and chaos. The violence emerged in this context as Khmer Rouge leaders were threatened by internal enemies, coup attempts, poor communication, a rival faction, and nonstop external intervention culminating in Vietnam's invasion. It is another variation of the denialist argument that Nuon Chea has been making for years.

A Manichean Narrative versus Truth

From the beginning of the trial, Nuon Chea's defense team argues, they have faced an uphill struggle against a "Manichean narrative" fashioned by Vietnam, its Soviet bloc allies, its "pitiful puppets in the PRK," and the current Cambodian government and reinforced by refugee accounts, the media, memorialization practices, academics, and "Anglo-French books, films, and exhibitions." This "historically inaccurate, and often plainly false and oversimplified narrative," Nuon Chea's C002/02 defense brief states, "presents DK as a monstrous regime sadistically intent in harming its people . . . [in] a simplistic black and white duality of 'Good versus Evil.'"[7]

Propaganda has normalized such a "hyperbolic depiction of the CPK," as Vietnam and its PRK lackeys "sought legitimacy *via* powerful and systematic efforts to reframe history by exaggerating DK's supposed atrocities . . . [and] attributing blame to a small group of CPK leaders" in order to deflect attention away from the fact that members of the PRK (and current government) are themselves former Khmer Rouge. Echoing Nuon Chea's long history of denials, the closing brief claims that Tuol Sleng is one among many examples of how the Manichean narrative is asserted.[8]

The reality of what happened, the Nuon Chea defense brief argues, is quite different. The DK regime was a legitimate government that implemented "lawful policies in response to the continual state of emergency in the DK period." This state of emergency was due to both the "unparalleled existential threat posed by Vietnam and its internal collaborators within the [CPK] and the dire conditions Cambodia faced when the CPK assumed power owing to the devastating impact of relentless US bombings and years of bloody civil war."[9]

Unfortunately, Nuon Chea's lawyers argue, the ECCC is not interested in the truth. The court's "national and international judges, prosecutors, and investigators [have] all bought the Manichean narrative 'hook, line and sinker' and are committed to upholding it in the name of 'justice.'" They do so because of both preexisting assumptions and political pressure. Their bias informs the court's rules of procedure, investigation, and trial proceedings. It skews the evidence deemed admissible and the choice of witnesses called to testify. It limits the defense's ability to adequately make its case. In other words, Nuon Chea has not received a fair trial. The tribunal, Nuon Chea's brief contends, is "a complete farce," mere victor's justice.[10]

Nevertheless, there is, the brief notes, a slight glimmer of hope. The Trial Chamber's Case 002/01 judgment had been critiqued by outside observers, including a Stanford report stating that the judgment offers "a poorly-organized, ill-documented, and meandering narrative in lieu of clearly structured legal writing, based upon a thorough and balanced analysis of the legal and factual issues in dispute."[11] The ECCC's Supreme Court Chamber has also critiqued the judgment and reversed some of the Trial Chamber's findings.

These critiques have "rewritten the 'rules of the game,'" opening the door to the defense's argument. "Breaking down Manichean 'accepted truths' is no easy feat," the Nuon Chea defense brief states, especially after "a 40-year process of reframing the truth of DK as the Manichean narrative" and making it part of "collective memory." The "new rules of the game," however, create fresh possibilities for the defense to reveal the truth as it "travelled a long road towards rewriting history."[12]

Rupture

These allegations and related tensions expressed in the brief date back to the early days of the court and were amplified by Khieu Samphan's international lawyer, Jacques Vergès, nicknamed "the Devil's Advocate." Vergès, who had defended notorious clients ranging from the terrorist Carlos the Jack to the Nazi Klaus

Barbie, pioneered the legal strategy of "rupture," which involves reframing trials to focus on the legitimacy of the court.[13] The ECCC is vulnerable to this strategy.

Early on, as corruption charges circulated, Vergès underscored bias, political interference, and corruption at the ECCC. After an early attempt to stop him from discussing such matters, Vergès responded, "If you believe that we should not talk about corruption here I shall not impose that debate upon you." He added, "It's not good to [shoot] on ambulances and victims and the wounded . . . [or] dying people or institutions."[14]

Although Vergès died in 2013, his tactics continued to be used by other lawyers, including Michael Vercken, who sought to foreground historical context, arguing that DK didn't "spring from nothing." In his Case 002/01 closing statements, Vercken argued, "We should add to those in the dock the American government, [which] started the bombings. We talk of the American bombings as if it is just an anecdote, but how do you explain the famine from 1975 to 1979 without talking of those years of destruction?"[15]

Vercken resigned in 2015, leaving Anta Guissé and her Cambodian counterpart, Sam Onn, to defend Khieu Samphan during Case 002/02. While less flamboyant than Vergès and Vercken, Guissé and Sam Onn continued to question the legitimacy of the court and highlight the role of the United States, including in questions they would ask me on the last day of my testimony.[16]

Nuon Chea's defense team increasingly turned to "rupture" as they grew convinced of the court's political bias and unfairness, referring to it as "the elephant in the room" at the ECCC.[17] This perception was fueled by corruption scandals and accusations of political interference, underscored by government statements, judicial decisions, and irregularities in the judicial process, including a major scandal involving the Office of the Co-Investigating Judges in 2012.[18]

By this time, Nuon Chea's defense lawyers had grown increasingly outspoken and contemptuous, leading to a Trial Chamber reprimand.[19] In response, several of Nuon Chea's international lawyers resigned. Then, on July 17, 2013, Nuon Chea announced he would no longer speak in court, following a Trial Chamber decision to limit his team's questioning of a key witness.[20] Nuon Chea's defense team would later unite with Khieu Samphan's to stage a boycott. Although the defense teams later rejoined the proceedings, they remained contemptuous of the court—especially Koppe.

Amid these tensions, and to robustly mount Nuon Chea's defense, Koppe acknowledges deploying the strategy of rupture, "operating within this [juridical] structure [while] at the same time heavily criticizing that power structure." He explains, "The central goal of any trial is to ascertain the truth, to determine whether the accused is guilty . . . [but] the ECCC is not about finding the truth," but instead implementing victor's justice.[21]

Koppe likens himself to Atticus Finch from *To Kill a Mockingbird*, struggling to defend an innocent man accused of horrific crimes in the face of systemic bias comparable to racism in the 1930s US South.[22] Against the odds, Koppe likewise claims to be fighting to reveal the truth that, as opposed to carrying out a Nazi-like genocide, the Khmer Rouge, supported by China, were locked in a fierce struggle with an equally powerful faction allied with Vietnam. It was the members of the rival faction who "acted independently to commit the crimes for which Nuon Chea was charged." It is the same denialist argument, mixing truth and lies, that the Khmer Rouge told after DK and that Nuon Chea recounted to journalist Thet Sambath.

Koppe takes it as his personal mission to challenge the prevailing historical view. He has even named his two dogs "Nhim" and "Phim," after two key leaders of the rival faction, a play on a DK refrain warning of "running dogs of all stripes," including Vietnamese agents.[23] Ultimately, Koppe states, "My job is to be an advocate for my clients, to make sure their perspectives are getting across. . . . Nuon Chea's position is quite clear, and much of what we do is derived from what he tells us."[24]

This defense includes foregrounding US culpability and war crimes. Nuon Chea's team has emphasized this point from the start. On the opening day of the trial, one of his lawyers asked, "Why were the terrible American bombings of Cambodia . . . not investigated, and their lasting impact [on] the people in this country? Is this Court trying to bury history?"[25]

Nuon Chea, Koppe suggests, believes in much of the defense narrative, as well as the good of the Khmer Rouge revolutionary cause, even if he acknowledges "moral responsibility" for its excesses. Koppe says he admires Nuon Chea's conviction and desire to fight power, although Koppe believes in "radical individualism" as opposed to Nuon Chea's collectivism. Nuon Chea's belief that he was doing good in the name of the revolutionary cause is, "exactly the same [as] the guy who sits in the desert in Nevada operating a drone . . . [and] gets the instruction to shoot a rocket on a wedding in south Yemen, to execute [a] terrorist. . . . This military person, right now as we speak, is killing people, is convinced of the righteousness of his cause."[26]

Expert Bias and the Standard Total View

The questions Koppe poses to me are made in the context of this defense. I am, he wants to claim, biased, like most of the expert witnesses—even as key expert witnesses the defense has proposed are not being called to testify. This claim of bias is important in part because of my testimony about my fieldwork research in Region 41, where Muslim Chams and ethnic Vietnamese were targeted and which the prosecution has foregrounded in its arguments supporting a conviction for genocide. Koppe knows that I can't reveal my sources due to university human subjects protocols, and he presses the point, asking for verification. Koppe seeks to have my testimony dismissed as unsubstantiated, with "magical Teap" as a prime example.

More broadly, Koppe wants to demonstrate that my scholarship and testimony reflect the "standard total view" that reduces historical complexity to Manichean narrative form. To this end, Koppe questions me about my repeated use of "paranoia" to describe the DK leaders. As opposed to acting in a "paranoid" manner, Koppe states, the DK regime acted reasonably and rationally in response to an enemy threat from Vietnam that was "absolutely real."[27] This sort of language, Koppe suggests, is part of a larger pro–United States, anti-communist narrative.

In response, I use Koppe's argument against him. Invoking the standard total view framing, I reply that "it's a standardized reductive manner of speaking to simply say that Vietnam was a real threat as if that [threat] existed from 1975 to 1979 everywhere for all people . . . with no nuance, no change." The situation was, I continue, more fluid and changed as the DK regime responded to challenges and threats, real and imagined. There is "abundant evidence that this regime had a paranoid element to it," even if it was part of "a larger process." Accordingly, it is important to examine "temporal flow and spatial flow over time and not draw standardized uniform conclusions about a situation that was more fluid, dialogic, dynamic, and varied."[28]

Wednesday morning, March 1, ECCC courtroom (defense questioning)

"Yesterday, I think about four or five times," Koppe states, "you made a comparison to Nazi Germany."[29] He pauses. "Isn't it true there is a huge difference between on the one hand, how Nazi Germany viewed Jews, and how they were treated as opposed to how DK saw Vietnam and how DK ultimately treated its Vietnamese citizens?"

"Thank you." I reply. Koppe has opened a door he tried to shut on the first day of my testimony, an analysis of the origin of the term "genocide." I seize the opportunity and begin a discussion of Raphael Lemkin, the Polish jurist who coined the term. Lemkin, I note, envisioned genocide as encompassing a wide range of victim groups—not just the racial, ethnic, religious, and national groups protected under the UN genocide convention but also political, social, and economic groups who suffered physical, biological, and cultural destruction.

When most people think of genocide, they imagine the Holocaust: state-sponsored mass murder, ghettos, Nazi fanatics, concentration camps, and Auschwitz. Although history and context are essential, comparisons can still be made by examining the dynamics of the genocidal process, as illustrated by the process of priming and manufacturing difference, which I had discussed during prosecution questioning. If one does consider such comparisons, parallels between Nazi Germany and the Khmer Rouge are evident—as is the fact that the DK regime committed genocide, regardless of whether you use a narrow or broad definition.

"I find the comparison very unpractical." Koppe seems displeased by my long reply.[30] He takes a different tack, tries to confound me with more ambiguous cases. "[Do] you believe, as a genocide scholar . . . [that] mass deportations or mass confinements are also [genocide]?" He asks me to consider "the mass internment of Japanese people in 1941 and subsequently in the United States" that involved dehumanizing "Japanese citizens. Do you consider that genocide?"

"It depends on what definition you use to begin to make a determination," I reply.

"Well, let me interrupt you," Koppe cuts in. "The problem with your opinions is that the word 'genocide' is all over the place. It is mass killings, political violence. It doesn't seem to matter. So my question to you . . . [is whether Japanese internment] was an act of genocide in the US."[31]

"Your Honour," Smith intervenes. "I have no objection to the question, but [do object to] the critiquing and criticizing of the expert prior to asking a question."

Finally, I'm allowed to answer. Notwithstanding his intent, Koppe has focused on a case that is underexamined. In December 1941, after Pearl Harbor, the US government had begun to register and round up Japanese living in its territories, regardless of whether they were citizens or had lived in the country for many years.[32]

Perhaps 120,000 Japanese Americans were imprisoned in concentration camps and had their assets frozen as they lived in difficult conditions and were subject to suspicion and abuse—including "Yellow Peril" invectives that had a long history in the United States and previously had helped fuel anti-Asian prejudice and discriminatory polices such as the Chinese Exclusion Act of 1882. Some people viewed Japanese Americans as part of the enemy side in a "race war." Many faced prejudice even after their release following the war. It wasn't until 1988 that the United States apologized and paid reparations to Japanese American victims.

"You raise a very interesting question," I say to Koppe, "and one that deserves further study." While I am not an expert on Japanese American internment and detailed research would be needed to make an accurate assessment, I continue, genocidal priming appears to have been underway. In the context of war and upheaval, a group was rounded up and confined (the organization of difference) and depicted as a threat and dehumanized through "Asian Peril" discourses (the marking and crystallization of difference). There is little doubt that the forced removal and incarceration of Japanese Americans at this time constitutes an atrocity crime. The case for genocide is less clear. Regardless, Japanese internment was a situation in which the possibility of genocide rose, one that would warrant a genocide alert today.

Wednesday afternoon, March 17, 2016

"Isn't it true that Vietnam was a real enemy?" Koppe asks me as he turns to the last main topic of his questioning, Vietnam. "And [isn't it true] that the fear of DK and the CPK were real?"[33]

His objectives are twofold. First, Koppe explains, he seeks to establish that Vietnam was a "very clear, and at that time, present danger to Cambodia's sovereignty, independence, [and] national security." Thus, when the DK regime used the term *yuon*, it was "not, in fact, to use your terms, dehumanizing people, but they were clearly speaking about Vietnam's policy and Vietnam's threat."[34] In other words, the DK texts Smith had earlier quoted about "the *yuon*" were directed externally, toward Vietnam, not ethnic Vietnamese.[35]

Moreover, Koppe says, arriving at his second key point, the people the DK regime "suspected of collaborating with Vietnam . . . were understandably and quite rightfully regarded as potential traitors." The actions taken by the DK regime to combat this very real threat, he emphasizes, were not the result of "paranoia on their side," but a legitimate response to a very real threat, "just as today the United States or France consider ISIS or al-Qaeda as their enemy."[36]

Koppe has arrived at the heart of the Nuon Chea defense. If U.S. bombing had helped fuel the DK flames, the defense contends, Vietnam first set the fire and eventually created the conflagration that destroyed the DK regime. This argument, Nuon Chea's team emphasizes, runs counter to the standard total view and has been silenced by power.

The Crocodile Defense

As noted earlier, Nuon Chea has been making this argument in one form or another for years. During DK, he and his Khmer Rouge inveighed against Vietnamese perfidy as they were beginning to lose their grip on power. They continued to do so afterward when fighting against the Vietnamese-backed PRK regime.

Nuon Chea made this contention during his interviews with Thet Sambath, and he articulated it once again when he first took the stand at the start of Case 002/01. Wearing oversized glasses, Nuon Chea began with a defiant greeting, as he paid "respect to our ancestors who sacrificed their flesh, blood, bones, and life to defend our motherland for so many years," especially those who fought the "incursion, annexation, land grabbing, and racial extermination from the Vietnamese Socialist Republic and other neighboring countries."[37]

"I, Nuon Chea," he continued, "have been given an opportunity today which I have been waiting for so long. That is, to explain to my beloved Cambodian people and the Khmer children [about] the facts that occurred in Cambodian history."[38] He wanted to tell them, he claimed, "proper history," not an account that was biased. Unfortunately, he warned, he was unable to do so because "this court has been unfair to me from the start" due to its temporal jurisdiction, which limits the discussion to the DK period and thereby erases what transpired before and after the DK regime.

To underscore this point, Nuon Chea invoked a metaphor that his defense team would subsequently make the center of their pleadings. The court, Nuon Chea stated, was only examining the DK "body of the crocodile . . . not its head or tail which are important parts of its daily activities."[39] In other words, he explained, the court focuses only on DK (the body of the crocodile), while ignoring the pre-1975 "root causes" (the head) of the conflict and the post-1979 aftermath (the tail).

FIGURE 5.1. Nuon Chea giving testimony near the start of Case 002/01, ECCC courtroom, December 5, 2011.

Photo courtesy of ECCC.

Nuon Chea selected this metaphor for a reason. While it can be used to highlight US perfidy, the analogy more directly invokes Vietnam. In Cambodian cosmology, the crocodile may connote savagery and treachery and is used as a metaphor for Vietnam, sometimes in tandem with the term *yuon*.

Indeed, Koppe at one point sought to challenge my testimony by recalling King Sihanouk's 1979 use of this phrase, putting me in the position of potentially having to impugn the reputation of the recently deceased king by maintaining that the language he had used—"land-swallowing Vietnamese" and "*yuon* crocodile"—had racist connotations.[40]

The defense invokes Nuon Chea's statement and metaphor throughout his trial and in their submissions, which have headings like "The Crocodile: What Really Happened before, during, and after the DK Period."[41] Nuon Chea states that while he wants to help the court accomplish its goals of "obtaining justice" and "ascertaining the truth," the head and tail of the crocodile also need to be examined.[42]

On his first day of testimony, Nuon Chea laid out his case against Vietnam, arguing that Vietnam had a long history of seeking to dominate Cambodia, with its "policy of incursion, annexation, land grabbing, [and] racial extermination." Nuon Chea began his narrative in the 1930s, when, he claimed, Ho Chi Minh created the Indochinese Communist Party to take control of the Cambodian and Lao revolutionary movements and dominate a future Indochinese Federation.[43]

Vietnam's attempt to co-opt the Khmer Rouge revolution was part of Vietnam's historical "March to the South" to colonize Cambodia and take its land. Nuon Chea gave highlights in court, arguing that "from 1960 to 1979, Vietnamese employed every trick available to destroy the Kampuchean revolution." Vietnam discouraged the armed struggle and critiqued the Khmer Rouge party line even as Vietnam was building networks within the Khmer Rouge ranks. In a mid-1974 CPK Standing Committee meeting, Nuon Chea stated, the Khmer Rouge leaders agreed that "Vietnam [had] never abandoned its ambition to manage Indochina" and that the revolutionaries would need to respond accordingly.[44]

Vietnam, Nuon Chea contends, is the "main factor" behind the DK "confusion."[45] Vietnam had taken a two-pronged approach to reassert its control over Cambodia. First, Vietnam mobilized its hidden networks as it sought to subvert the revolution and overthrow the DK regime. Nuon Chea's defense team would call this "Plan A."[46] When this plan failed, Vietnam turned to "Plan B," armed force. From the start, the two countries had border disputes. Fighting broke out in 1977 and included, Nuon Chea stresses, a massive Vietnamese strike at the end of the year.

The late 1978 Vietnamese invasion of Cambodia was the culmination of this conflict, enabling the Vietnamese to topple the Khmer Rouge and create a new government headed by its minions, including East Zone soldiers who had fled the purges. "On what grounds did Vietnam justify its incursion of Cambodia?" Nuon Chea asked the court. "Was Vietnam's incursion of Cambodia legal under international law?"[47]

This invasion and its aftermath constituted the core of the "tail" of "the crocodile": Vietnam's fulfillment of its imperialist ambitions, "unchanged for centuries," to dominate Cambodia and ultimately "occupy, annex, swallow Cambodia, and rid Cambodia of her race and ethnicity and bring further Vietnamese illegal immigrants to live in Cambodia." He likened Vietnam's strategy to "a python suffocating a young deer," which will only "swallow its prey after [the prey has] suffocated."[48] Vietnam, Nuon Chea warned, continues this strategy in the present.

Nuon Chea's defense team has built their case around these claims about "the crocodile." The gist of the argument, which the Khmer Rouge have been asserting for years, is largely spelled out in DK's 1978 *Black Paper* tract and defense arguments and briefs have given it legal form.[49] The crocodile, they claim, "absolves Nuon Chea of individual criminal responsibility," though ultimately, "Nuon Chea has no case to answer as the evidence is insufficient." Given the bias of the court, however, "the primary purpose" of the defense is to present to the public "Nuon Chea's insight into the head, body, and tail of the Crocodile."[50]

I have been critiquing this argument throughout Koppe's questioning. Nuon Chea will confront me with this crocodile defense again on the last day of my testimony, when I will face the challenge of responding directly to a person who has been using such arguments as part of a long-standing campaign of genocide denial.

6

DENIAL

Thursday late morning, March 17, 2016, ECCC courtroom

"Our client is quite upset with Mr. Hinton's testimony," Victor Koppe suddenly informs the court. Nuon Chea, who has been listening to the proceedings from his holding cell as part of his unofficial boycott of the court, wants to make a statement and have me respond. He is about to break his long silence.

Koppe glances at me with a half-smile. He has been attacking my testimony from the start. Now he is bringing out the defense team's secret weapon, Nuon Chea's dagger tongue. I have no idea that Nuon Chea will try to implicate me in atrocity crimes.

We wait. Minutes stretch like hours.

Yet, there is also energy in the court. Anticipation. It's expressed in whispered conversations and fidgeting, as if we have reached the climax of a drama three and a half days long.

For the court personnel, much of what takes place is procedure. They have been here long enough that they can predict how the other parties will act. Nuon Chea's appearance is unexpected. No one is sure what this loose cannon will say—or how I will respond to his oratorical fire.

Suddenly, the courtroom falls silent. There is movement in the defense section. A back door swings open.

I watch as Brother Number Two is rolled into the courtroom in a wheelchair.

I had imagined him as a towering presence, a man whose mere glance would render a person mute. Instead, he's wrinkled and in his late eighties, someone who needs to be helped into his seat by two guards.

For a moment, I feel sorry for him. Then I glance at the civil parties and think of how they and millions of other Cambodians suffered during DK. I wonder what they are thinking as Nuon Chea whispers to his lawyers, shuffles his papers, gets ready to speak.

Of course, he claims to be their champion, a man who had spent a lifetime fighting for the Cambodian masses.

Nuon Chea stresses that, while carrying out Pol Pot's orders, he gave up everything for a revolution that served "the interests of the nation and people." He has been playing it both ways, hero and pawn, even as he assumes the airs of a courtroom sage.

Now, as he settles into his seat and speaks briefly to his team, Nuon Chea is readying to reveal more of his truth that blames others for a righteous path turned terribly wrong. He is so close that I can make out the high slope of his forehead, a face weathered from years in the sun, his balding head. He sits a row behind Koppe and his national defense lawyer counterpart, Son Arun.

"I would like to give the floor now to Nuon Chea so that he can react to the testimony of the expert," Judge Nil announces.

"Mr. Expert," Judge Nil continues, looking at me, "please listen to the reaction by Nuon Chea to your testimony during the last three and a half days, and if it is necessary, you will be given the floor to respond." Now, one of only a few times during Case 002/02, Nuon Chea is about to speak.

"Nuon Chea," Judge Nil finishes, "you have the floor."

Nuon Chea looks up. Our eyes lock. Then he furrows his brow and begins reading a statement.

"Thank you, Mr. President, for permitting me to come provide clarification on this matter," Nuon Chea starts, his voice steady, well paced. "I am uneasy with the testimony given by the expert."

"I looked in the 1967 Khmer dictionary," he continues, his voice rising. "On page 955, line 5, the term *yuon* is defined as a noun to refer to those who resided in Tonkin, Annam, Cochinchina," he says, referring to different parts of French colonial Vietnam. As he speaks, he stresses certain words, starting with *yuon*, pausing for emphasis.

The meaning and use of this term, about which both the defense and prosecution have questioned me, is central to demonstrating that genocide against ethnic Vietnamese took place during DK. In international law, genocidal intent is difficult to prove, especially in situations like DK where there is less documentation. Intent, however, may be gleaned from other evidence, such as demographic data, testimony, and a context of incitement.

The demographic data is compelling: almost all the two hundred thousand or so ethnic Vietnamese living in Cambodia in 1975 were expelled or killed. In this context, the Khmer Rouge use of *yuon* is critical because it suggests genocidal incitement. Koppe returned to this issue again and again. Now Nuon Chea feels compelled to do so himself.

Nuon Chea stops reading and stares at me while saying dismissively, "So Democratic Kampuchea did not mean to incite anyone. The term is clearly defined in that dictionary." He shakes the single page of text in his right hand as he finishes.

"Further," Nuon Chea continues, now looking around the room as if speaking to a captive audience. "Pol Pot gave instructions that we should not regard them as our hereditary enemy because the Vietnamese were our friends."

He clears his throat, then goes on, "Cambodian people may consider *yuon* a hereditary enemy, but for Pol Pot, he said only that we were friends but had contradictions with them. This is the point I want to clarify." Then he adds, "In no way is there any incitement in this term."

Nuon Chea no longer reads prepared text; he just stares at me as he speaks. His voice commands attention, has the edge of unwavering belief. He modulates his tone, emphasizes key words and phrases as if, instead of speaking inside a courtroom, he is back behind the podium at a Khmer Rouge political meeting inveighing against "hidden enemies burrowing from within."

Except now I am the enemy.

Then Nuon Chea refers to a controversial Pol Pot speech, given in 1978 as war with Vietnam raged, which called for the mass killings of "yuon."

"This is also wrong," Nuon Chea states, arguing that the speech referred to military tactics necessitated by the far smaller number of DK troops. "It did not in any way refer to the killing of any 'Yuon' civilians. This is what I want to clarify."

For a moment, I think he is finished. Then he says, "Now we come to questions."

"Questions?" I think to myself, startled. I am about to be interrogated by a man accused of genocide.

"I would like to please ask Mr. Expert," he begins, his tone cloying, as he reads from his prepared remarks once again, "if, from the past all the way to the present, has Vietnam ever abandoned its ambition to swallow Cambodia?" He doesn't use the word *yuon*.

"Second," he continues, "Mr. Expert, you are an American citizen and you know that the United States dropped three million tons of bombs on Cambodia for three hundred days and nights. As a result, many houses, pagodas, and infrastructure were destroyed along with the lives of gentle Cambodian people. Do you consider that a war crime and genocide?"

The distance between us shrinks. The accusation hangs in the air. How do I refute this genocidal extremist who distorts the truth, tries to finger me for his crimes?

"Mr. Expert," President Nil says, "if you wish, you may respond to the two questions put to you by Nuon Chea."[1]

I pause, feel the weight of his words, his accusation, the historical implications of a reply. I try to gather my thoughts, formulate a response to Nuon Chea's accusations. On a notepad, I circle the word "genocide."

President Nil pauses. Bill Smith is standing, an objection. "But before that, I'd like to give the floor to the International Deputy Co-Prosecutor." A reprieve, time to collect my thoughts.

"Thank you, Your Honor," Smith begins, his arms clasped behind his back. "Many of the statements made by Nuon Chea do not tally with what the Prosecution says is the evidence." Smith contends that I shouldn't be asked to comment without consulting the case file. He manages to read part of a DK statement.

"He's pleading, Mr. President!" Koppe breaks in. "I would like you to stop the Prosecution."

"Your Honor, I'm about to get to my question," Smith replies, unmoved. "Unfortunately, I was interrupted by my friend," Smith goes on. "And if we're talking about speeches, I think we've heard many of them—many, many of them—from our friend yesterday."

Smith and Koppe are having their final fight as Nuon Chea sits down in his chair.

Smith quotes a Khmer Rouge statement: "Kampuchea's people are against Vietnam which is the hereditary enemy." This, he contends, "is a complete contrast to what Nuon Chea [just] stated."

"Mr. President, if I may. I really do object to these remarks from the Prosecution," Koppe complains. "He is feeding the expert the answers!" He adds, baiting me, "Mr. Hinton is man enough to be able to give a reaction."[2]

President Nil navigates the conflict, moving the proceedings toward their conclusion. "The matters have been extensively discussed," he says. "It is up to

Mr. Expert whether he wishes to respond. And now I'd like to hand the floor to the expert."

The court falls silent. Everyone is watching. What do you say to a genocidal extremist who denies his crimes and suggests you are partly to blame?

Before I respond, I glance down at the third image I had brought with me to court, the cover sheet of a S-21 confession written by Long Muy after torture and interrogation. In addition to containing basic identifying information, the confession is covered with annotations, including comments written by Duch, the commandant of S-21.

During his trial, Duch sought to use Long Muy's confession to prove that he was just a cog in the machine. Duch claimed that he merely conveyed information gleaned by his interrogators to his superiors—at first Son Sen and later Nuon Chea—who then gave him instructions that he relayed back to his interrogators. Long Muy's confession was of particular note because at the very top of the page, it included an annotation from Pol Pot, which Duch contended illustrated that the top leaders reviewed such documents and controlled everything that went on at S-21, including torture and execution.

To further support his argument that he lacked command responsibility, Duch pointed to a key March 30, 1976, Central Committee document assigning "the right to smash," a common Khmer Rouge euphemism for execution. S-21, Duch noted, was not among those given authorization to execute people. "It was not S-21, it was not me, it was the upper echelon who made decisions," he told the court. "So when there's an order, we had to follow. If we failed to do that, we would be beheaded."[3]

Like the image of the DK national emblem that I brought with me to court each day, the cover sheet of Long Muy's confession is a reminder of the DK regime's centralized control over the decision making, including the authorization of torture and execution. And like the copy of Bou Meng's painting, this image reminded me of the devastating impact the authorization of violence had on people on the ground. I know Bou Meng well, and I also traveled to the countryside to visit Long Muy's brother. He was quite aware of Duch's testimony and viewed it as a ruse: "People who do wrong don't admit it; they point their finger at someone else to escape the charges."[4]

I had brought the cover sheet of Long Muy's confession with me to remind me of this point as I testified. And indeed, Nuon Chea has at times pointed the finger at Pol Pot, suggesting that he himself had little control—even as at other times he stated that the two worked hand in hand to formulate DK policy.

Now, as I sit in the witness stand and prepare to respond to Nuon Chea, I think of the importance of rebutting the half-truths, lies, and denials of perpetrators like Nuon Chea, who seek to avoid responsibility for the mass human rights violations they have committed. Nuon Chea's remarks reiterate claims he has long made to present an alternative narrative denying his crimes. Vietnam stands at the center of his story, with the United States close at hand: the two culprits Nuon Chea singles out. My task now is to counter his "crocodile argument" denials.

Ultimately, Nuon Chea's defense is built on a weak foundation. Like many denialist arguments, Nuon Chea's defense mixes fact and fiction to manufacture a seemingly reasonable alternative account. It is true that the Vietnamese-backed PRK regime asserted a Manichean narrative after DK. So, too, have scholars and members of the media and international community sometimes bought into the account and vilified the DK regime, albeit understandably, given the mass deaths and suffering. And Nuon Chea is right to stress that the focus on the DK regime masks the culpability of geopolitical actors including the United States.

But, ultimately, the Nuon Chea defense does exactly what it claims to critique: it reduces a massive and nuanced scholarly and historical literature down to an overly simplified framing centered on "the crocodile." Scholars have for years recognized there were different factions within the Khmer Rouge, some with sympathies to Vietnam. The crocodile simply reverses the logic, creating a different Manichean "evil" (the United States and especially Vietnam) to which the "good" (the well-intentioned DK regime, which had liberated the country from oppression, only to be betrayed by internal enemies and toppled by Vietnam) was opposed.

And then there are the deaths. Nuon Chea's defense makes almost no mention of them. Nor has Nuon Chea offered an unconditional apology or shown more than halting remorse. The most Nuon Chea offered was his remark to Thet Sambath that he accepted "all the mistakes that other people had made. I blame them but I am the leader . . . [and] must accept responsibility for what happened." But, he added, "I am not a killer." The DK regime had targeted only "bad cadre and traitors" who "wanted to destroy us and make problems . . . [and] killed our people and we only killed [these people] who killed our people. Why should we keep them?"[5]

Nuon Chea was quick to blame others. While he acknowledged being "in charge of the legislative body and education, [the] killing was the problem of government administration, which was the responsibility of Pol Pot and Son Sen."[6] Lower-level, "bad" cadre, he asserted, did the killing and hid the fact they were overworking the people while sometimes giving them only starvation rations.[7]

International actors like Kissinger were also to blame. Nuon Chea's defense further deploys a classic denialist strategy that the Khmer Rouge have been using for years, arguing that the number of DK deaths have been vastly exaggerated despite enormous evidence to the contrary.[8]

While the first page of his defense's Case 002/02 closing brief notes that Nuon Chea had accepted "moral responsibility" for DK suffering,[9] it quickly launches into a 550-page discussion of the crocodile and related matters that displace responsibility onto a long list of evil others, especially Vietnam and the Cambodian revolutionaries Vietnam allegedly controlled. The crocodile defense is written like a tragedy in which a valiant hero (Nuon Chea and his comrades who had liberated the country from oppression) is doomed by the machinations of an evil nemesis ("land-swallowing" Vietnam). Although the shortcomings of the Cambodian government's Manichean atrocity narrative are clear, Nuon Chea's defense also relies on a Manichean narrative that is ultimately a form of genocide denial.[10] This is a point my reply to Nuon Chea must underscore.

"Thank you, Mr. President," I begin. "I'd like to thank the Accused for coming here to express his views."[11] His voice, I state, thinking of his boycott, has been "too absent" and "his perspective should be aired." Although as the defendant he should have the last word, I say, I will make a brief reply since he has asked me questions.

The first question was predictable, linked to his defense argument that Vietnam is responsible for all that went wrong, part of the unseen "head and tail of the crocodile" that has been ignored in favor of the "standard total view."

But the defense's use of this argument has a flaw, exposing it to being hoisted by its own petard. I had noted this during the proceedings and do so again now. "In terms of the question about the Vietnamese fulfilling a long-standing goal," I tell the court, looking at the defense, Nuon Chea's remarks provide "a very standardized, reductive, teleological view of what occurred." It ignores "historical and temporal and spatial variation. It reduces a complex historical and political situation in a reductive manner."[12] The Nuon Chea defense itself, I state, is premised on a "standard total view."

Now, I have to get out of Nuon Chea's "blame the United States" trap.

While Vietnam was central to the events that were taking place, Nuon Chea contended, so too was the United States. In his initial remarks to the court, Nuon Chea traced the history of how, in its Cold War attempt to combat communism, the United States gradually built up its military presence in Southeast Asia as the Vietnam War escalated. By the late 1960s, the United States was already bombing targets in Cambodia—both Khmer Rouge forces and North Vietnamese supply routes.

In 1973, Nuon Chea stated, the United States greatly increased its bombing of Cambodia while there was a cease-fire during peace negotiations with North Vietnam. "From February 1973 until mid-August 1973," Nuon Chea told the court, the United States used B-52s to carpet-bomb Cambodia, resulting in many deaths and extensive damage to "villages, pagodas, schools, [and Cambodia's] economy."[13]

Nuon Chea's defense lawyers highlighted this US part of "the head of the crocodile" throughout their pleadings, underscoring that during 230,516 sorties from 1965 to 1973, "the Americans dropped 2,756,941 tons of bombs on Cambodia, more than the total used by all the Allied Forces combined during the entirety of World War II including the nuclear bombs that struck Hiroshima and Nagasaki."[14]

Even as Nuon Chea noted that the destructiveness of this bombing was inestimable, his lawyers argued that the revolutionaries alone "lost an estimated 16,000 men and women," while hundreds of thousands of Cambodian civilians died, up to two million were displaced, and the economic infrastructure was devastated.[15] The Nuon Chea Case 002/01 defense brief quotes a study that states Cambodia may well be the most heavily bombed country in history.

As Koppe had suggested, B-52s are still wreaking havoc from the skies. As I testify in March 2016, bombs are falling on enemies old (the Taliban and al-Qaeda) and new (ISIS and the Assad regime). The day before I took the stand, the United States announced that B-52s are being sent to join the ongoing bombing campaign against ISIS, Operation Inherent Resolve.

Henry Kissinger, an architect of the bombing of Cambodia, has also been back in the news. In 2014 on National Public Radio, he recommended attacking ISIS with "superior air power" while claiming, "I bet if one did an honest account, there were fewer civilian casualties in Cambodia than there have been from American drone attacks."[16] He is engaging in his own form of denial.

The next year, in a 2015 Senate Armed Services Committee hearing, CodePink protestors tried to stage a citizens' arrest of Kissinger for crimes committed in Cambodia, Vietnam, and East Timor, among other places.[17] Their actions were part of a long-standing campaign to hold the United States accountable for atrocity crimes, efforts that famously included the 1967 Russell International War Crimes Tribunal.[18]

It was to this line of argumentation that Nuon Chea has returned. He wants to make me, a US citizen, a stand-in for these US crimes, a scapegoat onto whom he can displace blame for his crimes against humanity.[19]

All tribunals are founded on the fault lines of jurisdiction—who to try, for what crimes in which place, and for what period of time. In the case of the ECCC, the jurisdiction had been especially tricky because two permanent members of the UN Security Council, the United States and China, held veto power over the establishment of the ECCC. The result was a truncated temporal jurisdiction for the court, which covers only the years of DK, not what occurred before and after. In this regard, the missing "head and tail of the crocodile" argument of the defense foregrounds important silences in the proceedings.

As defense lawyers have repeatedly pointed out, this limited jurisdiction both diminishes the historical understanding that will emerge from the tribunal and precludes accountability for superpower crimes. China long provided support for the Khmer Rouge, including during DK. The United States, as Nuon Chea emphasizes, rained bombs on the Cambodian countryside.

Did the United States commit war crimes? Almost certainly. The bombing was too often indiscriminate, unconcerned for civilians on the ground. Over fifty thousand people—some say more—are thought to have been killed during the attacks. The displacement and property loss were enormous. Though the bombing may have forestalled the Khmer Rouge victory, it also provided the Khmer Rouge with a stream of new peasant recruits angered by the death and devastation wreaked on their homes and villages.

Yet now I am in an international court of law and wary of Nuon Chea's intentions. Why does he ask this? I know Nuon Chea is pandering to his dwindling number of supporters as well as Cambodians who blame foreign powers for what took place during DK. But I know his question is also part of his genocide denial, as he seeks to obscure his own responsibility and to blame others. He depicts Pol Pot as the culprit, himself as an obedient follower. He suggests Vietnam and the United States are the ones who should be convicted. And he implicates me as a US citizen to further minimize his guilt.

"With regard to the second question about the US Bombing," I acknowledge, the United States "might have violated international law." No one, I add, would contest that the bombing "had an awful impact."[20] But the United States did not cause the genocide.

I return to the model of the genocidal process I discussed earlier in the trial, which provides a way to account for the role of US bombing, but more importantly, for Nuon Chea's own crimes. Most genocides, I noted on my first day of testimony, emerge from the tumult of upheaval, including war. Particularly in the twentieth century, this situation has provided fertile ground for demagogues who offer a blueprint for renewal, ranging from Hitler's notion of the new Aryan *volk* community to Pol Pot and Nuon Chea's vision of a pure new revolutionary society. Such a vision is also evident in the rhetoric of more contemporary groups like ISIS.

The problem is that only certain types of people are viewed as worthy of membership in the promised new community. These pure groups are juxtaposed to the contaminating enemies who threaten their survival. To counter the threat, genocidal regimes take extreme actions, stigmatizing and disempowering the group they depict as dangerous, even as members of the victim group are regulated, registered, and controlled. Moral inhibitions against these targets are not just lifted but replaced by norms making such destruction a seemingly necessary good. Genocide may quickly emerge in such a situation, with ready targets at hand, as had been the case during DK.

Although the US bombing contributed significantly to the tumult that preceded DK, it was not responsible for the decisions Nuon Chea and his Khmer Rouge comrades later took. It is a point I need to underscore.

"The bombing was part of a process of upheaval," I continue, that, "combined with the CPK's [radical] vision of society, ultimately and unfortunately, once people were labeled as class enemies, as subversives, as counterrevolutionaries burrowing within, led to genocide." The onus is back on Nuon Chea.

To conclude, I return to the issue with which Nuon Chea had begun, his denial that the term *yuon* has animus. He knows that it does. So, too, do the Cambodians in the court. Now I have the chance to put it on the record in front of Nuon Chea.

Nuon Chea has been clever, seeking to strip the term of its vitriol using a dictionary definition. As part of his subterfuge, he cites a publication date, 1967, close to the DK revolution. He fails to mention that the dictionary was created by a monk during the French colonial era and later reprinted.

As I had noted at length during my testimony, the term *yuon* is racially charged, linked to a set of stereotypes characterizing the Vietnamese as thieving, lying, corrupting, and covetous of Cambodian land. The 1978 DK publication *Black Paper* recounted the famous legend of the Master's Tea, which "recalls the barbarous crime committed by the 'Yuons' in 1817" when the Vietnamese buried several Cambodian laborers "up to their necks and used [their] heads as a stand for a wood stove to boil water for their master's tea." As the victims screamed and suffered, "the Yuon torturers said to them: 'Be careful not to spill the master's tea.'" A footnote in the tract states that the word "Yuon" means "savage."[21]

Like so much DK propaganda, *Black Paper* is filled with invective, beginning with the first chapter, "The Annexationist Nature of Vietnam," which states that Vietnam seeks to "swallow" Cambodian land. It is exactly the language Nuon Chea used in his first question. It is how he thought then and still thinks today.

"In the end," I say, "I stand strongly by my stance that the term *yuon* can be a very incendiary word. It's a word that can incite hatred and violence. And in the context of DK, it was an incitement to genocide."[22]

I glance at Nuon Chea, who scowls.

Genocide. With this word, my testimony is over. I am also relieved to have escaped unscathed from what felt like a modern-day coliseum. As the court clerk leads me out of the courtroom, a few people nod.

Exhausted, I descend a steep flight of stairs to the ground floor, eager to return to my hotel. When I reach the landing, I glimpse a movement to my right. It is Nuon Chea. He's back in his wheelchair. Two guards are helping him into a waiting ambulance, which will drive him fifty yards across the field where the Lord of the Iron Staff stands to the detention compound.

I pity him for a moment. I think of Cambodian Buddhists who pray even for the soul of a mass murderer, expressing compassion for another human being whose actions will likely lead to a tormented rebirth, perhaps deep in the Buddhist hells. For them, Nuon Chea is like all of us, a human being blinded by ego, desire, and ignorance.

Then I remember Bou Meng's painting depicting him and his wife just before they were marched through the gates of S-21. Large black blindfolds cross their eyes. He never saw her again, another victim of the Khmer Rouge. I wonder what Bou Meng would say if he knew I feel pity for the person who had oversight of S-21, where his wife disappeared and he was tortured. Yet, as a devout Buddhist, Bou Meng might understand. He told me many times how he sought to understand the actions of Khmer Rouge like Duch and Nuon Chea through a Buddhist lens. But he also said he sometimes "overwhelmingly" desired revenge.

I do know that as they struggle with such complicated thoughts and emotions, Bou Meng and other survivors still want answers. To find them, we need to acknowledge the humanity of perpetrators, even those who commit genocide. Their choices provide a warning but also lessons for the present.

Suddenly, I realize Nuon Chea is gone. The midday sun blazes, the humid air still. Tire tracks fade into the distance, impressions left on a dirt field blotched by dead grass and uncut weeds.

7

JUDGMENT

November 16, 2018, Phnom Penh, ECCC Courtroom (Trial Chamber verdict)

Now I sit on the other side of the glass as the curtains draw open at the ECCC. The first thing my eyes rest on is the witness stand where I sweated it out two and a half years ago.

Then I see Nuon Chea. He wears a black jacket and a blue dress shirt, top button unfastened. Oversized tinted sunglasses rest on his forehead. He looks older. Days before, rumors circulated that he might be too ill to attend the hearings, or might even die. He sits with a furrowed brow I remember well, his lip lines forming a frown. He pushes his sunglasses down, glances at the crowd.

The courtroom is packed. There's excitement in the air as people await the court's decision about whether Nuon Chea and Khieu Samphan will be found guilty of crimes against humanity, war crimes, and the charge about which I testified, genocide.

Cambodians have waited for this moment for forty years.

When I arrived two hours earlier, the court parking lot was already packed. A string of saffron-robed monks was being led in, skipping the long queue as a mark of their social status. I stood in line amid dozens of civil parties and high school students, some of the hundreds who have arrived for this last act in "the show."

Busloads of villagers are attending, packing the five-hundred-seat public gallery to capacity. I am given a badged marked "A" for "academic" and seated in the middle of the gallery. Dark-suited VIPs, including foreign embassy staff and Cambodian government officials, sit behind me. Civil parties line the rows to my front.

Once the observed, I am again an observer.

I notice Koppe staring into the public gallery, his expression flat. The night before, I attended a local screening of a new documentary focused on him, *Defending Brother No. 2*. It recounts the twists and turns of his defense of Nuon Chea, including his growing frustration with the court. In one scene, Koppe sobs quietly. In another, he walks his dogs, Nhim and Phim, in the streets of Phnom Penh.

The film is largely fawning, portraying Koppe as a sensitive man who lost much, including his wife, to defend a client deemed guilty before his trial had begun. Koppe is depicted as trying, despite the long odds, to reveal a truth buried by the Cambodian government, foreign powers, and academics intent on whitewashing the past. He fancies himself an amateur historian who can courageously set the record straight.

The screening room was packed with Cambodians and foreigners, many from the court, including members of Koppe's team. When the film concluded, Koppe strode to the front of the room to take questions. He got some hard ones, including challenges to his characterization of the tribunal as a political farce. At the end of the screening, Koppe and I crossed paths for a moment. Awkwardly, we shook hands. "Alex Hinton, right?" he said, then turned abruptly and walked into the bar.

"All rise," the loudspeaker instructs. Everyone stands while the Trial Chamber enters the courtroom in a line. The courtroom is silent as President Nil shuffles his papers and begins reading a summary of the court's judgment.

Like most legal documents, the summary judgment is dry and filled with legal vernacular, which is accentuated by President Nil's monotone delivery. Emotion would undercut the dispassionate airs of justice and the reason that is supposed to inform it. But the verdict is also a political document, asserting the authority and legitimacy of the court and creating a history that has its own silences, as Nuon Chea's defense lawyers relentlessly underscore.

The judgment begins with a procedural history of the case before detailing the scope of the Case 002/02 hearings, which began on October 17, 2014, and ended on January 11, 2017. Closing arguments were given in June 2017. "Over the course of 24 months of evidentiary hearings," President Nil states, "the

Chamber heard the testimony of 185 individuals, including 114 fact witnesses, 63 Civil Parties and 8 experts."

During this period, he continues, "close to 5,000 evidentiary documents were subjected to examination and admitted, totaling over 82,000 pages," a number that, when Case 002/01 materials were added in, rose to "more than 10,000 [documents], totaling over 304,000 pages."[1] These evidentiary details further buttress the court's legitimacy, which is asserted in more detail in the full 2,259-page judgment that also includes discussion of the court's jurisdiction, legal principles and procedures, and adherence to fair trial rights.[2]

Having established the court's legal authority, President Nil turns to the charges. Nuon Chea and Khieu Samphan, he states, are accused of being part of a "joint criminal enterprise" (JCE) operated by the senior DK leaders as they sought to rapidly achieve a socialist revolution that would be defended "against enemies by whatever means necessary."

To this end, President Nil continues, this joint criminal enterprise implemented five criminal policies: "(1) the repeated movement of the population from towns and cities to rural areas, as well as from one rural area to another; (2) the establishment and operation of cooperatives and worksites; (3) the establishment of security centres and execution sites."

Judge Nil tone never changes as he continues reading: "(4) the targeting of specific groups, including the Cham and Vietnamese, Buddhists and former Khmer Republic officials . . . and (5) the regulation of marriage." After a slight pause, President Nil adds, "It is further charged that the Accused planned, ordered, instigated, aided and abetted the aforementioned crimes against humanity, grave breaches and genocide."

In addition to being part of a joint criminal enterprise, President Nil says, Nuon Chea and Khieu Samphan "are also charged on the basis of superior responsibility." He proceeds to list the specific charges for each of the five policies in question. The charges for the attack on Chams and Vietnamese, he notes, include genocide.

"The Chamber's Main Findings," Nil announces. President Nil starts by listing the elements required for a conviction for crimes against humanity and war crimes. During DK, he notes, "there was a widespread and systematic attack against the civilian population of Cambodia" involving, among other things, "enslavement, forced transfer, murder, extermination, enforced disappearances, attacks against human dignity and political persecution." The accused are both implicated in these crimes against humanity. In addition, President Nil states, Nuon Chea and Khieu Samphan were aware that the DK regime was battling Vietnam and that civilians and soldiers were being targeted. The attack on these protected groups constitutes grave breaches of the Geneva Conventions.

After giving historical background centered on the formulation of the Khmer Rouge principles that drove their joint criminal enterprise, President Nil turns to the policies related to the aforementioned crimes. Because the first DK policy in question, population movements, had largely been adjudicated in Case 002/01, he starts with the second, cooperatives and worksites. The DK regime, Nil states, viewed cooperatives and worksites "as the primary instrument for waging class struggle and intended to create a labour and production force of strictly controlled people." They were characterized by a "climate of control, threats, fear, hunger and discrimination," and people died in large numbers—some from overwork, starvation, and disease, others by execution. Accordingly, President Nil states, the court finds that a variety of crimes against humanity were committed at the cooperatives and worksites.

"Security Centres and Execution Sites," President Nil states, transitioning to the third policy. "The Chamber finds that during the Democratic Kampuchea period there existed a policy to establish and operate security centres to identify, arrest, isolate and 'smash' those considered the most serious types of enemies." At the S-21 security center, President Nil continues, prisoners "were brought to interrogation rooms handcuffed and blindfolded, their legs chained during questioning."

I think of Bou Meng's painting of himself and his wife at the gates of S-21, just before their ordeal began. Nil lists the interrogation methods, some of which Bou Meng had endured: "beatings with sticks, rods, electrical wire, whips and other tools; electroshocks; suffocation through covering the head with a plastic bag; covering the mouth and nose with a towel and pouring cold water from a kettle; and the extraction of toenails and fingernails." Some prisoners, he adds, died after having the blood drained from their bodies.

"At the very least," President Nil continues, "11,742 prisoners were executed . . . [many] by a blow to the neck with an iron bar, after which their throats were slit with a knife and their bodies disemboweled—and buried in mass graves." Nuon Chea, President Nil states, was directly involved in the chain of command that ordered these executions. At one point, he notes, Nuon Chea oversaw the running of the prison, working directly with Duch to manage the interrogations, torture, and confessions of prisoners.

Nuon Chea suddenly raises his hand as President Nil pronounces that such acts carried out at security centers and execution sites constitute crimes against humanity. Nuon Chea requests to listen to the remainder of the proceedings from his holding cell. A few minutes later, Khieu Samphan asks for a restroom break.

By the time President Nil turns to the section on "the targeting of specific groups," which includes the genocide charge, Koppe has swiveled his chair, turning his back to the Trial Chamber and gazing at the public gallery.

The DK regime, President Nil continues, targeted a number of groups as they sought "to establish an atheistic and homogeneous society without class divisions by abolishing all ethnic, national, religious, racial, class and cultural differences." The targeted groups included Chams, Vietnamese, Buddhists, and personnel from the previous government.

President Nil begins with the Cham. They faced discrimination and their religious practices were forbidden. Some were forced to eat pork. Many were forced to relocate, and large numbers of Cham were killed. The judgment singles out Region 41, where I did my doctoral research, as particularly severe. I think of "magical Teap" and Grandmother Yit when President Nil confirms "that orders targeting the Cham in the Center (old North) Zone, and specifically in Region 41, came from the upper echelon." The Cham, President Nil concludes, were victims of genocide and crimes against humanity.

"Regarding the Vietnamese," President Nil states, shifting to the topic on which much of my testimony had focused, "the Chamber finds that from 1975 until the end of 1976, there was a nationwide policy to expel people of Vietnamese ethnicity living in Cambodia." The DK regime organized transports and more broadly sought to identify Vietnamese, in part by the use of "lists and biographies [that] were prepared by the lower echelons and then communicated back to the upper echelons for further action."

This process of organization helped lay the groundwork for the mass murder of Vietnamese based on their group membership, a key criterion for reaching a genocide verdict. These actions, President Nil continues, took place "under the umbrella of the CPK's policy to specifically target the Vietnamese, including civilians, as a group. Until late 1976, the Vietnamese were targeted for expulsion, from April 1977, for destruction as such." Accordingly, President Nil announces, "The Chamber thus finds that the crime of genocide and crimes against humanity of murder, extermination, deportation and persecution on racial grounds were committed regarding the Vietnamese."

After determining that the Khmer Rouge also committed crimes against humanity against Buddhists and former Khmer Republic officials, President Nil turns to the fifth and last policy under consideration, forced marriage. During DK, President Nil states, "there existed a nationwide policy to regulate family-building and marriage" as the DK regime went about "replacing the role of parents in the selection of a suitable spouse, forcing couples to marry and forcing the production of children for the purpose of increasing the country's population within 10 to 15 years." Newlyweds often slept in "an assigned location, monitored by militiamen, specifically to have sexual intercourse." These DK policies on forced marriage and the rape that took place therein, President Nil concludes, also reach the threshold of crimes against humanity.

Having found that the DK policies resulted in these various crimes, the judgment next examines the culpability of the accused. Nuon Chea and Khieu Samphan, President Nil goes on, were part of the DK regime's senior leadership, which "personally oversaw the implementation of the various policies and used direct perpetrators to commit the crimes involved in the furtherance of their common purpose." Accordingly, President Nil states, the Trial Chamber "finds that these crimes are properly imputed to the members of the joint criminal enterprise."

In addition to being implicated in this joint criminal enterprise, President Nil goes on, the accused also bear individual criminal responsibility. Nuon Chea, he notes, "played a leading role in laying the foundations" for DK policies, beginning with his election as deputy secretary of the party in September 1960 and continuing with his DK role as Pol Pot's "right-hand man." Together, they "exercised the ultimate decision-making power of the Party."

Nuon Chea, President Nil continues, "participated in all key meetings and was involved in all major decisions of the Party." He also served as the regime's chief propagandist, helping to disseminate Khmer Rouge policy and also urging "that enemies be uncovered and eliminated." Nuon Chea was also involved in the purges that took place, including in his oversight of S-21 after August 15, 1977. In his capacity as Duch's supervisor, Nuon Chea gave orders, read confessions, and "was among those who decided who was arrested and sent to S-21." Nuon Chea also ordered executions. Given his superior responsibility and key role in the DK joint criminal enterprise, President Nil states, Nuon Chea is implicated in crimes against humanity and the genocide of Vietnamese and Chams. So, too, he states, is Khieu Samphan implicated in these crimes, with the exception of genocide against the Chams.

Before turning to sentencing, President Nil addresses the issue of civil party reparations. On behalf of the 3,865 admitted civil parties, the civil party lead co-lawyers had proposed fourteen reparations projects. The Chamber, he states, endorses twelve of them. Some focus on education and prevention, while others center on documenting the experience of particular groups, including "the treatment of the Cham, the treatment of the Vietnamese, and the regulation of marriage." A last set of projects relate to commemoration, seeking to make their accounts accessible to society at large, thus providing "appropriate measures of satisfaction." A last project is related to civil party healthcare and "rehabilitation."

"Disposition and Sentence," President Nil announces, reaching the final section of the Trial Chamber judgment. In the public gallery, where I had noticed a few villagers dozing during the reading, everyone sits up. President Nil orders Khieu Samphan brought to the dock. Two guards hoist him by the belt to help him stand.

"The Trial Chamber finds the Accused Nuon Chea to be GUILTY," President Nil states. President Nil notes Nuon Chea's crimes against humanity and war crimes. Then President Nil names it: "genocide by killing members of the Vietnamese and Cham groups." There is a murmur in the public gallery. I wonder what Nuon Chea is thinking as he lies on the cot in his holding cell.

Khieu Samphan stands unsteadily as President Nil convicts him of crimes against humanity and war crimes. In contrast to Nuon Chea, who held far more power, Khieu Samphan is convicted of genocide only against ethnic Vietnamese.

President Nil pronounces their sentence: "life imprisonment."

As the curtains close, everyone is on their feet and the courtroom is abuzz. Many commentators contend that it is the last judgment the court will deliver because the Cambodian government wants the court to shut down, a genocide conviction achieved.

In the public grounds just outside the court, journalists swarm, looking for a story. Some stand interviewing civil parties, asking for their reaction to the verdict. Many victims are pleased. So, too, are human right experts and court personnel. David Scheffer, a former US ambassador-at-large for war crimes issues, likens the significance of the verdict in Cambodia to the Nuremberg judgment on Nazi crimes. "That is worth the money and effort," he tells the *Guardian*. Later in the same article, Koppe, unsurprisingly, voices a different view, calling the court unfair and politically compromised. "In 10 or 20 years from now, when the dust has settled," he states, "people will look back on this as a complete waste of time and energy and resources."[3]

In a month, Koppe will be in the news again when a story breaks that he has been working unlicensed since 2016, when his Amsterdam Bar Association membership was not renewed. Another ECCC lawyer will note that Koppe "was effectively practicing without a license."[4] Some will wonder if this issue upends the entire case. Koppe will threaten to sue the court for $1 million in damages, arguing that he had permission to defend Nuon Chea and has fulfilled the requirements.[5] Meanwhile, the court will terminate Koppe's contract. He will not return. In less than a year, Nuon Chea will die in agony.

Conclusion

THE PUBLIC SCHOLAR

Saturday, November 17, 2018, Noir & Blanc Café, Phnom Penh

"How does my testimony fit into the legal chess match of the case?"[1]

The day after the judgment, I pose this question—which seeks to unpack the strategies of the parties and epistemological assumptions underlying the courtroom "field" in which they are acting—to ECCC prosecutor Bill Smith as we sit in a sleek coffee shop, one of many that have sprung up around Cambodia over the last five years. Whereas Koppe quickly showed his pique as the verdict was read, Smith seemed nonplussed, even calm, confident in the prosecution's case.

Smith relaxes on one of Noir & Blanc's plush black chairs in a t-shirt and shorts. When I arrive, he smiles as we shake hands, no doubt pleased at a conviction that he had worked to achieve at the court for over a decade.

"That was a quite a day," I say.

"Yes," he replies. "And we weren't sure Nuon Chea would make it." He is referring to reports that Nuon Chea had been quite ill, some say on the brink of death, just days before the verdict.

"Your office must have marked the occasion."

"We held a small ceremony," Smith acknowledges. "I spoke briefly about the importance of the trial and how the human rights issues raised are now part of the record in Cambodia."

When I mention some of the controversies at the court, Smith's smile fades briefly. He details some of its major accomplishments, ranging from the groundbreaking civil party participation to justice achieved at last for mass human rights violations, an accounting important to victims, the rule of law, reconciliation, and deterrence. Noting such accomplishments, Smith wonders if a "first-world bias" might underlie the quick dismissal of this hybrid court by critics.

The Courtroom Chess Match

"For the prosecution," Smith begins, in response to my question about the courtroom chess match that informed the questioning during my testimony, "we had these charges of genocide, crimes against humanity, and war crimes against Nuon Chea and Khieu Samphan, and we needed to make sure that we prove them with facts. Ultimately, it's the proof of facts that's most important."

The prosecution's case was focused on the argument that the Khmer Rouge operated a highly centralized joint criminal enterprise that carried out these crimes with top-down control. To return to the metaphor I used earlier, the prosecution is like a construction team that builds their argument piece by piece with evidence, and expert witnesses help provide mortar that makes the pieces of evidence—which in the end, they hope, are successfully tested and verified as facts by the Trial Chamber—cohere, thereby solidifying the structure of the joint criminal enterprise argument.

Smith states that the Office of the Co-Prosecutors (OCP) recommended me as a witness for several reasons, including my ability to shed light on the case from both "a factual perspective and a theoretical perspective." One reason is evidential. Smith points to my interviews with victims and perpetrators including "former Khmer Rouge cadre that made admissions to policies to kill Cham and Vietnamese." This is "actually quite powerful evidence" because my research was carried out relatively close in time to the events and for nonlegal purposes, and it "corroborated other information we had in the case." I wonder if Smith is referring to Teap.

But first and foremost, Smith notes, the prosecution wanted me to explain the mechanics and motivations of genocide and thereby help the facts of the case connect, cohere, and become more legible. While the prosecution only needs to prove criminal intent, he adds, "motive is also really important because motive can make sense of why all of that mass criminality happened. Because if you can't make sense of it, then it's harder to believe it, perhaps no matter how many witnesses there are." Along these lines, he notes, my testimony about how the Khmer Rouge used local knowledge, including Buddhism, to make their ideology and the violence more acceptable to their followers is also important.

By having me explain "how it is that a government . . . can make people commit mass killing," Smith says, the prosecution hoped the judges would better see the links between the facts of the case. "And I think that's what happened," he adds. Though the question of "how does genocide happen" was not expected to be a central theme, "as you testified, the judges were more interested in that perhaps than anything else."

"What made you think they were interested?" I ask.

"I could see from their body language," Smith replies, "particularly when we were starting to talk about the different phases that lead to mass killing. And particularly when those phases sort of tracked the evidence."

At the time of my testimony, there had been extensive evidence presented about DK crimes, but, Smith said, "no one was explaining why it could happen . . . but it needs to be explained. And that's the whole point of having that in-depth academic bringing that [sort of explanation] forward." Smith says that he could tell "from the way the judges were leaning forward and by their eyes that they were very interested . . . because they hadn't heard that angle before."

Especially in large trials like Case 002, Smith notes, courts bring in experts precisely to help them "interpret a large amount of facts, which is quite difficult to get on top of, and . . . to [make] links in evidence. Now whether the judges take them or not, that's ultimately up to them. But it can be very, very helpful when you're dealing with a large amount of information."

Of course, Smith points out, defense lawyers seek to disrupt such linkages that support the prosecution case and make things more "clear as to your client's guilt." The two defense teams took different tacks in doing so. As was evident in Koppe's many challenges to my testimony, Smith said, Nuon Chea's defense attacked my testimony frequently because "you made it a lot more understandable how all of this evidence can click together in terms of the theory of how genocide happens and [related] it to the different stages and the different unique factors of Cambodian society."

Besides seeking to undermine evidence supporting the prosecution's case, Nuon Chea's defense presented their alternative "crocodile" explanation centered around the idea that because of Vietnam, the DK regime was in a perpetual state of emergency as they were attacked from within and without. As a result, the Khmer Rouge leaders lacked control, and the violence was more haphazard even if, in response to the threat, they sometimes had to implement "some more draconian policies that are more acceptable in times of a state of emergency. And I think they were looking to you to try and get you to make concessions as to Vietnam's alleged intention to take over Cambodia."

While Nuon Chea's defense centered on "the crocodile," Khieu Samphan's lawyers depicted him as a puppet. This "puppet" defense contended that Khieu Samphan "didn't really know much about what was going on, he didn't have any power to affect what was going on, and he certainly wasn't involved in anything that was going on." As a result, his lawyers felt less of a need to challenge every prosecution claim about the DK regime's centralized control and criminal policies than Nuon Chea's lawyers did. Instead, they engaged in "the very normal and regular legal role of testing the evidence," which, during my testimony, included challenging my expertise and statements about issues like incitement, since Khieu Samphan had given speeches exhorting the fight against enemies.

Finally, Smith states, the civil parties' goal in the courtroom chess match often centered on "bringing out the pain and suffering of the victims" and how DK policies like forced marriage destroyed the fabric of family and social life. The prosecution hadn't focused on these topics during my questioning because they knew that the civil parties would do so—even as these issues were an important part of the prosecution's case, as illustrated by their closing brief, which cites my testimony on topics like "persecution of Buddhists."[2]

The Technological Chess Match

The chess match that produces legal knowledge is most visible on the courtroom floor, but contestations also take place behind the scenes in filings, motions, briefs, and investigations that are driven by information management and technology. Sometimes this background battle between the parties becomes visible, such as when, during Case 001, Duch's defense team objected to detailed witness summaries that, it suggested, were overly complicating the case. In response, Smith, who was representing the prosecution at the time, noted that such evidential summaries ensure "the focus is kept on key issues so that all the parties, including the Chamber, do not become lost in a sea of evidence. In effect, these tools are a road map to assist the Trial Chamber and the parties to understand the key issues."[3]

Smith was here referring to the prosecution's attempt to technologically organize the evidence, making it easier for the Trial Chamber to link the facts of the case to the crimes in question. While everyone has partial access to the larger Zylab database at the court, each party uses its own platforms, such as CaseMap, which facilitate this sort of legal coding.

Within the OCP, such legal data management is sometimes referred to as an "issues tree," a metaphor connoting a legal trunk (the prosecution's central legal argument), a crown (the particular crimes in question), and branches (the legal elements for these crimes). "As each piece of evidence comes in, a document, transcript, or whatever," a OCP legal officer told me, a case manager will "create an entry in CaseMap" that is subsequently "tagged for all of the various branches to which it relates." When someone clicks on a given "branch," he noted, CaseMap will show which of the ten thousand to twenty thousand pieces of evidence have "been assessed as relevant to that issue."[4]

Each court office, the OCP officer stated, works with such databases, which are now common in international criminal law. Indeed, CaseMap and other databases provide a digital infrastructure to the legal articulation of the case, taking shape with the introductory submission and then modified as needed during the trial. Thus, the OCP jurist noted, when the Case 002 closing order was issued, the OCP had to retag everything, a task that took several months. In many ways, the closing order and OCP closing brief resemble just this type of an "issues tree."

As these comments suggest, in parallel with the courtroom contestations, there is a behind-the-scenes attempt to win the case through information management. Like the other offices, the Office of the Co-Investigating Judges and the Trial Chamber have legal officers who use the same or similar databases. While rules separate the offices so they can't directly share databases, the OCP can seek to influence them by transferring Excel lists of facts that the other offices can then import into their own version of CaseMap or whatever database they use.

More broadly, the OCP legal officer noted that one of the most important things in prosecuting a case is to present "a clear theory of the case. What do you say happened and how did it happen? Because it's only once you have that clear in your head that you can start to pitch it and to present it." CaseMap coding and data transfer constitutes one part of the "pitch and presentation"; so, too, do simplified summaries facilitating the analysis of evidence. One example is the creation of charts encapsulating enormous amounts of information in clear form. The witness summaries constitute a second example, particularly given that the judges select witnesses. "So, we have to convince them," the OCP jurist told me, that certain "witnesses should be heard, or otherwise we can't get to the proof of things." It is critical to be "highly organized," which is why the OCP spends so much time translating "all that material . . . into something the judges can actually use."[5]

These legal technologies and databases distill the juridical logics undergirding trial proceedings, which are geared to test the facts and assess whether such evidence proves the accused's guilt. This logic structures the process from start to finish and informed the questions I was asked on the stand. It is also evident in Trial Chamber judgment.

Expert Witness and the Production of Legal Truth

The juridical production of knowledge, then, takes place on multiple levels, ranging from the procedural to the technological, and is informed by a distinct legal epistemology. The prosecution, for example, seeks to link the evidentiary "facts" to the elements of each crime to demonstrate the accused's guilt to the Trial Chamber and thereby achieve a conviction and appropriate sentence. The rules governing this process are specified in the law that established the ECCC and the court's internal rules, which provide the foundation of the proceedings and the verdict that results from it.

In its discussion of "Preliminary Issues," the Case 002/02 judgment devotes more than fifty pages to specifying the fair trial rights and "Evidentiary and Procedural Principles" that structured the proceedings, including issues like "Burden and Standard of Proof," "Admissibility of Evidence," "Sources of Evidence Put Before the Chamber," "Final Assessment of the Evidence," and "Considerations Regarding Specific Witnesses, Civil Parties and Experts."

These rules also inform the Trial Chamber's decisions about my testimony and sources. Their judgment states, "With regard to evidence provided by experts, the Chamber must scrutinize carefully the sources relied upon by the experts in making their conclusions. Where factual findings rely upon an expert's work, precise indications must be made to the specific and verifiable sources underpinning the expert's opinion." When this can't be done, as was the issue with my testimony, due to human subjects protocols, "diminished weight is attributed to expert evidence derived from them."[6] It then provides a list of the expert witnesses, including me.

While these procedures provide the framework within which testimony is given and evidence is introduced, challenged, and assessed for truth value as "fact," the contestations take place with an eye on the elements of the crimes in question: crimes against humanity, grave breaches of the Geneva Conventions of 1949 (war crimes), and genocide. The elements of each of these crimes are discussed at length in the judgment in a sixty-seven-page section titled "Applicable Law: Crimes."

With regard to genocide, the Case 002/02 judgment, echoing ECCC law and the pretrial closing order (the preliminary findings of the Office of the Co-Investigating Judges), centers on the 1948 UN Genocide Convention, which was ratified by Cambodia in 1949. Article 2 of the convention defines genocide as acts carried out with "the intent to destroy, in whole or in part, a national, ethnical, racial or religious group." The closing order identifies Chams and Vietnamese as such protected groups.

The Genocide Convention specifies five genocidal acts, including "killing members of the group," causing them "serious bodily or mental harm," imposing "conditions of life calculated to bring about [the group's] physical destruction," preventing "births within the group," and "forcibly transferring children" to another group. If these acts have taken place, the Trial Chamber notes, the court must then "consider 'whether all of the evidence, taken together, demonstrated a genocidal mental state' . . . [and this specific intent] must be the only reasonable inference available on the evidence."[7] This determination, it goes on, can be made based on factors such as context, scale, policy, and propaganda.

The goal of the prosecution, then, is to introduce relevant evidence that will lead the Trial Chamber to make such a determination that the criminal elements were present and warrant a conviction. As Smith underscored, the prosecution sought to have my testimony make the links between the evidence and criminal elements clearer and more understandable. The defense, in turn, sought to undermine such connections, in part by casting doubt on this evidence, as Koppe tried to do with my research, methods, and sources. This battle between the prosecution and the defense took place every day, just as it did throughout my testimony.

Indeed, the back-and-forth about my testimony that I observed on the courtroom floor continued long after I left the stand, with the defense presenting motions challenging the value of my testimony and the prosecution countering.

Nuon Chea's defense team reiterated many of their critiques in their 2017 closing arguments.[8] On the one hand, they contended, my testimony was biased, reflecting my preexisting opinion that genocide took place in Cambodia and a "deep confirmation bias" that echoes the view of other scholars, especially historian Ben Kiernan, who holds that the Vietnamese had been targeted. My comments about the term *yuon*, they say, followed from this lack of objectivity.

On the other hand, the Nuon Chea defense continued to critique my methods and sources. Once again, they argued that my perspective is too microlevel, largely derived from a single village in Cambodia and based on informant "hearsay." Moreover, their brief asserts, my sources are unverifiable. It uses "magical Teap" as a prime example. The Supreme Court Chamber, the brief continues, has opined "that 'careful scrutiny of the sources from which experts infer their conclusions' was a 'key factor in the assessment' of the reliability and probative value of their evidence. Abiding by these new 'rules of the game' accordingly necessitates disregarding the totality of Hinton's evidence."[9]

Doing so is important, the defense brief claims, because my testimony is "central to the Co-Prosecutors' case." And indeed, the prosecution's closing brief cites my testimony as well as my book *Why Did They Kill?* many times.[10] It does so in relation to several of the issues I discussed during my civil party questioning, such as the impact of the DK transformations on family and religion—including the attack on Buddhism and disruption of ritual transactions with the spirits of the dead. But most of the prosecution's closing brief references to my testimony center on the issue of genocide.

Together with other evidence, the prosecution brief notes my assessment that the term *yuon* is often used to express animus toward Vietnamese and, in the context of DK, suggests genocidal incitement. The brief also references my remarks about how the attack on Chams emerged over time as opposed to being part of a preordained plan, and how this process played out in the Region 41 area around Banyan. And it refers to Teap and Grandmother Yit, who also testified during the proceedings.

In the verdict, the Trial Chamber takes a middle ground on my testimony. Likely with an eye on the appeals that will inevitably follow, the Trial Chamber finds that my "sources are not fully accessible and verifiable, which diminishes the weight of his conclusions" and leads them to treat my "evidence with due caution."[11] In doing so, the Trial Chamber references the Supreme Court Chamber appeals ruling about sources, which the Nuon Chea defense team invokes and Koppe calls the "new rules of the game."

At the same time, the judgment notes that expert witnesses "provide clarification, context or additional assistance for the purpose of a Chamber's assessment of the evidence. They are not expected 'to testify on disputed facts or about the acts, conduct, or criminal responsibility of an accused as would a fact witness.'" In other words, as opposed to drawing on the source-based evidence I had given, the Trial Chamber limits its use of my testimony to "assessing the appropriate interpretation of established facts and placing them in context."[12]

The Trial Chamber does so most significantly on the issue of genocidal intent. After quoting a 1976 *Revolutionary Flag* tract inveighing against the Vietnamese and praising the way in which many of them had been "swept clean" from DK, the judgment states, "The Chamber concurs with Expert Alexander Hinton that, within the broader historical context, this text refers to ethnic Vietnamese who were living in Cambodia at the time and that the message was one of 'purification' of ethnic Vietnamese." Quoting my testimony directly, the judgment states that this message "was based on a 'long-standing animosity and vitriol toward ethnic Vietnamese in Cambodia that was mobilized almost from the start' [of DK] and intensified with the escalation of the armed conflict with Vietnam."[13] This finding speaks to the heart of the genocide conviction as well as the way my testimony is clipped, pruned, and incorporated into the culminating legal truth produced at the ECCC in accordance with the epistemology of law.

The Clash of Epistemologies

When I first received the summons to testify at the ECCC, I was concerned about the divergences between the epistemologies of law and anthropology. My experience testifying confirms what I knew from my research on the ECCC: testimony is constrained in the courtroom setting and reshaped by legal epistemology and practices like the "issues tree" that underpin the juridical rendering of truth as expressed in the verdict. This is precisely the sort of situation about which historian Henry Rousso worried.

In his reply to the French court that summoned him to testify in the trial of an accused Nazi collaborator in Vichy France, Rousso declines largely on the procedural grounds. Historical expertise, he states, "is poorly suited to the rules and objectives of juridical proceedings. It is one thing to attempt to understand history in the context of one's research or teaching, with the intellectual freedom these activities presuppose, and quite another to pursue the same aim, under oath, when the fate of a particular individual is being determined." At the end of the letter, he adds that he fears "that my 'testimony' will merely serve as a pretext to exploit historical research and interpretations that were elaborated and formulated in a context entirely alien to [your] Court. The discourse and argumentation of the trial, moreover, are certainly not of the same nature as those of the university."[14]

These kinds of legal minimalist concerns about the "class of epistemologies" have some merit.[15] Amid the structural constraints of the court, testimony is highly regulated and inevitably involves a degree of loss and coercion as it is regulated by juridical logics and translated into legal code. At the ECCC, this canalization of testimony was perhaps most glaring when rural civil parties who had little familiarity with legal conventions took the stand. They wanted to tell their stories in ways that didn't speak "to the facts" directly and succinctly, which created a problem in the courtroom setting, where time is strictly limited. And when they did speak, their narratives, like my testimony, were thereafter clipped and pruned to fit the juridical logic of evidence and relevance to the criminal elements in question.

While serving the mandated purpose of international justice, this process also involved an appropriation partly at odds with the desires, intentions, and meanings of the speaker. This was evident when Bou Meng testified about his torture at S-21 during Duch's trial (Case 001). At one point, for example, Bou Meng was asked to raise his shirt and show the scars on his back, which were the result of whippings he had received during interrogation. Bou Meng's lawyer objected to this public display, and eventually his scars were photographed and put into the court record. The ECCC thereby took possession of Bou Meng's scars, transforming his personal signifiers of memory, emotion, suffering, and trauma so that they fit the juridical logics of evidence and criminality.

His scars, in turn, became part of the legal "issues tree." In the Duch verdict, "scars" are designated as an outcome of "beatings" that constitute "torture techniques" (each category and subcategory is given a number, in this case, 2.4.4.1.1), which is itself a subcategory of "The use of torture within the S-21 complex" (2.4.4.1) and "Torture, including rape" (2.4.4). The subcategories are part of the broader criminal category "Crimes against Humanity" (2.4), which also encompasses "Murder and extermination" (2.4.1), "Enslavement" (2.4.2), "Imprisonment" (2.4.3), "Other inhumane acts" (2.4.5), and "Persecution on political grounds" (2.4.6). Bou Meng's display of scars is referenced in a footnote and includes a specific court record number for the photographs.[16] His experience is also described in paragraphs illustrating "Specific incidents of torture" (2.4.4.1.2).[17] What began as a complicated testimonial narrative about torture and interrogation, then, was clipped, pruned, and truncated into legal idiom and form.

This dynamic is constantly operative in the court, just as it was when I testified. One early example was my desire to talk about Raphael Lemkin, the origin of the term "genocide," different ways the term has been defined, and how these issues bore on the crimes committed by Nuon Chea and the Khmer Rouge. Koppe immediately intervened, stating that I was in a court of law where the legal definition holds sway. He continued to complain about my invocations of genocide, leading me at one point to note that if I were to stop using the term, which was necessary since I was discussing the genocidal process, I would be engaging in a form of self-censorship.

As was the case with Bou Meng, my testimony was clipped and pruned into legal form to bear on "the facts" of the case and how the evidence related to the elements of the crimes in question. In the judgment, my extensive testimony on Buddhism was whittled down to a handful of citations. Likewise, my testimony on the Vietnamese was folded into an "issues tree" as part of the DK regime's policy of genocide: "Treatment of Targeted Groups" (13), "Treatment of the Vietnamese" (13.3), "Targeting of the Vietnamese" (13.3.5), and "Evidence of a Policy Targeting the Vietnamese" (13.3.5.2).

Epistemological Convergence

So, in light of the challenges, is there a place for the public scholar in the courtroom?

Based on my research and experience testifying at the ECCC, my answer is an emphatic, but cautious, "yes." As Rousso and other critics warn, and as I discussed above, there are important differences between legal epistemology, which is focused on linking evidence to criminality, and the epistemologies that inform scholarship in the humanities and social sciences. These differences were underscored at different moments during my testimony, such as when the juridical need to identify my sources clashed with anthropological ethics and my university human subjects protection requirements regarding research that is carried out on topics like genocide and which involves interviewing not just victims but also perpetrators who might be endangered if their identities were revealed. The debate over "magical Teap" underscored the tension.

As this example illustrates, important differences exist between the epistemological assumptions and goals of law and those of anthropology. Juridical logics focus on the assessment of guilt or innocence, while those of anthropology and related academic fields are directed toward explanation. But these different orientations are not insurmountable. To say so is to make totalizing assumptions about law and anthropology and related humanistic and social scientific disciplines and to overlook the narrative, performative, and restorative dimensions of law. In this respect, Rousso and legal minimalists get it wrong.

As well as epistemological divergences between law and anthropology, there are also areas of convergence. This point emerged in my meeting with Smith after the verdict. After noting the importance of my testifying about the mechanics of genocide and helping "make sense of why all that mass criminality happened," Smith noted that my testimony was also important "for historical purposes and for purposes of looking forward to the future, having someone to be able to explain how mass abuses can occur."

In a 2013 interview, Smith had told me that, epistemological differences notwithstanding, there is also a synergy between historical truth and truth seeking in the court. "The court can't deliver the detail that many academics do in their books," Smith noted. "But maybe it can deliver some fundamental truths which, perhaps, are more difficult for academics to achieve, because you don't have that challenge or debate between the accused and the accusers." The legal process, he explained, is sometimes able to "tease out the truth, bring out a truth that just doesn't happen without that sort of direct challenge, particularly in the real somberness of a courtroom—although it can't bring all of the years and years of research that academics build. So it's a complementary process."[18]

Smith stated that this process of truth seeking is important not just for the accountability and rule of law reasons that legal minimalists foreground, but also for some of the things legal maximalists emphasize, including healing, reconciliation, education, and the strengthening of human rights and democracy. In this regard, he pointed to the involvement of civil parties in the ECCC legal process and how this involvement is the culmination of the process of victim empowerment that has taken place over the past few decades and now affords them the right to participate in trials and seek the truth.

Rousso failed to recognize how expert witness testimony may also directly or indirectly speak to such explanatory truth seeking, in addition to the legalistic truth seeking that remains privileged in the proceedings. Rousso is certainly correct that there are important epistemological differences between history and law, just as there are with anthropology and other explanatory-driven academic fields. But he makes this conclusion using a narrow conception of both academic scholarship and law while taking what Richard Wilson has critiqued as a "clash of epistemologies" approach that ignores spaces of epistemic convergence.[19]

Negotiation, Agency, and the Field of Law

These spaces, it is true, have limits. Smith points this out, even as he emphasizes the importance of expert witness explanation. "The court is not set up to be a historian," he cautions. "The court, it has to, for legacy purposes, it has to find out why. That's why we wanted you there." Nevertheless, he adds, a court is focused on "the criminal history. It's not the history. People write PhDs forever and a day. That's a different discourse. There is an intersection. But there's a limit to that."

It is useful to return to Bourdieu's metaphor of the "field" as a way to consider these epistemic limits. As the legal production of knowledge plays out in court, the participants, including expert witnesses like me, navigate their way amid the structural constraints.[20] As suggested earlier, these constraints include such things as jurisprudence, legal codes, the rules of evidence and procedure, legal technologies, jurisdiction, enforcement mechanisms, courtroom conventions, and training in law schools and clerkships. These structures are enmeshed with power in ways large (for example, sentencing, policing, political authority, and incarceration) and small (for example, the regulation of who sits where in the courtroom space and the control over who speaks and when).

While subject to these disciplines, each party decides how to act amid the constraints. Bourdieu likens the field to a game. It is played on a field, regulated by rules, and oriented toward a competitive end. This backdrop structures action even as the participants vary in terms of their expertise, strategies, positions, roles, and personal histories, knowledge, and motivations. Though there are limitations to such metaphors,[21] they nevertheless serve to highlight how courtroom proceedings are informed by juridical logics, structure, and agency. While other metaphors, such as performance, are of use in thinking about courtroom dynamics, the metaphor of the field captures much of my own experience on the stand and what I observed during my research on the ECCC.[22]

Having studied the tribunal and written on the juridical production of knowledge, I was aware of epistemological limits and how witness testimony is clipped and pruned. While my goals in testifying overlapped with those informing the juridical logics of the court, they also differed in certain respects and were informed by social scientific and anthropological logics. As an anthropologist, I wanted to make a small return and help give voice to the lived experience of the Banyan villagers and others, like Bou Meng, who spent hours sharing their stories and views with me.

The questions from the civil party lead co-lawyer spoke directly to the issue of lived experience, enabling me to convey anthropological insights about how DK policy impacted everyday life during DK and caused enormous social suffering. At the same time, the experience of Banyan villagers and other people who had lived in Region 41 during DK were relevant to the charges, especially the allegations of genocide of the Chams and ethnic Vietnamese. I was therefore glad to have the opportunity to convey this evidence, even if it was outside the purview of much of my expert witness testimony.

My main goal, however, was to help explain the genocidal process and answer, before the Cambodian public, the question so many people, including Banyan villagers, still ask to this day: *why?* Smith's questioning raised this issue directly, and I was able to discuss at length the explanations I had given in *Why Did They Kill?* and how the genocidal process related to comparative genocide studies more broadly. While the dynamics of this process played out differently across time and space during DK, they were centrally organized by Pol Pot, Nuon Chea, and the other Khmer Rouge leaders.

Nuon Chea's defense arguments, echoing claims the Khmer Rouge had made for years, sought to deflect blame and rewrite history. I had brought the DK emblem and Long Muy's confession to remind me of this centralized control as I critically unpacked misleading defense contentions—like the Nuon Chea defense team's monolithic, totalizing, and self-contradictory reworking of Vickery's "standard total view" argument—that masked the long-standing Khmer Rouge project of genocide denial. I had the opportunity to do this not just during my testimony, but also in my reply to Nuon Chea.

These were some of the objectives I sought to fulfill—ones that intersected and diverged from the those of other parties—within the limits of the courtroom "field." Yet, such limits are somewhat elastic, with the degree of latitude negotiated in real time by various actors. This process is influenced by a range of factors, including affective ones, as illustrated by Smith's remarks about how the Trial Chamber judges showed particular interest in my testimony and, through their rulings, gave me leeway to speak at length in court. "So," Smith commented, "that's a decision by the Chamber and we were in that parameter."

To illustrate how these "parameters" of the proceedings are negotiated in the courtroom, Smith noted that the Trial Chamber overruled defense objections seeking to circumscribe the purview of my expertise and expert testimony. The court, Smith said, had effectively told the defense, "No, we want to hear this."

Smith's discussion of this negotiation of courtroom "parameters" reminded me of two moments. The first was Koppe's attempt to dismiss my testimony by complaining that I was "just an anthropologist." The second moment was from Ieng Sary's pretrial hearing. His lawyer, Michael Karnavas, had argued that the standards applied in courtrooms "are rather malleable. It depends on where you are. It depends on who you have on the bench. It depends on who's defending and who's prosecuting. It depends on the resources available."[23]

Even at the International Criminal Tribunal for the former Yugoslavia, where Karnavas had practiced, "six trials are being held, one in the morning and one in the afternoon [and] in all [three] courts, you'll see six different procedures." Though exaggerated, Karnavas's remarks underscore the point that there is latitude within the courtroom, shaped by the participants involved—the same point that Smith made in relation to my testimony.

This latitude is a space of contestation between the parties, including expert witnesses like me who give testimony that, if constrained by the rules of procedure and applicable law, may also be enabled. The error of legal minimalists is to focus primarily on the epistemic constraints and not the epistemic convergences and even overlap between the goals of law and those of expert witness academics. The public scholar in the courtroom is an active participant—albeit one among many in the courtroom in which the judges have the most powerful position—in the negotiation of the expansion or contraction of this overlap.

Politics, Power, and Silence

These possibilities for academic witness in the courtroom notwithstanding, public scholars must nevertheless remain cautious, since they are participating in legal processes enmeshed with politics, power, and silences. Indeed, politics and power are an important part of the structural backdrop that informs the action taking place within the juridical field. This is certainly the case at the ECCC, just as it is at other international courts.[24] Power and politics, for example, shape the jurisdiction of the ECCC, leading to a narrow temporal purview (the period of Khmer Rouge rule in Cambodia) that silences consideration of the involvement and culpability of foreign actors like China, Vietnam, and the United States.

Operating within the constraints of the juridical field, Verges and other ECCC defense lawyers, including Koppe, use the strategy of rupture to undermine the proceedings by making this truncated jurisdiction an issue and vocalizing it often inside and outside the court. Koppe's questions, as well as Nuon Chea's remarks to me, were informed by this strategy. Defense lawyers highlight other issues as well, including allegations of corruption and political interference. Koppe's complaints about the court only delivering victor's justice point to yet another issue—the use of international courts to enhance the legitimacy of governments. There is no doubt they may do so, and this was certainly the case in Cambodia since, as I discussed in chapter 1, the ruling party has long used its toppling of the DK regime to enhance its legitimacy.

In addition to decrying this political use of the court, commentators also critique the ECCC for giving the Cambodian government human rights credibility that masks a lack of judicial independence in Cambodian courts and ongoing attacks on the human rights community, including a major crackdown in 2017 ahead of the 2018 election. Some people even suggest that the date of the Nuon Chea verdict was meant to distract from a "Death of Democracy" anniversary of the crackdown—the dissolution of the main opposition party on November 16, 2017.[25]

I was aware of and had written about such issues when I testified, and I wondered if I would be questioned about them by the defense. This ended up not being the case, perhaps because there appeared to be an agreement to limit the questions to my work on genocide, not my research on transitional justice and the court itself.

When interviewed by the media about the ECCC, I also was careful to acknowledge the controversies surrounding the court. For example, in the same *Guardian* article in which Scheffer and Koppe made their (highly positive and negative, respectively) remarks about the Nuon Chea verdict, I also commented, "These tribunals are political through and through, and this one more than most. It has been plagued by accusations of corruption, political interference, and at times less than robust law. But in the end the court delivered. . . . I expect most Cambodians will take this court, warts and all."[26] As actors who are not directly invested in the process, academics have a distance that enables them to make these kinds of more nuanced remarks highlighting both the strengths and weaknesses of international justice.

It would be misguided, however, to claim that "ivory tower" scholarship is apolitical. That line of thinking has long been debunked, including by Bourdieu, who has written on the operation of power in the field of the academy. There are many other examples, such as professional association resolutions and the involvement of scholars in state-sponsored projects ranging from systemic white supremacy to, in the case of German anthropologists in the Nazi regime, genocide.[27]

Despite these histories and political enmeshments, sometimes extreme ones, scholars nevertheless have expertise and institutional distance that enable them to productively speak out on public issues like genocide and in public forums like international tribunals. The key is to always keep an eye on one's reasons for engagement, goals, and disciplinary ethics, logics, and epistemologies. The latter are, after all, the source of the public scholar's expertise.

Ultimately, scholars have a choice. They can remain safe and seemingly untainted by politics on an ivory tower perch. Or they can engage with major public issues in ways that are highly visible and therefore risky. When the public scholar takes the stand in the courtroom, their scholarship and reputation come under attack and may be impugned. This position does not have the safety of a circumscribed class lecture. Being questioned on the stand lacks such predictability and control. And the answers one gives in court are frozen in time, as they are recorded, videotaped, and placed online.

I understand the caution and concern of those who decide to avoid this sort of exposure and the messiness of processes that are politicized. But for me, at least, there is an obligation to engage with public issues, given the right circumstances. My view is no doubt informed by my long-term research on genocide, my public anthropology orientation, and, as Hannah Arendt underscored, my view that it is imperative to engage with—and thereby help ensure the vitality and thoughtfulness of—the public sphere. My position is also inflected by my critical theory perspective and related recognition of the importance of contributing to "education after Auschwitz" and prevention efforts by raising awareness about structures of domination that lead to the mass violence in places like Nazi Germany and Cambodia under the Khmer Rouge.

In fact, the day after my testimony at the ECCC concluded, I participated in a genocide education teacher-training program run by DC-Cam.[28] My lecture focused on critical thinking about the concept of genocide, including discussion of its origins, Lemkin, the debates that gave the UN Genocide Convention its ultimate form, and the inclusions and exclusions that resulted, including the removal of political groups from the list of protected groups in the final text—issues I sought to discuss in court.

The work of nongovernmental groups like DC-Cam illustrates ways in which the ECCC, while informed by juridical logics and legal epistemology, also has an impact beyond the courtroom and facilitates understanding of the past. While the court has its own outreach program, it also works with groups like DC-Cam to bring Cambodian villagers, students, teachers, and others to the court. By doing so, it helps open up pedagogical spaces beyond the courtroom, even when these efforts are ultimately led by outside actors, especially DC-Cam.[29] Some of the reparation projects admitted in the judgment also contributed to this end, including a DC-Cam–led program, Khmer Rouge History Education through Teacher and University Lecturer Training and Workshops. Such efforts illustrate a point that Rousso, legal minimalists, and other skeptics downplay—that tribunals can serve didactic, explanatory, narrative, and reparative ends, including ones that extend beyond the confines of the courtroom.[30]

Though he was focused first and foremost on accountability and the rule of law during our meeting after the verdict, Smith also acknowledged such legal maximalist goals and how expert witness testimony helps achieve them. A year after my testimony, for example, Smith gave a keynote address at an international genocide conference in which he discussed how academics can contribute to tribunals through their research and by serving as expert witnesses. He used my testimony as an example, noting my discussion of "the mechanics of genocide" and incitement.

Smith also recounted my exchange with Nuon Chea, which he said was notable given Nuon Chea's unofficial boycott of the proceedings. "Sitting at the prosecution bench as this exchange was unfolding," Smith recalls, "I thought to myself, would Alex Hinton ever have thought that, when he was a 31-year-old PhD research student sitting in a village in Kompong Cham province in the middle of Cambodia collecting evidence on the genocide of the Khmer Rouge, that twenty-five years later he would be discussing his findings [directly] with Nuon Chea" at an international tribunal charging Nuon Chea with this very crime.[31]

"All Dr. Hinton's prior hard work had paid off," Smith finished, "and he was able to make his contribution to the accountability and reconciliation process in Cambodia in one of the most salient possible ways."[32] Smith is correct. At the time, it was almost inconceivable that I would have an opportunity to serve as an anthropological witness in the courtroom, let alone have a direct exchange with a mastermind of the Cambodian genocide.

EPILOGUE

July 8, 2019 (Newark, New Jersey, USA)

"Karma!"

Four years after receiving the summons to testify at Nuon Chea's trial, I receive an e-mail from Youk Chhang, the head of DC-Cam, which ends with this exclamation. Chhang writes that Nuon Chea has been hospitalized, his toes turning black with rot. "Karma is Justice in the mind of Cambodian people," he explains. "You just cannot escape it."[1]

From this Buddhist perspective, Nuon Chea's bad deeds have come full circle, in keeping with the karmic principle of cause and effect. Detention. Conviction. A life sentence. Now excruciating suffering. A toe ulcer, then an infection slowly spreading through his body. His choice: amputation or death.

A photograph of Nuon Chea appears in the Cambodian press. He lies, grimacing and emaciated, on a hospital bed with green sheets, his bare feet protruding. Three of his toes are black.

Like Chhang, I think of the ways in which Cambodians suffered and died under the Khmer Rouge: starvation, imprisonment, torture, beatings, forced labor, illness, family separations, malnutrition, and execution. Some, like Nuon Chea now, contracted infections that ravaged their bodies, rotted their flesh, inflicted pain. "Do good, receive good," Cambodians say. "Do bad, receive bad." Karma.

Nuon Chea's suffering continues for weeks, until he dies on the evening of August 4, 2019. His death is marked by headlines like "Nuon Chea, Khmer

Rouge's Infamous 'Brother Number Two,' Dies at 93" and "World's Most Evil Man Dies; He Hated Education and Pushed Ethnic Supremacy." Radio Free Asia highlights worries that Nuon Chea's recent conviction will be vacated, since his appeal has not concluded: "Nuon Chea Dies at 93, Ending Hopes of Closure for Cambodia's Victims of the Khmer Rouge." The article quotes Bou Meng, who complains that Nuon Chea took "the truth with him to the grave."[2]

Ironically, Nuon Chea is given a lavish Buddhist funeral seven days after his death.[3] His elaborate funeral pyre is raised high and draped with blinking lights. Fireworks fill the sky when it is lit. Ninety-three monks, one for each year of his life, perform rites to facilitate the rebirth of his soul.[4]

The ceremony takes place in Pailin, the longtime Khmer Rouge stronghold that Nuon Chea made his home and where Thet Sambath interviewed him for years after the Khmer Rouge movement finally imploded. Hundreds of people attend the funeral, including another ECCC defendant, Meas Muth, who smokes a cigar.

Meas Muth, who is charged in Case 003 with genocide, among other crimes, will likely never stand trial, after the international and Cambodian judges split over whether the case should proceed. Two months earlier, the ECCC announced that the investigating judges were also divided on Case 004. In both cases, the national judges voted not to proceed, providing critics with further evidence of political interference, even as it suggested to all that the ECCC would begin to shut down after Khieu Samphan's appeal.

While Meas Muth says little to reporters at Nuon Chea's funeral, others are more outspoken. Nuon Chea's daughter contends that her father was "a good man" who did "nothing wrong. He struggled for the people."[5] A former Khmer Rouge soldier calls Nuon Chea a "nationalist" and a "hero," explaining, "I love him because his leadership was protecting the country's territory from invasion."[6]

Unsurprisingly, many survivors have a different perspective. Some bitterly note the irony of Nuon Chea's long life and elaborate funeral, given that the DK regime banned Buddhism and precisely these sorts of rituals for the dead. Others are more detached, including one person who states, "I no longer hate him because it's been a long time."[7]

Over the years, I have heard many Cambodians, especially older Buddhists who increasingly spend their days at the pagoda, express such sentiments regarding the Khmer Rouge leaders. Karma often informs their view. Human beings like Nuon Chea commit bad deeds because they are blinded by delusion, aversion, and attachment. There is no direct Khmer-language translation of "evil"; such acts are viewed as an extreme manifestation of sin.

From this perspective, victims who are vindictive are themselves committing a sin, one that will impact their own karma. While difficult, the best path is to let go of one's anger and recognize how attachment and desire lead people like Nuon Chea to commit bad deeds. In the end, they will receive their due, the karmic return on their sins—being reborn in the worst of the Buddhist hells—as Chhang suggested when Nuon Chea's toes began to turn black.

For Buddhists, awareness comes with being present in a world conditioned by karma and impermanence. Such understanding provides the basis for forgiveness, or at least letting go of vindictiveness while seeing the reasons that lead someone like Nuon Chea to commit horrible crimes. Along these lines, Chhang states that Nuon Chea was "born innocent but he committed sin and so died with sin," one manifestation of which were his black toes. "The crimes he has committed," Chhang adds, "will always be a lesson for us."[8]

Such awareness is difficult. And, in Buddhism, the consequences for those who kill are severe. This point is underscored in Thet's film, *Enemies of the People*, which also features lower-level perpetrators. In perhaps the most sensationalist segment of the film, one of them, Comrade Suon, uses a plastic knife to demonstrate—on another person—how he killed people by holding their heads back and cutting their throats.

In other parts of the film, Suon shows remorse, including a scene in which he makes offerings to monks at a pagoda. "I don't know what I'll be reborn as in the next life," Suon laments. "How many holes of Hell must I go through before I can be reborn as a human being again? I feel desperate, but I don't know what to do. I will never again see sunlight as a human being in this world. This is my understanding of Buddha's dharma. I feel desolate."[9]

Nuon Chea shows little such remorse. The scene of Suon at the pagoda is juxtaposed to one in which Nuon Chea tells him and another former cadre not to worry about the violent acts they committed during DK. "Who killed the people?" he asks them, rhetorically. "It was USA and Vietnam." Nuon Chea uses the word *yuon* for Vietnam. "We preserved the country and stopped it falling into the hands of the enemy," he continues. "You should be proud."[10]

Turning to Buddhism, Nuon Chea tells Suon and the other man, "You had no intention, you were just following orders. So according to Buddha's teachings, you need fear no punishment. If there is no intention, there can be no sin, you understand? You did not have the intention, therefore you did not commit any sin. You can start life again."[11]

It took years for Thet to nudge Nuon Chea, a man known for secrecy, beyond such rationalizations. When Thet finally gets Nuon Chea to take some responsibility for the violence, Nuon Chea adds caveats, claiming that counterrevolutionaries were killed only after warnings, reeducation, and censure. "If they still could not be corrected," Nuon Chea says, "they had to be solved. These people were categorized as criminal." When Thet asks what happened to them, Nuon

Chea explains, "They were killed and destroyed. If we had let them live, the party line would have been hijacked. They were enemies of the people."[12]

"It was the correct decision," Nuon Chea adds, invoking his usual blame "the crocodile" denial strategy. "The country was in danger of being taken over by the Vietnamese." The Khmer Rouge leaders had to act quickly, he says, "to solve the traitor problem . . . so it didn't get out of control and infect the innocent people lower down. . . . If we had shown mercy to these people the nation would have been lost." In a voiceover, Thet comments, "This is the first time a top Khmer Rouge leader has admitted the killings like this."[13]

Nuon Chea is careful to specify that "it was Pol Pot who made the decision"—despite the fact that Nuon Chea at other times stresses that he and Pol Pot "were equal" and jointly involved in the decision-making.[14] Nevertheless, Thet's interviews with Nuon Chea were admitted as evidence in Case 002/02 and foregrounded by the prosecution, which even used an excerpt as an epigraph to start their closing brief.[15] Smith also told me that Nuon Chea's "admissions to that journalist Thet Sambath over the ten years, I mean, in criminal law terms, it's a confession. It's the biggest confession you can get. Not that the case needed that, but it certainly was an explicit manifestation of all the other evidence."[16]

Thet also eventually gets Nuon Chea to express a modicum of remorse. When Thet asks Nuon Chea if he feels regret for the killings, Nuon Chea acknowledges, "I made mistakes. I am regretful and I have remorse. I am sorry for our regime, I am sorry." But his apology wanders as he appears to be expressing remorse that the DK regime was toppled. "We won the war, we beat the enemy," Nuon Chea goes on, "but then we were defeated. The people were left still poor and suffering."[17]

Nuon Chea held tightly to his denials and rationalizations until the end of his life. In an interview with a Cambodian member of his defense team during the trial, Nuon Chea fondly remembered the Khmer Rouge struggle to liberate the poor from oppression and their attempt to create a "clean regime, a bright regime, a peaceful regime"—a goal he again claimed was subverted by Vietnam.[18]

As for the DK deaths, Nuon Chea repeated his assertion that there were two types. With regard to the first type, Nuon Chea said he knew little about the killing of innocent people and that Pol Pot gave the orders anyway. On the other side, he said the killing of "traitors" was legitimate given the real threat posed by Vietnam. Therefore, he had "no regrets" about their elimination.

After the Case 002/02 verdict, Nuon Chea complained to a member of his defense team about the politicization of the tribunal and the current Cambodian government. He offered "condolences" to the victims, even as he qualified this remark by invoking the "CPK's guidelines which were trying to help the poor to have enough to eat, proper clothes and escape from the oppressors." In the end, he stated, "I am a patriot and I was right to struggle for the nation." For this reason, he refused to apologize, stating: "I was not wrong."[19]

Meanwhile, discussions over the status of his case continued. Some wondered if Nuon Chea's genocide conviction would be vacated since his case had not gone through the appeal process as intended. In the end, the ECCC terminated his case while ruling that his conviction would stand, even as Khieu Samphan's appeal moved forward.[20]

Amid such developments, commentators will continue to debate the legal achievements of the ECCC. Regardless, the court had a broader impact on the Cambodian public, not just in terms of holding accountable those who caused so much death and suffering, but with regard to helping to answer the question *why?* that so many Cambodians still ask today. This question is even more salient given the long history of Khmer Rouge genocide and the lack of apology and acknowledgement by former senior leaders like Nuon Chea. My opportunity to help answer this question while serving as an expert witness demonstrates that, politics and the constraints of legal epistemology notwithstanding, there is a crucial place for the public scholar in the courtroom.

ECCC Timeline

1953	Cambodian independence from France Prince Sihanouk dominates Kingdom of Cambodia until 1970
1967	Khmer Rouge begin armed struggle against Prince Sihanouk
1973	US carpet-bombing of Cambodian countryside spikes
1975	Khmer Rouge, led by Pol Pot, topple Khmer Republic Democratic Kampuchea (DK) established
1979	Vietnamese-backed army overthrows DK regime People's Republic of Kampuchea (PRK) established New Cambodian civil war begins
1989	Vietnamese troops withdraw from Cambodia
1991	Paris Peace Agreement
1993	UN Transitional Authority in Cambodia (UNTAC) elections Royal Government of Cambodia formed Proliferation of democracy and human rights NGOs begins
1997	Discussions on holding a tribunal commence
1999	Khmer Rouge movement ends following Pol Pot's 1998 death
2003	UN and Cambodia sign agreement to hold tribunal
2006	ECCC commences operation
2007	Case 001 and 002 suspects detained by ECCC
2009	Case 001 trial proceedings held
2010	Case 001 Trial Chamber judgment
2011	Case 002/01 commences Ieng Thirith deemed unfit to stand trial due to dementia
2012	Case 001 Supreme Court Chamber final decision Duch sentenced to life
2013	Ieng Sary dies
2014	Case 002/01 Trial Chamber judgment Nuon Chea and Khieu Samphan sentenced to life
2015	Case 002/02 commences Case 003 defendants charged
2016	Case 002/01 Supreme Court Chamber final decision Life sentences for Nuon Chea and Khieu Samphan upheld
2017	Case 002/02 trial proceedings conclude
2018	Case 002/02 Trial Chamber judgment Nuon Chea and Khieu Samphan sentenced to life
2019	Nuon Chea dies
2021	Khieu Samphan appeals hearing
2021	Announcement that ECCC will wind down operations during next three years
2022	Case 002/02 Supreme Court Chamber final decision expected

Notes

INTRODUCTION

1. Witness/Experts Support Unit, Extraordinary Chambers in the Courts of Cambodia (ECCC), e-mail message to author, September 22, 2015.

2. For overviews of the rise of the Khmer Rouge and their Democratic Kampuchea regime, see Elizabeth Becker, *When the War Was Over: Cambodia and the Khmer Rouge Revolution* (New York: PublicAffairs, 1998); David P. Chandler, *The Tragedy of Cambodian History: Politics, War and Revolution since 1945* (New Haven, CT: Yale University Press, 1991); Ben Kiernan, *The Pol Pot Regime: Race, Power, and Genocide in Cambodia under the Khmer Rouge, 1975–79* (New Haven, CT: Yale University Press, 2008).

3. The legal minimalism and maximalism contrast is adapted from Richard Ashby Wilson, *Writing History in International Criminal Trials* (New York: Cambridge University Press, 2011).

4. Hannah Arendt, *Eichmann in Jerusalem: A Report on the Banality of Evil* (New York: Penguin, 2006), 253.

5. Henry Rousso, *The Haunting Past: History, Memory, and Justice in Contemporary France* (Philadelphia: University of Pennsylvania Press, 2002), 62. For discussions of Rousso's perspective, see Richard J. Evans, "History, Memory and the Law: The Historian and Expert Witness," *History and Theory* 4, no. 3 (2002): 326–45; Rebecca Gidley, "Judicializing History: Mass Crimes Trials and the Historian as Expert Witness in West Germany, Cambodia, and Bangladesh," *Genocide Studies and Prevention* 3, no. 9 (2018): 52–67.

6. Author e-mail message to Witness/Experts Support Unit, ECCC, September 28, 2015.

7. Lawrence Douglas, *The Memory of Judgment: Making Law and History in the Trials of the Holocaust* (New Haven, CT: Yale University Press, 2001); Gidley, "Judicializing History"; Mark Osiel, *Mass Atrocity, Collective Memory and the Law* (New Brunswick, NJ: Transaction, 2000); Wilson, *Writing History.*

8. Pierre Bourdieu, *Outline of a Theory of Practice* (New York: Cambridge University Press, 1977). See also Pierre Bourdieu, "The Force of Law: Toward a Sociology of the Juridical Field," *Hastings Law Journal* 38 (1987): 814–53.

9. Didier Fassin and Samuel Lézé, eds., *Moral Anthropology: A Critical Reader* (New York: Routledge, 2014); Jarrett Zigon, *Morality: An Anthropological Perspective* (New York: Routledge, 2008).

10. See, for example, Pierre Bourdieu, *Homo Academicus* (Stanford, CA: Stanford University Press, 1988); Aisha M. Beliso-DeJesús and Jemima Pierre, "Introduction: Toward an Anthropology of White Supremacy," *American Anthropologist* 12, no. 1 (2020): 65–75.

11. Kamari M. Clarke, "Toward Reflexivity in the Anthropology of Expertise and Law," *American Anthropologist* 122, no. 3 (2020): 584–87.

12. Theodor W. Adorno, *Critical Models: Interventions and Catchwords* (New York: Columbia University Press, 1998), 191. Theodor Adorno, Else Frenkel-Brunswik, Daniel J. Levinson, and R. Nevitt Sanford, *The Authoritarian Personality* (New York: Norton, 1950); Max Horkheimer and Theodor W. Adorno, *Dialectic of Enlightenment* (Stanford, CA: Stanford University Press, 2007). See also Stephen Eric Bronner, *Of Critical Theory and Its Theorists* (New York: Routledge, 2002).

13. Alexander Laban Hinton, *It Can Happen Here: White Power and the Rising Threat of Genocide in the US* (New York: New York University Press, 2021).

14. See, for example, Tracy Kidder, *Mountains beyond Mountains: The Quest of Dr. Paul Farmer, a Man Who Would Cure the World* (New York: Random House, 2004).

15. E-mail message to author, Witness/Experts Support Unit, ECCC, January 28, 2016.

16. Marlie Waserman, March 4, 2016, quoted in Angelique Haugerud, "Public Anthropology in 2015: Charlie Hebdo, Black Lives Matter, Migrants, and More," *American Anthropologist* 118, no. 3 (2016): 586.

17. This tradition dates back at least as far as Zora Hurston's 1937 classic *Their Eyes Were Watching*, was solidified into a subfield of sorts by Clifford and Marcus' *Writing Culture*, and continues to be explored in a number of recent texts. See, for example, Zora N. Hurston, *Their Eyes Were Watching God* (New York: Amistad, 2006); James Clifford and George E. Marcus, eds., *Writing Culture: The Poetics and Politics of Ethnography* (Berkeley: University of California Press, 1986); Carole McGranahan, ed. *Writing Anthropology: Essays on Craft and Commitment* (Durham, NC: Duke University Press, 2020); Alissa Waterston and Maria D. Vesperi, eds., *Anthropology off the Shelf: Anthropologists on Writing* (Malden: Wiley-Blackwell, 2011); Helena Wulff, "Writing Anthropology" *Cambridge Encyclopedia of Anthropology*, February 26, 2021, https://www.anthroencyclopedia.com/entry/writing-anthropology, accessed November 20, 2021.

18. Given that the story I tell is centered on Nuon Chea, I only minimally discuss Khieu Samphan and his defense team in the pages that follow. For an account of a courtroom encounter with Khieu Samphan, see Theary C. Seng, *Daughter of the Killing Fields: Asrei's Story* (London: Fusion Press, 2005).

1. TRUTH, POLITICS, AND THE ACCUSED

1. On S-21 and the DK purges, see David Chandler, *Voices from S-21: Terror and History in Pol Pot's Secret Prison* (Berkeley: University of California Press, 1999); Alexander Laban Hinton, *Man or Monster? The Trial of a Khmer Rouge Torturer* (Durham, NC: Duke University Press, 2016).

2. ECCC, "The Situation of Interrogating Ke Kim Huot alias Sot, July 22," E3/369, 9–10. See also Chandler, *Voices from S-21*, 110; Hinton, *Man or Monster?*, 48, 150–51.

3. Trial Chamber (TC), "[Case 001] Judgement," E188, July 26, 2010, 48 (hereafter "Case 001 Judgement"); TC, "Case 002/02 Judgement," E456, November 16, 2018, 1103 (hereafter "Case 002/02 Judgment").

4. TC, "Case 001 Judgement"; TC, "Case 002/02 Judgement."

5. Chandler, *Voices from S-21*, 2.

6. Dinh Phong, interview with author, Phnom Penh, Cambodia, April 8, 2009.

7. Nate Thayer, "Death in Detail," *Far Eastern Economic Review*, May 13, 1999, 21; TC, "Case 002/02 Judgment," 1295.

8. Nic Dunlop, *The Lost Executioner: A Story of the Khmer Rouge* (London: Bloomsbury, 2005), 17.

9. Dinh Phong, interview with author.

10. Thayer, "Death in Detail," 21.

11. TC, "Transcript of Trial Proceedings," E1/63.1, April 18, 2012, 3.

12. Julia Wallace, "Nuon Chea Claims No Role at Tuol Sleng," *Cambodia Daily*, April 19, 2012, 15.

13. The details of this meeting are from Gina Chon and Sambath Teth, *Behind the Killing Fields: A Khmer Rouge Leader and One of His Victims* (Philadelphia: University of Pennsylvania Press, 2010), 125. On the 1979 Vietnamese invasion, see Chandler, *Tragedy of Cambodian History.*

14. Voice of Democratic Kampuchea, "[December 18] Statement of the Joint Congress [maha sanibat ruom] of the Standing Committee of the Kampuchean People's Representative Assembly, the Government of Democratic Kampuchea, Representatives of the National Army of Democratic Kampuchea and Representatives of Various Government Ministries," Foreign Broadcast and Information Services (FBIS) Asia & Pacific, December 26, 1979. See also Democratic Kampuchea, *Black Paper: Facts and Evidences of the Acts of Aggression and Annexation of Vietnam against Kampuchea* (Phnom Penh: Ministry of Foreign Affairs, 1978).

15. Voice of Democratic Kampuchea, "[December 18] Statement."

16. Voice of Democratic Kampuchea.

17. Henry Kamm, "Aide Says Pol Pot Regime Is Ready to Join Old Foes against Vietnam," *New York Times*, June 1, 1979, A6, https://www.nytimes.com/1979/06/01/archives/aide-says-pol-pot-regime-is-ready-to-join-old-foes-against-vietnam.html, accessed November 21, 2021.

18. "Milan Paper Interview Khieu Samphan," *Corriere della Sera* (Milan), FBIS Asia & Pacific, November 3, 1980.

19. Chon and Thet, *Behind the Killing Fields*, 128f.

20. Chon and Thet, 128.

21. Chon and Thet, 133.

22. Seth Mydans, "Cambodian Leader Resists Punishing Top Khmer Rouge," *New York Times*, December 29, 1998, https://www.nytimes.com/1998/12/29/world/cambodian-leader-resists-punishing-top-khmer-rouge.html, accessed November 21, 2021.

23. Seth Mydans, "Under Prodding, 2 Apologize for Cambodian Anguish," *New York Times*, December 30, 1998, A3, https://www.nytimes.com/1998/12/30/world/under-prodding-2-apologize-for-cambodian-anguish.html, accessed November 21, 2021; Seth Mydans, "Former Khmer Rouge Leader Arrested," *New York Times*, September 20, 2007, https://www.nytimes.com/2007/09/20/world/asia/20cambodia.html, accessed November 21, 2021.

24. Peter Maguire, *Facing Death in Cambodia* (New York: Columbia University Press, 2005), 22. On the creation of the map, see also Judy Ledgerwood, "The Cambodian Tuol Sleng Museum of Genocidal Crimes National Narrative," *Museum Anthropology* 21, no. 1 (1997): 82–98. See also Hanoi Domestic Service, "No Place under the Sun for Genocidal Clique," FBIS Asia & Pacific, September 17, 1983.

25. (Clandestine) Radio of the Provisional Government of National Union and National Salvation of Cambodia, "KR Tuol Sleng Bones Belong to Vietnamese," FBIS Asia & Pacific, December 16, 1994.

26. Nate Thayer, "On the Stand," *Far Eastern Economic Review*, October 30, 1998, 17.

27. Duong Sokha, "Testimony of Vietnamese Makers of First Documentary Shot in S-21 after Fall of Khmer Rouge," *Ka-Set*, February 16, 2009, http://khmernz.blogspot.com/2009/02/testimony-of-vietnamese-makers-of-first.html, accessed August 7, 2021.

28. Hanoi VNA, "Film on Kampuchea," FBIS Asia & Pacific, April 7, 1979, K18.

29. On Mai Lam's February 1979 arrival, see Tom Fawthrop and Helen Jarvis, *Getting Away with Genocide: Cambodia's Long Struggle against the Khmer Rouge* (London: Pluto, 2004), 9 and Chandler, *Voices from S-21*, 4. On Mai Lam's legal background, see Maguire, *Facing Death in Cambodia*, 89.

30. The narrative about Ong's experiences is based on his C002 testimony in August 2012 and on an excerpt of his memoir: Ong Thong Hoeung, "Tuol Sleng, S21," November 28, 2010, http://ongthonghoeung.over-blog.com/article-tuol-sleng-s21-61888124.html, accessed August 7, 2021.

31. Ong.

32. Ong.
33. Ong.
34. TC, "Transcript of Trial Proceedings," E1/107.1, August 14, 2012, 45.
35. Ong, "Tuol Sleng, S-21."
36. Ong.
37. Ong. On the attempt to make a connection S-21 and the Nazi camps, see Chandler, *Voices from S-21*, 7.
38. "PRK Foreign Ministry Statement Defends Legitimacy," FBIS Asia & Pacific, June 1, 1979.
39. "PRK Foreign Ministry Statement," H1.
40. Ramses Amer, "The United Nations and Kampuchea: The Issue of Representation and Its Implications," *Bulletin of Concerned Asian Scholars* 22, no. 3 (1990): 52–60. See also Fawthrop and Jarvis, *Getting Away with Genocide.*
41. Paris Peace Accords, Article 3, 15; Fawthrop and Jarvis, *Getting Away with Genocide.*
42. Michel-Rolph Trouillot, *Silencing the Past: Power and the Production of History* (Boston: Beacon, 1995), 26, emphasis in the original.
43. Michelle Caswell, *Archiving the Unspeakable: Silence, Memory, and the Photographic Record in Cambodia* (Madison: University of Wisconsin Press, 2014).
44. Youk Chhang, e-mail message to author, July 5, 2021. John D. Ciorciari and Youk Chhang, "Documenting the Crimes of Democratic Kampuchea," in *Bringing the Khmer Rouge to Justice: Prosecuting Mass Violence before the Cambodian Courts*, edited by Jaya Ramji and Beth Van Schaak (Lewiston, NY: Edwin Mellen Press, 2005), 226–27.
45. Julia Wallace, "DC-Cam Seeks Recognition for Role at KRT Tribunal," *Cambodia Daily*, May 14, 2010, https://english.cambodiadaily.com/news/dc-cam-seeks-recognition-for-role-at-krt-tribunal-96575/, accessed November 21, 2021.
46. For a detailed discussion of DC-Cam's efforts in this regard, see Caswell, *Archiving the Unspeakable.* On DC-Cam and transitional justice, see also Alexander Laban Hinton, *The Justice Facade: Trials of Transition in Cambodia* (New York: Oxford University Press, 2018).
47. "Genocide: The Importance of Case 002," Documentation Center of Cambodia, 2010, http://d.dccam.org/Archives/Photographs/Exhibition_TSL.htm, accessed July 28, 2021. See also Jaya Ramji-Nogales and Anne Heindel, *Genocide: Who Are the Senior Khmer Rouge Leaders to Be Judged?* (Phnom Penh: Documentation Center of Cambodia, 2010).
48. TC, "Case 002/02 Judgement," 1095.
49. Sok Sidon, "KR Victim Now Ready to Defend Nuon Chea," *Cambodia Daily*, September 26, 2007, https://english.cambodiadaily.com/news/kr-victim-now-ready-to-defend-nuon-chea-78219/, accessed November 21, 2021.
50. Daniel Otis, "Khmer Rouge Tribunal: The Devil's Advocates," *Diplomat*, December 20, 2013, https://thediplomat.com/2013/12/khmer-rouge-tribunal-the-devils-advocates/, accessed August 8, 2021.
51. Minh Bui Jones, "Victor's Justice," *Mekong Review* 1, no. 2 (2016): 9–10.
52. The biographical details that follow are from Chon and Teth, *Behind the Killing Fields*, 18f; Rob Lemkin and Thet Sambath, *Enemies of the People*, Dogwoof Pictures, 2009; and Chandler, *Tragedy of Cambodian History.* Parts of this section are adapted from Alexander Laban Hinton, "What Makes a Man Start Fires?," in *Pre-Genocide: Warnings and Readiness to Protect*, edited by Anders Jerichow and Cecilie Felicia Stokholm Banke (Copenhagen: Humanity in Action, 2018), 83–93, some of which appear in revised form in Hinton, *It Can Happen Here*, 62f.
53. Chon and Teth, *Behind the Killing Fields*, 20.

54. Chon and Teth; Chandler, *Tragedy of Cambodian History.*

55. See Chon and Teth, *Behind the Killing Fields*; and David P. Chandler, *Brother Number One: A Political Biography of Pol Pot* (Boulder, CO: Westview Press, 1999).

56. This paragraph is based on Chon and Teth, *Behind the Killing Fields*, 61.

57. Chandler, *Voices from S-21*; Chon and Teth, *Behind the Killing Fields*; Pol Pot, *Long Live the Nineteenth Anniversary of the Communist Party of Kampuchea: Speech by Pol Pot, Secretary of the Central Committee of the Kampuchean Communist Party Delivered on September 29, 1977* (Phnom Penh: Democratic Kampuchea Ministry of Foreign Affairs, 1977).

58. Pol Pot, *Long Live*, 21–22.

59. Pol Pot, 28.

60. Pol Pot, 28.

61. Pol Pot, 57.

62. Pol Pot, 33, 38.

63. Chandler, *Voices from S-21*, 59.

64. Chandler.

65. Lemkin and Thet, *Enemies of the People*, 14:13f.

2. ANTHROPOLOGICAL WITNESS

1. Rebecca Gidley, "Trading a Theatre for Military Headquarters: Locating the Khmer Rouge Tribunal," *Contemporary Southeast Asia* 40, no. 2 (2018): 279–300.

2. On the history, structure, controversies, and trial proceedings at the ECCC, see Fawthrop and Jarvis, *Getting Away with Genocide*; John D. Ciorciari and Anne Heindel, eds., *Hybrid Justice: The Extraordinary Chambers in the Courts of Cambodia* (Ann Arbor: University of Michigan Press, 2014); Craig Etcheson, *Extraordinary Justice: Law, Politics, and the Khmer Rouge Tribunals* (New York: Columbia University Press, 2020).

3. See "Transcript of Trial Proceedings," E1/401.1, March 14, 2016 (hereafter Hinton Testimony [HT], Day 1), 5.

4. On anthropology and epistemology, see Henrietta L. Moore and Todd Sanders, "Anthropology and Epistemology," in *Anthropology in Theory: Issues in Epistemology*, edited by Henrietta l. Moore and Todd Sanders (Malden, MA: Blackwell, 2014), 1–22. For discussions of the epistemologies of anthropology and law in relation to expert witness testimony, see Wilson, *Writing History*; and Nigel Eltringham, *Genocide Never Sleeps: Living Law at the International Criminal Tribunal for Rwanda* (New York: Cambridge University Press, 2019).

5. Trouillot, *Silencing the Past.*

6. HT, Day 1, 6f. At points in this book, as is the case here, I begin with direct quotations from my testimony before providing a synopsis of what I said, due to space constraints and differences in the flow of speech versus written prose.

7. Bronislaw Malinowski, *Argonauts of the Western Pacific: An Account of Native Enterprise and Adventure in the Archipelagoes of Melanesian New Guinea* (London: Kegan Paul, 1922), 25.

8. Clifford Geertz, "'From the Native's Point of View': On the Nature of Anthropological Understanding," *Bulletin of the American Academy of Arts and Sciences* 28, no. 1 (1974): 26–45.

9. Clifford Geertz, *Local Knowledge: Further Essays in Interpretive Anthropology* (New York: Basic Books, 1983), 59.

10. On ideological palimpsests, see Hinton, *Why Did They Kill?*, 23.

11. Dorothy Holland and Naomi Quinn, eds., *Cultural Models in Language and Thought* (New York: Cambridge University Press, 1987); Bradd Shore, *Culture in Mind: Cognition, Culture, and the Problem of Meaning* (New York: Oxford University Press, 1996). See Hinton, *Why Did They Kill?*, 25.

12. Anthony Giddens, *The Constitution of Society* (Berkeley: University of California Press, 1984).

13. Fredrik Barth, *Cosmologies in the Making: A Generative Approach to Cultural Variation in Inner New Guinea* (New York: Cambridge University Press, 1990); Fredrik Barth, "An Anthropology of Knowledge," *Current Anthropology* 43, no. 1 (2002): 1–18.

14. HT, Day 1, 11.

15. Evelyne Shuster, "Fifty Years Later: The Significance of the Nuremberg Code," *New England Journal of Medicine* 337 (1997): 1436–40.

16. HT, Day 1, 14.

17. Richard A. Wilson, "The Trouble with Truth: Anthropology's Epistemological Hypochondria," *Anthropology Today* 20, no. 5 (2004): 14–17.

18. Robert Borofsky, *Why a Public Anthropology?* (Kailua, HI: Center for a Public Anthropology, 2011); Didier Fassin, ed., *If Truth Be Told: The Politics of Public Ethnography* (Durham, NC: Duke University Press, 2017); Setha M. Low and Sally Engle Merry, "Engaged Anthropology: Diversity and Dilemmas," *Current Anthropology* 51, supplement 2 (2010): S203–14. For overviews of the literature on public anthropology, see various public anthropology "year in reviews" published in *American Anthropologist*, and Robert Borofsky and Antonio De Lauri, "Public Anthropology in Changing Times," *Public Anthropologist* 1 (2019): 3–19.

19. Arendt, *Eichmann in Jerusalem*; Hannah Arendt, *The Life of the Mind* (New York: Harcourt, 1978).

20. It is worth noting that some anthropologists have been very active in these sorts of domains. See, for example, Catherine Besteman and Hugh Gusterson, eds., *Why America's Top Pundits Are Wrong: Anthropologists Talk Back* (Berkeley: University of California Press, 2005); Roberto J. González, ed., *Anthropologists in the Public Sphere: Speaking Out on War, Peace, and American Power* (Austin: University of Texas Press, 2004).

3. THE GENOCIDAL PROCESS

1. HT, Day 1, 16.

2. TC, "Case 002/02 Judgement," 2234f.

3. HT, Day 1, 17.

4. HT, Day 1, 18–19.

5. HT, Day 1, 21.

6. Official from Office of the Co-Prosecutors, interview with author, Phnom Penh, Cambodia, February 26, 2013.

7. Office of the Co-Prosecutors (OCP), "Co-Prosecutors' Closing Brief [in Case 002/02]," E457/6/1, May 2, 2017. See also William Smith, "Justice for Genocide in Cambodia: The Case for the Prosecution," *Genocide Studies and Prevention* 12, no. 3 (2018): 20–39.

8. Smith, "Justice for Genocide."

9. Lars Olsen, "The Role of Expert Witnesses," ECCC, October 5, 2013, https://www.eccc.gov.kh/en/blog/2013/05/10/role-expert-witnesses, accessed May 17, 2019.

10. Witness/Experts Support Unit, ECCC, e-mail message to author, October 16, 2015.

11. HT, Day 1, 24.

12. Alexander Laban Hinton, ed., *Annihilating Difference: The Anthropology of Genocide* (Berkeley: University of California Press, 2002); Alexander Laban Hinton, ed., *Genocide: An Anthropological Reader* (Malden, MA: Blackwell, 2002).

13. Alexander Laban Hinton, "Critical Genocide Studies," *Genocide Studies and Prevention* 7, no. 1 (2012): 4–15. See also Jens Meierhenrich, ed., *Genocide: A Reader* (New York: Oxford University Press, 2014); and Adam Jones, *Genocide: A Comprehensive Introduction* (New York: Routledge, 2017).

14. A. Dirk Moses, "Genocide: Critical Concepts in Historical Studies," in *Genocide: Critical Concepts in Historical Studies*, edited by A. Dirk Moses (New York: Routledge, 2010), 1–23.

15. HT, Day 1, 39. On prosecution strategy for my testimony, see Smith, "Justice for Genocide," 37f.

16. HT, Day 1, 42.

17. HT, Day 1, 42.

18. HT, Day 1, 44; Hinton, *Why Did They Kill?*, 281.

19. HT, Day 1, 44; Hinton, 281.

20. HT, Day 1, 46.

21. HT, Day 1, 48.

22. HT, Day 1, 49–51.

23. HT, Day 1, 52.

24. HT, Day 1, 53–54.

25. HT, Day 1, 56, Hinton, *Why Did They Kill?*, 33.

26. HT, Day 1, 83–84.

27. HT, Day 1, 82.

28. HT, Day 1, 110.

29. HT, Day 1, 112.

30. HT, Day 1, 86.

31. See "Transcript of Trial Proceedings," E1/402.1, March 15, 2016 (hereafter Hinton Testimony [HT], Day 2), 2–3.

32. Democratic Kampuchea, *Black Paper.*

33. Hinton, *Why Did They Kill?*, 215f; Penny Edwards, "Imaging the Other in Cambodian Nationalist Discourse before and during the UNTAC Period," in *Propaganda, Politics, and Violence in Cambodia: Democratic Transition under United Nations Peace-Keeping*, edited by Steve Heder and Judy Ledgerwood (Armonk, NY: M. E. Sharpe, 1996), 50–72.

34. HT, Day 2, 8. See Hinton, *Why Did they Kill?*, 216.

35. Hinton, *Why Did They Kill?*, 216.

36. HT, Day 2, 11. See also Kiernan, *Pol Pot Regime.*

37. HT, Day 2, 12.

38. Ian Kershaw, *The Nazi Dictatorship: Problems and Perspectives of Interpretation* (London: Arnold, 2000); Donald Bloxham, "The Armenian Genocide of 1915–1916: Cumulative Radicalization and the Development of a Destruction Policy," *Past & Present* 181 (2003): 141–91.

39. HT, Day 2, 18.

40. HT, Day 2, 18. See also Hinton, *Why Did They Kill?*, 154.

41. HT, Day 2, 22–23.

42. HT, Day 2, 23.

43. HT, Day 2, 45.

44. HT, Day 2, 49.

45. HT, Day 2, 51.

46. HT, Day 2, 54.

4. LIVED EXPERIENCE

1. HT, Day 2, 55.

2. HT, Day 2, 55.

3. This paragraph draws on Gary Jonathan Bass, *Stay the Hand of Vengeance: The Politics of War Crimes Tribunals* (Princeton, NJ: Princeton University Press, 2001).

4. Hannah Arendt and Karl Jaspers, *Correspondence 1926–1969* (New York: Harcourt Brace Jovanovich, 1992).

5. David Scheffer, "Genocide and Atrocity Crimes," *Genocide Studies and Prevention* 1, no. 3 (2006): 229–50.

6. For a discussion of several of these elements, see Jens Meierhenrich and Devin O. Pendas, "'The Justice of My Cause Is Clear, but There's Politics to Fear': Political Trials in Theory and History," in *Political Trials in Theory and History*, edited by Jens Meierhenrich and Devin O. Pendas (New York: Cambridge University Press, 2017), 1–64.

7. Arendt, *Eichmann in Jerusalem*, 253, 5.

8. Judith N. Shklar, *Legalism: Law, Morals, and Political Trials* (Cambridge, MA: Harvard University Press, 1986). On Arendt and legalism, see Douglas, *Memory of Judgment*, 111. On legal minimalism and maximalism, see Wilson, *Writing History*.

9. Douglas, *Memory of Judgment*, 5. See also Austin Sarat, Lawrence Douglas, and Martha Merrill Umphrey, eds., *The Limits of Law* (Stanford, CA: Stanford University Press, 2005).

10. Jack Donnelly and Daniel J. Whelan, *International Human Rights* (Boulder, CO: Westview, 2020); Kathryn Sikkink and Hun Joon Kim, "The Justice Cascade: The Origins and Effectiveness of Prosecutions of Human Rights Violations," *Annual Review of Law and Social Science* 9 (2013): 269–85.

11. Hinton, *Justice Facade*, 5f; Paige Arthur, "How 'Transitions' Reshaped Human Rights: A Conceptual History of Transitional Justice," *Human Rights Quarterly* 31, no. 2 (2009): 321–67; Ruti G. Teitel, "Transitional Justice Genealogy," *Harvard Human Rights Journal* 16 (2003): 69–94.

12. For a critique of the teleological, essentialist, and universalizing assumptions of this "transitional justice imaginary," see Hinton, *Justice Facade*, 10f.

13. United Nations Secretary-General, *The Rule of Law and Transitional Justice in Post-Conflict Societies*, New York: United Nations Security Council, August 23, 2004, Doc. S/2004/616, paragraph 38.

14. ECCC, "Agreement between the United Nations and the Royal Government of Cambodia Concerning the Prosecution under Cambodian Law of Crimes Committed during the Period of Democratic Kampuchea," June 6, 2003.

15. Yasmin Naqvi, "The Right to Truth in International Law: Fact or Fiction?," *International Review of the Red Cross* 88, no. 862 (2006): 245–73.

16. "Statistics: Civil Party Applicants per Case File," ECCC, https://www.eccc.gov.kh/en/statistics-civil-party-applicants-case-file, accessed July 30, 2021.

17. See, for example, Hinton, *Justice Facade*; Caswell, *Archiving the Unspeakable*; Elena Lesley, "Lessons for the Future: Khmer Rouge Survivor Testimonies as Sites of Individual and Social Regeneration," *Ethnos* 86, no. 3 (2019): 570–91; Eric Stover, Mychelle Balthazard, and K. Alexa Koenig, "Confronting Duch: Civil Party Participation in Case 001 at the Extraordinary Chamber in the Courts of Cambodia," *International Review of the Red Cross* 93, no. 882 (2011): 505.

18. Hudson McFann and Alexander Laban Hinton, "Impassable Visions: The Cambodia to Come, the Detritus in Its Wake," in A *Companion to the Anthropology of Death*, edited by Antonius C.G.M. Robben (Malden, MA: Wiley-Blackwell, 2018), 223–35.

19. May Mayko Ebihara, "Revolution and Reformulation in Kampuchean Village Culture," in *The Cambodian Agony*, edited by David A. Ablin and Marlowe Hood (Armonk, NY: M. E. Sharpe, 1990), 16–61.

20. Lemkin and Thet, *Enemies of the People*, 48:00f.

21. "Nuon Chea on Year Zero" and "Nuon Chea on Revolution" (videos), in Rob Lemkin, "Nuon Chea Uncut: 1," Enemies of the People blog, June 30, 2011, https://

enemiesofthepeoplemovie.com/blog_2f96cda1-93fb-41eb-9506-bb4e08b23790.html, accessed August 13, 2021.

22. Communist Party of Kampuchea (CPK), “The Red Heart of Dam Pheng,” *Revolutionary Youth*, no. 3, 1973, reproduced in *Searching for the Truth*, Documentation Center of Cambodia, July 2012.

23. CPK, “Red Heart.”

24. CPK.

25. TC, “Transcript of Trial Proceedings—Kaing Guek Eav ‘Duch,’” E1/70.1, August 27, 2009, 88.

26. See Hinton, *Justice Facade*, 161f; Vannak Huy, *Bou Meng: A Khmer Rouge Survivor of S-21* (Phnom Penh: Documentation Center of Cambodia, 2010).

27. HT, Day 2, 56. On the DK attack on Buddhism, see François Ponchaud, *Cambodia, Year Zero* (New York: Holt, Rinehart and Winston, 1978); Ian Harris, *Buddhism under Pol Pot* (Phnom Penh: Documentation Center of Cambodia, 2007).

28. HT, Day 2, 56.

29. Pol Pot, *Long Live*, 48.

30. See Hinton, *Justice Facade*; Erik W. Davis, *Deathpower: Buddhism's Ritual Imagination in Cambodia* (New York: Columbia University Press, 2016).

31. Bou Meng, interview with author, Phnom Penh, July 2, 2008.

32. TC, “Transcript of Trial Proceedings—Kaing Guek Eav ‘Duch,’” E1/64.1, August 18, 2009, 109–10 (English), 84 (Khmer). See also Hinton, *Justice Facade*, 205–6.

33. Stover, Balthazard, and Koenig, “Confronting Duch,” 243.

34. Neth Phally, interview with author, Phnom Penh, February 28, 2015.

35. Stover, Balthazard, and Koenig, “Confronting Duch,” 505.

36. HT, Day 2, 58.

37. Neth Phally, interview with author, Phnom Penh, February 28, 2015. This paragraph is adapted from Hinton, *Justice Facade*, 245.

38. Bou Meng, interview with author, Phnom Penh, July 2, 2008.

39. Neth Phally, interview. This paragraph is adapted from Hinton, *Justice Facade*, 245.

40. HT, Day 2, 63–64.

41. Haing Ngor, *A Cambodian Odyssey* (New York: Warner Books, 1987), 199. See also Ponchaud, *Cambodia, Year Zero*; Hinton, *Why Did They Kill?*, 126f.

42. HT, Day 2, 66.

43. D. E. Hinton, A. L. Hinton, V. Pich, J. R. Loeum, and M. H. Pollack, “Nightmares among Cambodian Refugees: The Breaching of Concentric Ontological Security,” *Culture, Medicine, and Psychiatry* 33, no. 2 (2009): 219–65; Davis, *Deathpower*.

44. On the Lord of the Iron Staff, see Hinton, *Justice Facade*, 180–83.

45. Hinton, *Why Did They Kill?*, 106–7. On *neak ta*, see Ang Choulean, *Les êtres surnaturels dans la religion populaire khmère* (Paris: Cedoreck, 1987).

46. Hinton, *Why Did They Kill?*, 105f.

47. Hannah Arendt, *The Origins of Totalitarianism* (New York: Harcourt, Brace, Jovanovich, 1973); Arendt, *Life of the Mind*.

48. John Marston, “Metaphors of the Khmer Rouge,” in *Cambodian Culture since 1975: Homeland and Exile*, edited by May Ebihara, Carol A. Mortland, and Judy Ledgerwood (Ithaca, NY: Cornell University Press, 1994), 113, 114.

49. Youk Chhang, “How Did I Survive the Khmer Rouge?,” *Searching for the Truth*, special English edition, 2nd quarter 2005, 7.

50. Robert K. Headley Jr., Kylin Chhor, Lam Kheng Lim, Lim Kah Kheang, and Chen Chun, *Cambodian-English Dictionary* (Washington, DC: Catholic University of America Press, 1977), 113; Ponchaud, *Cambodia, Year Zero*, 89–90.

5. RUPTURE

1. HT, Day 2, 111.
2. HT, Day 2, 105.
3. HT, Day 2, 111.
4. HT, Day 2, 111.
5. Michael Vickery, *Cambodia 1975–1982* (Boston: South End Press, 1984). For a critique, see Ledgerwood, "Cambodian Tuol Sleng Museum."
6. Nuon Chea Defense Team [NCDT], "Nuon Chea's Closing Submissions in Case 002/01," E295/6/3, September 26, 2013, 6.
7. NCDT, "Nuon Chea's Closing Brief in Case 002/02," May 2, 2017, 15, 2, 18.
8. NCDT, 15–16, italics in original.
9. NCDT, 1–2.
10. NCDT, 1–2, 3, 42.
11. See NCDT, 4.
12. NCDT, 3, 42, 20, 42.
13. Stéphanie Giry, "Against the Law," *National*, August 14, 2009; Martti Koskenniemi, "Between Impunity and Show Trials," *Max Planck Yearbook of United Nations Law* 6 (2002): 1–35; Mikael Baaz and Mona Lilja, "Using International Criminal Law to Resist Transitional Justice: Legal Rupture in the Extraordinary Chambers in the Courts of Cambodia," *Conflict and Society: Advances in Research* 2 (2016): 142–59.
14. Khieu Samphan Pre-Trial Appeal Hearing, C26/5, April 3, 2009, 47.
15. TC, "Transcript of the Trial Proceedings," E1/234.1, October 25, 2013, 59.
16. As noted in the introduction, due to space constraints and my narrative focus on Nuon Chea, I only minimally discuss Khieu Samphan and the questioning by his defense lawyers in this text.
17. NCDT, "Nuon Chea's Closing Brief in Case 002/02," 15.
18. See Stéphanie Giry, "Necessary Scapegoats? The Making of the Khmer Rouge Tribunal," *New York Review*, July 23, 2012, https://www.nybooks.com/daily/2012/07/23/necessary-scapegoats-khmer-rouge-tribunal/, accessed August 15, 2021.
19. Trial Chamber [TC], "Decision on NUON Chea Defence Misconduct," E214, June 29, 2012.
20. NCDT, "Withdrawal of Notice of Intent Pursuant to Internal Rule 90," E287/2, July 30, 2013.
21. Jones, "Victor's Justice," 9.
22. Jones, 10.
23. Jones, 10.
24. Otis, "Khmer Rouge Tribunal."
25. TC, "Transcript of Initial Hearing—Nuon Chea, Ieng Sary, Ieng Thirith, Khieu Samphan Public," E1/4.1, June 27, 2011, 14.
26. Jones, "Victor's Justice," 9.
27. TC, "Transcript of Trial Proceedings," E1/403.1, March 16, 2016 (hereafter Hinton Testimony [HT], Day 3), 102.
28. HT, Day 3, 104.
29. HT, Day 3, 63.
30. HT, Day 3, 65.
31. HT, Day 3, 67–68.
32. "Japanese American Relocation," Holocaust Encyclopedia, United States Holocaust Memorial Museum, https://encyclopedia.ushmm.org/content/en/article/japanese-american-relocation, accessed July 30, 2021.
33. HT, Day 3, 60.

34. HT, Day 3, 74.

35. See, for example, HT, Day 3, 78.

36. HT, Day 3, 75.

37. TC, "Transcript of Trial Proceedings," E1/14.1, November 22, 2011, 77.

38. TC, 77.

39. TC, 77.

40. HT, Day 2, 135; HT, Day 3, 31. See also NCDT, "Nuon Chea's Closing Brief in Case 002/02," 339.

41. NCDT, "Nuon Chea's Closing Brief in Case 002/02."

42. TC, "Transcript of Trial Proceedings," E1/14.1, 77.

43. TC, 77. See also NCDT, "Nuon Chea's Closing Brief in Case 002/02," 59–61.

44. TC, "Transcript of Trial Proceedings," E1/14.1, 79, 105.

45. TC, 80, 81.

46. NCDT, "Nuon Chea's Closing Brief in Case 002/02."

47. TC, "Transcript of Trial Proceedings," E1/14.1, 100.

48. TC, 100, 101.

49. Democratic Kampuchea, *Black Paper*.

50. NCDT, "Nuon Chea's Closing Brief in Case 002/02," 13, 12.

6. DENIAL

1. See ECCC Trial Transcripts, March 17, 2016, 79f (hereafter Hinton Testimony [HT], Day 4).

2. HT, Day 4, 80, 79.

3. TC, "Transcript of Trial Proceedings—Kaing Guek Eav 'Duch,'" E1/35.1, June 22, 2009, 82–83; Central Party of Kampuchea, "Decision of the Central Committee Regarding a Number of Matters," E3/13, March 30, 1976. See Hinton, *Man or Monster?* 103–7, 270–72.

4. Long Tai, interview with author, Peareang district, Prey Veng province, March 24, 2014. For a detailed discussion of Long Muy, see Hinton, *Man or Monster?*

5. Chon and Teth, *Behind the Killing Fields*, 161–62.

6. Chon and Teth, 162.

7. Chon and Thet, 161, 76.

8. NCDT, "Nuon Chea's Closing Brief in Case 002/02"; Otis, "Khmer Rouge Tribunal."

9. NCDT, "Nuon Chea's Closing Brief in Case 002/02," 1.

10. See Hinton, *Justice Facade*.

11. HT, Day 4, 81.

12. HT, Day 4, 82.

13. TC, "Transcript of Trial Proceedings," E1/14.1, November 22, 2011, 94.

14. NCDT, "Nuon Chea's Closing Submissions in Case 002/01," 38; Taylor Owen and Ben Kiernan, "Bombs over Cambodia," *The Walrus*, October 12, 2006, 63, https://thewalrus.ca/2006-10-history/, accessed November 14, 2021.

15. TC, "Transcript of Trial Proceedings," E1/14.1, November 22, 2011, 94; NCDT, "Nuon Chea's Closing Submissions in Case 002/01," 38; NCDT, "Nuon Chea's Closing Brief in Case 002/02," 12.

16. Karen Coates and Jerry Redfern, "Henry Kissinger Is Not Telling the Truth about His Past. Again," *Washington Post*, September 18, 2014, https://www.washingtonpost.com/posteverything/wp/2014/09/18/henry-kissinger-is-not-telling-the-truth-about-his-past-again/, accessed August 15, 2021.

17. "CodePink Attempts to 'Arrest' Henry Kissinger for War Crimes in Vietnam, Laos, Chile, and East Timor," *Democracy Now!*, January 30, 2015, https://www.youtube.com/watch?v=5ApY-P6oAxU, accessed August 13, 2021.

18. Cody J. Foster, "Did America Commit War Crimes in Vietnam?," *New York Times*, December 1, 2017, https://www.nytimes.com/2017/12/01/opinion/did-america-commit-war-crimes-in-vietnam.html, accessed August 15, 2021.

19. NCDT, "Nuon Chea's Closing Submissions in Case 002/01," 38, citing Owen and Kiernan, "Bombs over Cambodia," 67.

20. HT, Day 4, 82.

21. DK, *Black Paper*, 9.

22. HT, Day 4, 83.

7. JUDGMENT

1. The Non Nil quotes in this chapter are taken from the text he read: Trial Chamber [TC], "Summary of Judgment, Case 002/02," November 16, 2018.

2. TC, "Case 002/02 Judgement."

3. Hannah Ellis-Petersen, "Khmer Rouge Leaders Found Guilty of Genocide in Cambodia's 'Nuremberg' Moment," *Guardian*, November 16, 2018, https://www.theguardian.com/world/2018/nov/16/khmer-rouge-leaders-genocide-charges-verdict-cambodia, accessed December 10, 2021.

4. Julia Wallace, "Lawyer's Status Throws Genocide Conviction of Khmer Rouge Leader into Doubt," *New York Times*, December 16, 2018, https://www.nytimes.com/2018/12/16/world/asia/cambodia-lawyer-khmer-rouge-genocide.html, accessed December 10, 2021.

5. Leonie Kijewski, "Lawyer for Khmer Rouge's Nuon Chea was Practicing Illegally, Says Cambodian Bar Association, Casting Mistrial Risk over Historic Verdict," *South China Morning Post*, December 15, 2018, https://www.scmp.com/news/asia/southeast-asia/article/2178118/lawyer-khmer-rouges-nuon-chea-was-practising-illegally-says, accessed December 10, 2021.

CONCLUSION

1. Unless otherwise specified, all the quotes from William Smith in this chapter are from my interview with him on November 17, 2018, in Phnom Penh, Cambodia. Smith also discusses my testimony in a conference keynote that was published as an article, Smith, "Justice for Genocide."

2. OCP, "Co-Prosecutors' Closing Brief [in Case 002/02]," 207f.

3. TC, "Transcript of Trial Proceedings—Kaing Guek Eav 'Duch,'" E1/80.1, November 25, 2009, 75, 24.

4. OCP staff member, interview with author, Phnom Penh, Cambodia, March 25, 2014. Parts of this section are adapted from Hinton, *Man or Monster?*, 209–10.

5. OCP staff member, interview with author.

6. TC, "Case 002/02 Judgement," 30.

7. TC, 408.

8. NCDT, "Nuon Chea's Closing Brief in Case 002/02."

9. NCDT, 320.

10. OCP, "Co-Prosecutors' Closing Brief [in Case 002/02]."

11. TC, "Case 002/02 Judgement," 1613.

12. TC, 1706.

13. TC, 1718–19.

14. Henry Rousso, "Letter to the President of the Bordeaux Assizes Court," October 6, 1997, in *The Papon Affair: Memory and Justice on Trial*, edited by Richard J. Golsan (New York: Routledge, 2000), 193–94. For a measured consideration of Rousso's arguments from another historian who has served as an expert witness, see Evans, "History, Memory, and the Law."

15. The legal minimalism and maximalism distinction and the phrase "class of epistemologies" are from Wilson, *Writing History*; Richard Ashby Wilson, "Expert Evidence on Trial: Social Researchers in the International Criminal Courtroom," *American Ethnologist* 43, no. 4 (2016): 730–44.

16. TC, "Case 001 Judgement," 85n444; Hinton, *Justice Facade*, 174.

17. TC, "Case 001 Judgement," 88.

18. William Smith, interview with author, February 26, 2013, Phnom Penh, Cambodia.

19. Wilson, "Expert Evidence."

20. Bourdieu, *Outline of a Theory of Practice*; Bourdieu, "Force of Law."

21. Yves Dezalay and Mikael Rask Masden, "The Force of Law and Lawyers: Pierre Bourdieu and the Reflexive Sociology of Law," *Annual Review of Law and Social Science* 8 (2012): 433–52.

22. See also Eltringham, *Genocide Never Sleeps*, on the field of law.

23. Ieng Sary Pre-Trial Detention Hearing, July 1, 2008.

24. See, for example, Kamari Maxine Clarke, *Fictions of Justice: The International Criminal Court and the Challenge of Legal Pluralism in Sub-Saharan Africa* (New York: Cambridge University Press, 2009).

25. Oliver Holmes, "'Death of Democracy' in Cambodia as Court Dissolves Opposition," *Guardian*, November 16, 2017, https://www.theguardian.com/world/2017/nov/16/death-of-democracy-cambodia-court-dissolves-opposition-hun-sen, accessed August 13, 2021.

26. Ellis-Petersen, "Khmer Rouge Leaders Found Guilty."

27. See, for example, Gretchen E. Schafft, *From Racism to Genocide: Anthropology in the Third Reich* (Champaign: University of Illinois Press, 2004).

28. "Genocide Research and Education," Documentation Center of Cambodia, http://dccam.org/genocide-education, accessed November 14, 2021.

29. See also Gidley, "Judicializing History," on this point. On nongovernmental organizations and ECCC outreach, see Hinton, *Justice Facade*.

30. Douglas, *Memory of Judgment*.

31. Smith, "Justice for Genocide," 38.

32. Smith, 38.

EPILOGUE

1. Youk Chhang, e-mail message to author, July 8, 2019.

2. William Branigin, "Nuon Chea, Khmer Rouge's Infamous 'Brother Number Two,' Dies at 93," *Washington Post*, August 4, 2019, https://www.washingtonpost.com/local/obituaries/nuon-chea-khmer-rouges-infamous-brother-number-two-dies-at-93/2019/08/04/06d5ecce-b6b7-11e9-a091-6a96e67d9cce_story.html, accessed August 13, 2021; Lincoln Green, "World's Most Evil Man Dies; He Hated Education and Pushed Ethnic Supremacy," *Daily Kos*, August 6, 2019, https://www.dailykos.com/stories/2019/8/6/1877197/-World-s-most-evil-man-dies-he-hated-education-and-pushed-ethnic-supremacy, accessed August 13, 2021; RFA Khmer Service, "Nuon Chea Dies at 93, Ending Hopes of Closure for Cambodia's Victims of the Khmer Rouge," Radio Free Asia, August 5, 2019, https://www.rfa.org/english/news/cambodia/death-08052019161903.html, accessed August 13, 2021.

3. The details of his funeral are based on Taryn Wilson, "Fireworks Light Up Cremation of Khmer Rouge's Chief Ideologue," *Efe-Epa*, August 9, 2019, https://www.efe.com/efe/english/destacada/fireworks-light-up-cremation-of-khmer-rouge-s-chief-ideologue/50000261-4040470, accessed December 11, 2021; Aun Chhengpor, "Nuon Chea's Family Remembers 'Pleasant' Father, 'Man of Secrets,'" VOA Khmer, August 15,

2019, https://www.voacambodia.com/a/nuon-chea-s-family-remembers-pleasant-father-man-of-secrets/5042125.html, accessed December 11, 2021.

4. Wilson, "Fireworks Light Up."

5. Wilson.

6. Suy Se, "Mourners Pay Final Respects to Khmer Rouge 'Brother Number Two,'" AFP, August 9, 2019, https://www.yahoo.com/now/mourners-pay-final-respects-khmer-rouge-brother-number-090117032.html, accessed December 11, 2021.

7. Suy Se.

8. News Wire, "Khmer Rouge 'Brother Number Two' Nuon Chea Dies," *France 24*, August 4, 2019, https://www.france24.com/en/20190804-khmer-rouge-brother-number-two-nuon-chea-dies-cambodia-court, accessed December 11, 2021; Mech Dara, "Khmer Rouge's Brother No 2 Dies," *Phnom Penh Post*, August 5, 2019, https://www.phnompenhpost.com/national-kr-tribunal/khmer-rouges-brother-no-2-dies, accessed December 11, 2021.

9. Lemkin and Thet, *Enemies of the People*, 1:13:00f.

10. Lemkin and Thet, 1:11:45f.

11. Lemkin and Thet, 1:11:45f.

12. Lemkin and Thet, 48:00f.

13. Lemkin and Thet, 50:00f, 1:02:30f.

14. Lemkin and Thet, 50:30; Chon and Teth, *Behind the Killing Fields*, 135.

15. OCP, "Co-Prosecutors' Closing Brief [in Case 002/02]," 1.

16. Smith, interview with author, November 17, 2018, Phnom Penh, Cambodia.

17. Lemkin and Thet, *Enemies of the People*, 1:05:00f.

18. Phalla Prum, "Talks beyond the Courtroom: The Life of Nuon Chea," *Khmer Times*, August 27, 2019, https://www.khmertimeskh.com/637362/talks-beyond-the-courtroom-the-life-of-nuon-chea, accessed December 11, 2021.

19. Prum, "Talks beyond the Courtroom"; Phalla Prum, "Did the Khmer Rouge's Nuon Chea Escape the Truth in Death?" *Phnom Penh Post*, August 29, 2019, https://www.phnompenhpost.com/opinion/did-khmer-rouges-nuon-chea-escape-truth-death, accessed December 11, 2021.

20. "Press Release from the International Co-Prosecutor and National Co-Prosecutor," ECCC, May 4, 2020.

Bibliography

Adorno, Theodor W. *Critical Models: Interventions and Catchwords.* New York: Columbia University Press, 1998.

Adorno, Theodor, Else Frenkel-Brunswik, Daniel J. Levinson, and R. Nevitt Sanford. *The Authoritarian Personality.* New York: W. W. Norton, 1950.

Amer, Ramses. "The United Nations and Kampuchea: The Issue of Representation and Its Implications." *Bulletin of Concerned Asian Scholars* 22, no. 3 (1990): 52–60.

Ang Choulean. *Les êtres surnaturels dans la religion populaire khmère.* Paris: Cedoreck, 1987.

Arendt, Hannah. *Eichmann in Jerusalem: A Report on the Banality of Evil.* New York: Penguin, 2006.

——. *The Life of the Mind.* New York: Harcourt, 1978.

——. *The Origins of Totalitarianism.* New York: Harcourt, Brace, Jovanovich, 1973.

Arendt, Hannah, and Karl Jaspers. *Correspondence 1926–1969.* New York: Harcourt Brace Jovanovich, 1992.

Arthur, Paige. "How 'Transitions' Reshaped Human Rights: A Conceptual History of Transitional Justice." *Human Rights Quarterly* 31, no. 2 (2009): 321–67.

Baaz, Mikael, and Mona Lilja. "Using International Criminal Law to Resist Transitional Justice: Legal Rupture in the Extraordinary Chambers in the Courts of Cambodia." *Conflict and Society: Advances in Research* 2 (2016): 142–59.

Barth, Fredrik. "An Anthropology of Knowledge." *Current Anthropology* 43, no. 1 (2002): 1–18.

——. *Cosmologies in the Making: A Generative Approach to Cultural Variation in Inner New Guinea.* New York: Cambridge University Press, 1990.

Bass, Gary J. *Stay the Hand of Vengeance: The Politics of War Crimes Tribunals.* Princeton, NJ: Princeton University Press, 2001.

Becker, Elizabeth. *When the War Was Over: Cambodia and the Khmer Rouge Revolution.* New York: PublicAffairs, 1998.

Beliso-DeJesús, Aisha M., and Jemima Pierre. "Introduction: Toward an Anthropology of White Supremacy." *American Anthropologist* 12, no. 1 (2020): 65–75.

Besteman, Catherine, and Hugh Gusterson, eds. *Why America's Top Pundits Are Wrong: Anthropologists Talk Back.* Berkeley: University of California Press, 2005.

Bloxham, Donald. "The Armenian Genocide of 1915–1916: Cumulative Radicalization and the Development of a Destruction Policy." *Past & Present* 181 (2003): 141–91.

Borofsky, Robert. *Why a Public Anthropology?* Kailua, HI: Center for a Public Anthropology, 2011.

Borofsky, Robert, and Antonio De Lauri. "Public Anthropology in Changing Times. *Public Anthropologist* 1 (2019): 3–19.

Bourdieu, Pierre. "The Force of Law: Toward a Sociology of the Juridical Field." *Hastings Law Journal* 38 (1987): 814–53.

——. *Homo Academicus.* Stanford, CA: Stanford University Press, 1988.

——. *Outline of a Theory of Practice.* New York: Cambridge University Press, 1977.

Bronner, Stephen Eric. *Of Critical Theory and Its Theorists.* New York, Routledge, 2002.

Caswell, Michelle. *Archiving the Unspeakable: Silence, Memory, and the Photographic Record in Cambodia.* Madison: University of Wisconsin Press, 2014.

Chandler, David P. *Brother Number One: A Political Biography of Pol Pot.* Boulder, CO: Westview Press, 1999.

——. *The Tragedy of Cambodian History: Politics, War and Revolution since 1945.* New Haven, CT: Yale University Press, 1991.

——. *Voices from S-21: Terror and History in Pol Pot's Secret Prison.* Berkeley: University of California Press, 1999.

Chhang, Youk. "How Did I Survive the Khmer Rouge?" *Searching for the Truth*, 2nd quarter 2005, 7.

Chon, Gina, and Sambath Teth. *Behind the Killing Fields: A Khmer Rouge Leader and One of His Victims.* Philadelphia: University of Pennsylvania Press, 2010.

Ciorciari, John D., and Youk Chhang. "Documenting the Crimes of Democratic Kampuchea." In *Bringing the Khmer Rouge to Justice: Prosecuting Mass Violence before the Cambodian Courts*, edited by Jaya Ramji and Beth Van Schaak, 226–27. Lewiston, NY: Edwin Mellen Press, 2005.

Ciorciari, John D., and Anne Heindel, eds. *Hybrid Justice: The Extraordinary Chambers in the Courts of Cambodia.* Ann Arbor: University of Michigan Press, 2014.

Clarke, Kamari Maxine. *Fictions of Justice: The International Criminal Court and the Challenge of Legal Pluralism in Sub-Saharan Africa.* New York: Cambridge University Press, 2009.

——. "Toward Reflexivity in the Anthropology of Expertise and Law." *American Anthropologist* 122, no. 3 (2020): 584–87.

Clifford, James, and George E. Marcus, eds., *Writing Culture: The Poetics and Politics of Ethnography.* Berkeley: University of California Press, 1986.

Communist Party of Kampuchea (CPK). *The Red Heart of Dam Pheng. Revolutionary Youth* no. 3, 1973. Reproduced in *Searching for the Truth*, July 2012.

Davis, Erik W. *Deathpower: Buddhism's Ritual Imagination in Cambodia.* New York: Columbia University Press, 2016.

Democratic Kampuchea. *Black Paper: Facts and Evidences of the Acts of Aggression and Annexation of Vietnam against Kampuchea.* Phnom Penh: Ministry of Foreign Affairs, 1978.

Dezalay, Yves, and Mikael Rask Masden. "The Force of Law and Lawyers: Pierre Bourdieu and the Reflexive Sociology of Law." *Annual Review of Law and Social Science* 8 (2012): 433–52.

Donnelly, Jack, and Daniel J. Whelan. *International Human Rights.* Boulder, CO: Westview Press, 2020.

Douglas, Lawrence. *The Memory of Judgment: Making Law and History in the Trials of the Holocaust.* New Haven, CT: Yale University Press, 2001.

Dunlop, Nic. *The Lost Executioner: A Story of the Khmer Rouge.* London: Bloomsbury, 2005.

Ebihara, May Mayko. "Revolution and Reformulation in Kampuchean Village Culture." In *The Cambodian Agony*, edited by David A. Ablin and Marlowe Hood, 16–61. Armonk, NY: M. E. Sharpe, 1990.

Edwards, Penny. "Imaging the Other in Cambodian Nationalist Discourse before and during the UNTAC Period." In *Propaganda, Politics, and Violence in Cambodia: Democratic Transition under United Nations Peace-Keeping*, edited by Steve Heder and Judy Ledgerwood, 50–72. Armonk, NY: M. E. Sharpe, 1996.

Eltringham, Nigel. *Genocide Never Sleeps: Living Law at the International Criminal Tribunal for Rwanda.* New York: Cambridge University Press, 2019.

——. "'Illuminating the Broader Context': Anthropological and Historical Knowledge at the International Criminal Tribunal for Rwanda." *Journal of the Royal Anthropological Institute* 19 (2013): 338–55.

Etcheson, Craig. *Extraordinary Justice: Law, Politics, and the Khmer Rouge Tribunals.* New York: Columbia University Press, 2020.

Evans, Richard J. "History, Memory and the Law: The Historian and Expert Witness." *History and Theory* 4, no. 3 (2002): 326–454.

Fassin, Didier, ed. *If Truth Be Told: The Politics of Public Ethnography.* Durham, NC: Duke University Press, 2017.

Fassin, Didier, and Samuel Lézé, eds. *Moral Anthropology: A Critical Reader.* New York: Routledge, 2014.

Fawthrop, Tom, and Helen Jarvis. *Getting Away with Genocide: Cambodia's Long Struggle against the Khmer Rouge.* London: Pluto, 2004.

Geertz, Clifford. "'From the Native's Point of View': On the Nature of Anthropological Understanding." *Bulletin of the American Academy of Arts and Sciences* 28, no. 1 (1974): 26–45.

——. *Local Knowledge: Further Essays in Interpretive Anthropology.* New York: Basic Books, 1983.

Giddens, Anthony. *The Constitution of Society.* Berkeley: University of California Press, 1984.

Gidley, Rebecca. "Judicializing History: Mass Crimes Trials and the Historian as Expert Witness in West Germany, Cambodia, and Bangladesh." *Genocide Studies and Prevention* 3, no. 9 (2018): 52–67.

——. "Trading a Theatre for Military Headquarters: Locating the Khmer Rouge Tribunal." *Contemporary Southeast Asia* 40, no 2 (2018): 279–300.

Giry, Stéphanie. "Necessary Scapegoats? The Making of the Khmer Rouge Tribunal." *New York Review of Books,* July 23, 2012.

González, Roberto J., ed. *Anthropologists in the Public Sphere: Speaking Out on War, Peace, and American Power.* Austin: University of Texas Press, 2004.

Harris, Ian. *Buddhism under Pol Pot.* Phnom Penh: Documentation Center of Cambodia, 2007.

Haugerud, Angelique. "Public Anthropology in 2015: Charlie Hebdo, Black Lives Matter, Migrants, and More." *American Anthropologist* 118, no. 3 (2016), 585–610.

Headley, Robert K., Jr., Kylin Chhor, Lam Kheng Lim, Lim Kah Kheang, and Chen Chun. *Cambodian-English Dictionary.* Washington, DC: Catholic University of America Press, 1977.

Hinton, Alexander Laban, ed. *Annihilating Difference: The Anthropology of Genocide.* Berkeley: University of California Press, 2002.

——. "Critical Genocide Studies." *Genocide Studies and Prevention* 7, no. 1 (2012): 4–15.

——, ed. *Genocide: An Anthropological Reader.* Malden, MA: Blackwell, 2002.

——. *It Can Happen Here: White Power and the Rising Threat of Genocide in the US.* New York: New York University Press, 2021.

——. *The Justice Facade: Trials of Transition in Cambodia.* New York: Oxford University Press, 2018.

——. *Man or Monster? The Trial of a Khmer Rouge Torturer.* Durham, NC: Duke University Press, 2016.

——. "What Makes a Man Start Fires?" In *Pre-Genocide: Warnings and Readiness to Protect,* edited by Anders Jerichow and Cecilie Felicia Stokholm Banke, 83–93. Copenhagen: Humanity in Action, 2018.

——. *Why Did They Kill? Cambodia in the Shadow of Genocide*. Berkeley: University of California Press, 2005.

Hinton, D. E., A. L. Hinton, V. Pich, J. R. Loeum, and M. H. Pollack. "Nightmares among Cambodian Refugees: The Breaching of Concentric Ontological Security." *Culture, Medicine, and Psychiatry* 33, no. 2 (2009): 219–65.

Holland, Dorothy, and Naomi Quinn, eds. *Cultural Models in Language and Thought*. New York: Cambridge University Press, 1987.

Horkheimer, Max, and Theodor W. Adorno. *Dialectic of Enlightenment*. Stanford, CA: Stanford University Press, 2007.

Hurston, Zora N. *Their Eyes Were Watching God*. New York: Amistad, 2006.

Jones, Adam. *Genocide: A Comprehensive Introduction*. 3rd ed. New York: Routledge, 2017.

Jones, Minh Bui. "Victor's Justice." *Mekong Review* 1, no. 2 (2016): 9–10.

Kershaw, Ian. *The Nazi Dictatorship: Problems and Perspectives of Interpretation*. London: Arnold, 2000.

Kidder, Tracy. *Mountains beyond Mountains: The Quest of Dr. Paul Farmer, a Man Who Would Cure the World*. New York: Random House, 2004.

Kiernan, Ben. *The Pol Pot Regime: Race, Power, and Genocide in Cambodia under the Khmer Rouge, 1975–79*. New Haven, CT: Yale University Press, 2008.

Koskenniemi, Martti. "Between Impunity and Show Trials." *Max Planck Yearbook of United Nations Law* 6 (2002): 1–35.

Ledgerwood, Judy. "The Cambodian Tuol Sleng Museum of Genocidal Crimes National Narrative." *Museum Anthropology* 21, no. 1 (1997): 82–98.

Lesley, Elena. "Lessons for the Future: Khmer Rouge Survivor Testimonies as Sites of Individual and Social Regeneration." *Ethnos* 86, no. 3 (2019): 570–91.

Low, Setha M., and Sally Engle Merry. "Engaged Anthropology: Diversity and Dilemmas: Introduction to Supplement 2." In "Engaged Anthropology: Diversity and Dilemmas," supplement, *Current Anthropology* 51, no. S2 (2010): S203–14.

Maguire, Peter. *Facing Death in Cambodia*. New York: Columbia University Press, 2005.

Malinowski, Bronislaw. *Argonauts of the Western Pacific: An Account of Native Enterprise and Adventure in the Archipelagoes of Melanesian New Guinea*. London: Kegan Paul, 1922.

Marston, John. "Metaphors of the Khmer Rouge." In *Cambodian Culture since 1975: Homeland and Exile*, edited by May Ebihara, Carol A. Mortland, and Judy Ledgerwood, 105–18. Ithaca, NY: Cornell University Press, 1994.

McFann, Hudson, and Alexander Laban Hinton. "Impassable Visions: The Cambodia to Come, the Detritus in Its Wake." In *A Companion to the Anthropology of Death*, edited by Antonius C.G.M. Robben, 223–35. Malden, MA: Wiley-Blackwell, 2018.

McGranahan, Carole, ed. *Writing Anthropology: Essays on Craft and Commitment*. Durham, NC: Duke University Press, 2020.

Mech Dara. "Khmer Rouge's Brother No 2 Dies." *Phnom Penh Post*, August 5, 2019.

Meierhenrich, Jens, ed. *Genocide: A Reader*. New York: Oxford University Press, 2014.

Meierhenrich, Jens, and Devin O. Pendas. "'The Justice of My Cause Is Clear, but There's Politics to Fear': Political Trials in Theory and History." In *Political Trials in Theory and History*, edited by Jens Meierhenrich and Devin O. Pendas, 1–64. New York: Cambridge University Press, 2017.

Merry, Sally Engle. "Anthropology and International Law." *Annual Review of Anthropology* 23 (2006): 99–116.

Moore, Henrietta L., and Todd Sanders. "Anthropology and Epistemology." In *Anthropology in Theory: Issues in Epistemology*, edited by Henrietta L. Moore and Todd Sanders, 1–22. Malden, MA: Blackwell, 2014.

Moses, A. Dirk. "Genocide: Critical Concepts in Historical Studies." In *Genocide: Critical Concepts in Historical Studies*, edited by A. Dirk Moses, 1–23. New York: Routledge, 2010.
Naqvi, Yasmin. "The Right to Truth in International Law: Fact or Fiction?" *International Review of the Red Cross* 88, no. 862 (2006): 245–73.
Ngor, Haing. *A Cambodian Odyssey*. New York: Warner Books, 1987.
Osiel, Mark. *Mass Atrocity, Collective Memory, and the Law*. New Brunswick, NJ: Transaction, 2000.
Owen, Taylor, and Ben Kiernan. "Bombs over Cambodia." *The Walrus*, October 12, 2006.
Ponchaud, François. *Cambodia, Year Zero*. New York: Holt, Rinehart and Winston, 1978.
Rousso, Henry. *The Haunting Past: History, Memory, and Justice in Contemporary France*. Philadelphia: University of Pennsylvania Press, 2002.
——. "Letter to the President of the Bordeaux Assizes Court" (October 6, 1997). In *The Papon Affair: Memory and Justice on Trial*, edited by Richard J. Golsan, 193–94. New York: Routledge, 2000.
Sarat, Austin, Lawrence Douglas, and Martha Merrill Umphrey, eds. *The Limits of Law*. Stanford, CA: Stanford University Press, 2005.
Schafft, Gretchen E. *From Racism to Genocide: Anthropology in the Third Reich*. Champaign: University of Illinois Press, 2004.
Scheffer, David. "Genocide and Atrocity Crimes." *Genocide Studies and Prevention* 1, no. 3 (2006): 229–50.
Seng, Theary C. *Daughter of the Killing Fields: Asrei's Story*. London: Fusion Press, 2005.
Shklar, Judith N. *Legalism: Law, Morals, and Political Trials*. Cambridge, MA: Harvard University Press, 1986.
Shore, Bradd. *Culture in Mind: Cognition, Culture, and the Problem of Meaning*. New York: Oxford University Press, 1996.
Shuster, Evelyne. "Fifty Years Later: The Significance of the Nuremberg Code." *New England Journal of Medicine* 337 (1997): 1436–40.
Sikkink, Kathryn, and Hun Joon Kim. "The Justice Cascade: The Origins and Effectiveness of Prosecutions of Human Rights Violations." *Annual Review of Law and Social Science* 9 (2013): 26–85.
Smith, William. "Justice for Genocide in Cambodia—The Case for the Prosecution." *Genocide Studies and Prevention* 12, no. 3 (2018): 20–39.
Stover, Eric, Mychelle Balthazard, and K. Alexa Koenig. "Confronting Duch: Civil Party Participation in Case 001 at the Extraordinary Chamber in the Courts of Cambodia." *International Review of the Red Cross* 93, no. 882 (2011): 505.
Teitel, Ruti, G. "Transitional Justice Genealogy." *Harvard Human Rights Journal* 16 (2003): 69–94.
Trouillot, Michel-Rolph. *Silencing the Past: Power and the Production of History*. Boston: Beacon Press, 1995.
Vickery, Michael. *Cambodia 1975–1982*. Boston: South End Press, 1984.
Waterston, Alisse, and Maria D. Vesperi, eds. *Anthropology off the Shelf: Anthropologists on Writing*. Malden: Wiley-Blackwell, 2011.
Wilson, Richard Ashby. "Expert Evidence on Trial: Social Researchers in the International Criminal Courtroom." *American Ethnologist* 43, no. 4 (2016): 730–44.
——. "The Trouble with Truth: Anthropology's Epistemological Hypochondria." *Anthropology Today* 20, no. 5 (2004): 14–17.
——. *Writing History in International Criminal Trials*. New York: Cambridge University Press, 2011.
Zigon, Jarrett. *Morality: An Anthropological Perspective*. New York: Routledge, 2008.

Index

Note: Photos are indicated by an *italicized* page number. Figures are indicated by f.

CPSIA information can be obtained
at www.ICGtesting.com
Printed in the USA
LVHW101638270922
729408LV00004B/480

9 781501 765698